Dear Reader: 7.5. B S

The book you are about to read is the latest bestseller from the St. Martin's True Crime Library, the imprint the *New York Times* calls "the leader in true crime!" Each month, we offer you a fascinating account of the latest, most sensational crime that has captured the national attention. St. Martin's is the publisher of bestselling true crime author and crime journalist Kieran Crowley, who explores the dark, deadly links between a prominent Manhattan surgeon and the disappearance of his wife fifteen years earlier in THE SURGEON'S WIFE. Carlton Smith's COLD-BLOODED details the death of a respected attorney—and the secret, sordid life of his wife. In Edgar Award–nominated DARK DREAMS, legendary FBI profiler Roy Hazelwood and bestselling crime author Stephen G. Michaud shine light on the inner workings of America's most violent and depraved murderers. In the book you now hold, ONE DEADLY NIGHT, veteran true crime author John Glatt details the murder of an Indiana family—was the father guilty?

St. Martin's True Crime Library gives you the stories behind the headlines. Our authors take you right to the scene of the crime and into the minds of the most notorious murderers to show you what really makes them tick. St. Martin's True Crime Library paperbacks are better than the most terrifying thriller, because it's all true! The next time you want a crackling good read, make sure it's got the St. Martin's True Crime Library logo on the spine—you'll be up all night!

Charles E. Spicer, Jr.
Executive Editor, St. Martin's True Crime Library

JUN 3 0 2005

St. Martin's True Crime Library Titles
by John Glatt

For I Have Sinned

Evil Twins

Cradle of Death

Blind Passion

Depraved

Cries in the Desert

Twisted

Deadly American Beauty

ONE DEADLY NIGHT

A State Trooper, Triple Homicide,
and a Search for Justice

By John Glatt

St. Martin's Paperbacks

For Chiquita from Split

ONE DEADLY NIGHT

Copyright © 2005 by John Glatt.

Cover photo credit: the Camm Family.

ISBN: 0-312-99309-9
EAN: 80312-99309-2

Printed in the United States of America

St. Martin's Paperbacks edition / May 2005

St. Martin's Paperbacks are published by St. Martin's Press, 175 Fifth Avenue, New York, NY 10010.

10 9 8 7 6 5 4 3 2 1

CONTENTS

ACKNOWLEDGMENTS

The long, labyrinthine saga of whether ex-Indiana State Trooper David Camm did or did not kill his wife, Kim, and two young children, Jill and Brad, is anything but a clear-cut case. In Summer 2004—two-and-a-half years after a jury found him guilty of their murders—the Indiana Court of Appeals unanimously overturned the verdict, declaring much of the evidence used against him inadmissible. The three appeals judges ruled that although the handsome former policeman may have been a serial adulterer that did not make him a killer.

In March 2005, while Camm was out on bail awaiting his second trial and his family members continued their fight to clear his name, an ex-con named Charles Boney was arrested and charged with Kim, Brad and Jill's murder. More than four years after the murders, investigators finally discovered that some mysterious DNA found on a sweatshirt at the scene was Boney's.

Now prosecutors plan to try David Camm and Boney together as co-conspirators.

At his first trial Camm's uncle and employer Sam Lockhart, as well as ten other witnesses testified under oath he could not have committed the murders, as he was playing basketball with them at the time. It appeared to be the perfect alibi but a prosecution blood spatter expert found eight microscopic drops of his daughter Jill's blood on his shirt, helping to persuade a jury he was guilty.

Out of the eight true crime books I have written this was

undoubtedly *the* most challenging one. Is David Camm guilty of one of the most horrible crimes imaginable, or is he an innocent man wrongfully convicted by overzealous detectives and prosecutors after having made the horrifying discovery that his wife and children had been murdered? As events unfold, this seems more of a real possibility than ever.

But one thing's for certain—Kimberly Camm, her seven-year-old son, Brad, and daughter, Jill, aged five, are all dead and someone is responsible.

I am indebted to the Lockhart and Camm families for their help and generosity, during my stay in New Albany in March 2004. I spent many hours with David Camm's brother Donnie, his sister, Julie, and their parents, Susie and Don, who shone some light into his troubled life. I would also like to thank his uncle Sam Lockhart and aunts Phyllis Rhodes and Debbie TerVree for their help and insight. Unfortunately, despite repeated attempts to interview Kim's parents, Frank and Janice Renn, and her sister, Debbie Karem, they declined, saying they were too upset to reopen old wounds.

I also met with Sean Clemons at ISP Post 45, but under strict orders from his superiors he declined from discussing his former boyhood friend David Camm.

My thanks also go to Floyd County Prosecutor Stan Faith, with whom I shared a memorable lunch at his club in Louisville, Kentucky, and Sheriff Randy Hubbard, whose insight into David's character was invaluable. Much gratitude also goes to Mat Herron of *Snitch*, whose unique and colorful coverage of the nine-week trial was exemplary.

As always I would like to thank my longtime editor at St. Martin's Press, Charles Spicer and his excellent team of Joseph Cleemann and Michael Homler. Also my literary lion of an agent, Peter Miller and his staff, Julie, Scott and Lisa for all their help.

Thanks also goes to: Gail, Jerry and Emily Freund, Debbie, Doug and Taylor Baldwin, Walter Nonnsen and Charlotte, Annette Witheridge, Jerry, Edie, Joanne and Stan at the Belleayre Plaza, Pine Hill, New York, Roger, Daphna and Lianna Hitts, Don, Doug and Bernie MacLeod, Doc and Gotham Gayley.

Prologue

Perched on his commode in a tiny six-by-eight-foot jail cell, David Camm stared down a fly on the ceiling. Then, slowly aiming his catapult, he fired, dispatching a soggy paper missile to score a bull's-eye. And as the fly fell dead to the ground, he raised his shackled wrists and gave himself a celebrative high-five.

In better days the former highly decorated Indiana State Trooper and expert marksman had been an avid deer hunter. But now, chained up in solitary confinement in a southern Indiana maximum security jail, David Ray Camm had invented a sport he called "pretend hunting." In place of a bow and arrow he used a rubber band, with chewed-over candy wrappers as ammunition.

So far on this cool mid-March morning in 2004, the boyish-looking, muscular six-foot-tall ex-policeman had killed three flies. It was a new record and he had triumphantly asked his father to mount their bodies on a plaque as a trophy.

Seventy-two-year-old Donald Camm had smiled, promising to do so. But as he left the cell, wiping a tear from his eye, he was still unable to believe the real life nightmare that had engulfed his family.

For 40-year-old David was serving 195 years for the cold-blooded murders of his beautiful wife, Kim, and their two little children—7-year-old Brad and 5-year-old Jill. It was, said prosecutor Stan Faith, a crime almost beyond comprehension, as he believed—though he could not prove it—that the ex-trooper had also sexually molested Jill, just hours before the September 28, 2000, bloody massacre in his garage in Georgetown, Indiana.

David Camm and his family had always vehemently protested his innocence, claiming he had been playing basketball in a church hall when the murders took place. Besides, he had the perfect alibi, with eleven witnesses testifying under oath they had been on the court with him the entire night.

But in 2002, a jury had not believed him and found him guilty of killing Kim, Brad and Jill. A superior court judge had sentenced him to the maximum penalty, making him eligible for parole when he turned 143 years old.

Everything changed in September 2004, when the Indiana Court of Appeals unanimously overturned the guilty verdict. Three appeals judges criticized the judge and prosecutor, ruling that a substantial amount of the evidence used against him at trial was inadmissible.

On November 5 the Indiana Supreme Court refused to reinstate the convictions and threw the case back to Floyd County, where new prosecutor Keith Henderson planned on retrying David Camm in late 2005. But everything changed when, in March 2005, another man—ex-con Charles Boney—was arrested and charged in the case after his DNA was identified on a sweatshirt found at the crime scene. At first, Boney denied any involvement in the killings. But prosecutors now say that Boney has admitted being at the Camm house during the killings, although they also say Boney claims it was Camm who was the actual killer. After dropping the original charges against Camm and issuing new charges against him, Keith Henderson now plans on trying Camm and Boney together as co-conspirators.

Meanwhile, the question remains, who is the real David Camm?—is he an innocent man wrongly convicted after suffering an unimaginable tragedy, or one of the most cold-blooded murderers in American criminal history?

1

Roots

David Camm's family traces its ancestors back to the fourteenth century and the legendary Scottish crusader Sir Symon Locard, who carried Robert the Bruce's heart into battle in the Holy Land. As the custodian of the key to the casket that contained Bruce's heart, Sir Symon was later honored by having his name officially changed to Lockheart, later abbreviated to the modern Lockhart.

One of his illustrious family's most treasured possessions is a bound volume called *Lockhart Roots*. It proudly bears their coat of arms, consisting of a lion, a cross and a sword, meaning defenders of Christian freedom. Written above is the family motto: "Corda Serata Pando"—Latin for "I Open Locked Hearts."

In 1683 Captain James Lockhart carried the family name to America, when he and his sons settled in Virginia and prospered. They made their money transporting new immigrants from England to Virginia.

The Lockharts lived in Russell County, Virginia, for the next two centuries, becoming frontiersmen. They were the first of a tough breed of pioneers who moved south, forcibly taking large areas of Virginia away from the Native Americans.

"They had such fear of God in their hearts that it left no room for fear of man," wrote David Camm's maternal grandfather, Amos Lockhart, in his 1989 self-published family history, *When We Were Young*. "Short in material goods, they were long on faith. They were taking God at his promise."

Amos' father, John Patton Lockhart, also known as "J. P.," was born near Honaker, Virginia, on May 7, 1881. At the age of 24 in September 1905, he married Elizabeth A. Thompson, who bore a son, Swanson Banner Lockhart, exactly ten months later.

On January 9, 1908, David's grandfather Amos H. Lockhart was born and three years later J. P. started his own ministry and began preaching all over the South. In 1916, J. P. moved his wife and children into a small train station in Artrip, West Virginia. And over the next few years he became a traveling minister, preaching on horseback through the mountains of Tennessee and West Virginia and setting up numerous ministries.

"Nothing stopped him," Amos wrote. "He kept going, hardly knowing the future results."

J. P., who had thirteen children, relied on collection plate proceeds at his revival meetings, or the good-will donations afterwards, where he could expect live chickens, canned goods or bacon to feed his growing family.

As Amos and his brothers and sisters were growing up they were constantly on the move as the family crisscrossed the South on revival tours, where J. P.'s mission was to convert people to his self-styled version of Scottish Presbyterianism. During their many trips all over the South, J. P. and young Amos would camp out in a tent and live rough.

Amos' father always carried his Bible, striking up conversations with any strangers they met.

"Soon they would know he was a preacher," wrote Amos. "And soon he was invited to a home or homes to sing, have prayer meetings and preach. What I liked about these religious services was the good woman home-cooked meals."

In the early 1920s Amos was a strong, strapping teenager and he and his friend Hollie Bloomer lived the hobo life, looking for work. Sometimes they jumped freight trains and got into many "mischievous" scrapes during their various adventures.

"We were not murderers nor the worst of people," Amos later wrote. "Neither were we saints."

In 1929, 21-year-old Amos moved to New Castle, Indiana, where he worked on the inspection line at the Chrysler car factory. But after losing his job in the Depression he moved to Boyle County, in Kentucky, where he met a tobacco farmer's daughter, a beautiful blue-eyed blonde named Daisy B. Belcher.

Just 15 years old, Daisy, whose family was originally from Germany, was one of seven children and her parents struggled to put food on the table. By the time 21-year-old Amos met Daisy, he had dated many "nice respectable young ladies." But soon after meeting "this Belcher damsel," they married.

Looking back on his November 1, 1930, wedding more than fifty-eight years later in his memoir, Amos would quote Chapter 18, Verse 22 of the book of Proverbs: "Whoso findeth a wife findeth a good thing, and obtaineth favor of the Lord."

Amos and Daisy would have nine children, starting with a son, Carlin, who was born on December 28, 1932. Just over two years later, on February 4, 1935, David Camm's mother, Delpha Susie, was born. And over the next twenty years Daisy bore a further seven children: Leland, Nelson, Gloria, Sam, Phyllis, Kathy and Deborah.

The Lockhart children always had a strong family bond, looking after each other in business and helping any member who might fall on hard times. Years later this would be put to the test with David Camm.

Delpha Susie's first memories are of the countryside around Danville, Kentucky. When she was a little girl she attended her grandfather J. P. Lockhart's church, where her father was also a lay minister.

"My father did everything you can think of," she remembered. "He sold insurance, he sold Bibles and he worked in the coal mines of eastern Kentucky."

The family lived on a small farm and Amos would travel to wherever the work was, once moving his dutiful wife and children to the Blue Diamond Coal Mining Camp for a year. Delpha Susie, who dropped her first name as a young girl, went to grade school in Junction City, Kentucky, with her older brother and sisters.

In the early 1950s Amos worked for Southern Railroad, finding a job as a fireman on the Louisville-to-Danville run. Eventually he found full-time work as an engineer with the L & N Railroad based in Louisville, moving the family 50 miles northwest across the Ohio River to New Albany, Indiana.

New Albany is a true slice of Americana, lying directly across the river from the more cosmopolitan Louisville. With just fifteen thousand families living there, the town embraced small-town American values, with everybody literally knowing everybody's business.

New Albany rests on the banks of the Ohio River, which the early French settlers first named "La Belle Rivière," meaning Beautiful River. Even today it has little in common with the twenty-first century, moving at its own pace with little thought of the outside world.

Before the French and English arrived in the seventeenth century, this scenic part of southern Indiana housed many Native American tribes, including the Wyandotte, Miami, Shawnee and Potawatomi. During the American Revolution in 1778, General George Rogers Clark led an expeditionary force across the Ohio River, capturing three key strategic forts from the British. Five years later, in recognition of the part he played in winning the war, the new Virginia legislature awarded Clark and his men 150,000 acres of land, which today houses Floyd and neighboring Clark Counties.

Since General Clark and his ancestors began settling southern Indiana two centuries ago, the Ohio River has shaped the area's economic and cultural development. Throughout the nineteenth century, steamboats glided along the river past the growing city of New Albany, bringing hordes of tourists to gamble. And in 1875 the first Kentucky Derby, across the river in Louisville, put the whole area on the map.

But in January 1937 disaster struck when heavy rain caused the Ohio River to break its banks, inflicting millions of dollars in damage on New Albany and its neighboring towns of Clarksville and Jeffersonville. To prevent another costly flood a network of floodwalls and levees was completed in 1945 and some years later an even more ambitious $8-million floodwall was constructed around Louisville.

To this day Floyd County is a rural throwback to a time when American life was simpler and far less commercial. It boasts many unspoiled nineteenth century farm houses, and Greek revival–influenced churches around, as religion plays a crucial role in the life of Floyd County.

By the time the Lockhart family arrived in 1954, Susie was an attractive 19-year-old girl. Like the rest of her large family, she attended the New Albany First Church of God and sang in the choir.

Soon after joining the church, Susie befriended another choir member named Margaret Camm, who was two years her senior.

"It just happened that I borrowed a suitcase from Margaret to go to my brother Leland," said Susie. "Donald Camm was there and I was introduced."

Don Camm was a handsome 24-year-old U.S. Air Force flight engineer, who was flying Typhoons out of Guam during the Korean War. Don's father, William Camm, hailed from Liverpool, England, having emigrated to America in the late 1920s, when he was 24 years old.

A couple of weeks after they met, Don had to return to his base in Massachusetts to complete his four-year service. On his release he returned to New Albany.

"He asked me to marry him," remembered Susie. "And we were married on February 9, 1956."

The newlyweds moved into a small house on the rural fringes of New Albany, with several relatives as neighbors. Don found a job as a mechanic with a chemical company called BF Goodrich, which made an assortment of rubber products, including car tires. Susie became a homemaker.

One year after they married, Susie became pregnant and in 1958 their first child, Donnie, was born. Three years later a daughter named Julie followed. And then on March 23, 1964, at Floyd Memorial Hospital, New Albany, David Ray made his entrance into the world.

2

Dirt Boy

Almost as soon as he could crawl David Camm would wander outside his parents' house to play in the dirt. The little blond-haired boy loved nothing better than amusing himself at the back of the house, digging holes and making roads.

"Dave insisted on digging the dirt," remembered his mother, Susie. "He'd play by himself for hours."

His elder sister, Julie, remembers how Dave stood out from the other children as a fiercely independent loner.

"Growing up he spent a lot of time outside," she remembered. "He was the quietest of us all."

When David was 1 year old his parents had a third son, Daniel, to complete the family. Then his mother found a job selling furniture in a local store, so a babysitter was hired to care for David and baby Daniel during the day.

All the Camm children's lives revolved around the Georgetown Community Church, one of the many churches that David's grandfather Amos had founded over the years.

"That was real important," said David's brother Donnie. "That was a very big part of growing up."

Every Sunday morning Susie Camm would dress up her four children in their best clothes and drive them the ten miles to the small church on State Road 64 outside Georgetown. In the afternoon, after the service, David and his many cousins would play together in the fields. Then they'd go their respective ways to spend the evening with their parents.

"The family is very close," said David's sister, Julie Hogue, "especially because my mom has a very large family. We were very proud of who we were as a family, my grandpa, my aunts and uncles and my cousins."

The Lockhart family patriarch, Amos, then in his early sixties, built a special playhouse for all his grandchildren in the garden of his house on Lockhart Road in Georgetown. Affectionately known to his family as "Pappaw," he had purchased the road a few years earlier, inviting members of his family to build houses on his land, naming it eponymously.

"Our cousins were like our brothers," explained Julie. "It went way beyond our nuclear family."

Don Camm was soon promoted into management at BF Goodrich, so in 1966 he moved his family into a larger house on Hausfeldt Lane in New Albany, where he and Susie Camm live to this day. In those days Hausfeldt Lane was still very rural, but now it has been developed by industry.

"There were a lot of cows and pastures and woods to play in," said Donnie. "We had a rural upbringing [with] bicycles, mini-bikes and go-carts and playing in the creeks, the trees and the woods."

A friend of the Camms owned a filling station and his little nephew Sean Clemons sometimes played ball with David Camm, who was a couple of years older. Growing up, the boys went to the same schools, becoming friends. Over thirty years later their lives would often intersect— with disastrous results for David.

The Clemons and Lockhart families went back several generations, and one of Sean Clemons' uncles helped build Amos Lockhart's Georgetown Community Church, whose current pastor is David's uncle Leland Lockhart. They were "Two big families who grew up on McDonald Street in New Albany," said David's aunt, Debbie TerVree. "Sean's family and our family were very close."

A few weeks before David was due to start at New Albany Elementary School, he had a serious accident on his bicycle. The injuries to his kidneys resulted in the highly dangerous viral infection mephritis, which caused his heart to enlarge. Mephritis, which can also be caused by strep throat, attacks and damages the membranes in the kidneys that allow blood to flow through, and can disable them permanently. It takes months of treatment for a patient to recover. David was hospitalized for four weeks and then had to spend a semester at home, being tutored.

"It had gotten in through the skin," said his mother. "The doctor thought he had gotten it from his bicycle accident."

David missed most of his first year of elementary school and when he eventually was well enough to start classes, he had difficulty reading and writing and was way behind his classmates.

David's small, spindly writing leaned backwards. "He had a little problem," said Susie Camm. "They didn't know it was dyslexia, but I could see it."

Although he was academically challenged, David was a natural athlete and an excellent basketball player.

Growing up, Donnie took special care of David, teaching him how to fish and going on long nature hikes with him. Every summer the Camm family spent several weeks in a cabin on their Uncle Ben's spread in Jefferson, Indiana.

"That was probably the biggest activity that we did as a whole family," said Donnie. "It was very secluded. [There was] fishing and you could swim in the lakes too and there was a boat."

Little David loved the outdoors and it was here that he learned to hunt deer, although his mother maintains that the first time he went hunting he could not bring himself to shoot his bow.

"He said, 'It looked at me with his big brown eyes and I couldn't shoot it,' " remembered Susie. "He was so tender-hearted."

David was also close to his uncle Sam Lockhart, who was just starting his foundation repair company, United Dynamics, Inc., which would end up employing many members of the Lockhart family.

"Actually, when he was three or four years old, I would take him on dates with me," remembered Lockhart. "He was such a pleasant little kid, smiled a lot and always laid-back."

Sam was also impressed with the boy's natural mechanical ability, which he had inherited from his father.

"He would like to do things and put things together," said Sam. "That type of little kid."

When he was 8 years old, David came home one day and told his mother he wanted to be a church minister, like his Uncle Leland.

"Mama, I want to be baptized," Susie remembers him saying, as he clutched his Bible. According to his mother, Dave was very serious about dedicating himself to God, by always trying to be "a good Christian boy."

But the other important influence on his life was his Uncle Nelson, who served twelve years with the Kentucky State Police, before ending his career as a lieutenant with the Jefferson County police department. As a young boy, David questioned his Uncle Nelson about law enforcement and the criminal cases he'd worked on. Then he would daydream about one day becoming a policeman and capturing the bad guys.

When David was in the third grade he began having acute migraine headaches, which would go on to plague him throughout his life. Susie Camm says migraine headaches run in the family and she suffers terribly, as did her mother, Daisy.

"When he was a little boy he started having headaches," said his mother. "But then I noticed his face began to sweat and his shoulders and all. You could tell something wasn't right."

Susie called in the doctor, who prescribed painkillers, but the migraines persisted, only getting worse.

"He'd just lay down in a dark room and lie quietly," said his mother. "It was the only thing he could do."

Every morning the four Camm children would board the school bus outside their front gate, taking Donnie and Julie to New Albany High, Dave to junior high school and little Dan to elementary.

Slowly David made progress at school but he would never get the top grades his brother Donnie did.

"[Dave] was an average student," said his mother, "getting Bs and Cs."

His sister, Julie, remembers Dave always having to struggle to keep up with his classmates. For years he appears to have had an inferiority complex, until he became a state trooper and finally gained some self-confidence.

But his natural athleticism made up for his academic failures, and he was on New Albany High School's basketball and football teams for several years in the late 1970s.

He could also be very charming and made friends easily, although he always seemed to distance himself from people.

"He was very popular and well-liked," said Donnie, who always felt protective towards his kid brother. "A leader among his friends, but he probably would not have run for school council, just because I don't think those kinds of things were important to him."

Donnie describes his brother as reserved and extremely quiet. He would never strike up a conversation unless somebody spoke to him first.

"He didn't stand out in a crowd or call attention to himself," explained Donnie.

And the teenager had little experience with girls, as he was too shy to initiate conversations. While other boys went out on dates he worked in his garage, taking car engines apart and then reassembling them.

"I think he gets that from my dad," explained Donnie. "David was able to build engines, build cars, do bodywork. It was pretty natural. He just had a mind for those things."

One of the Camms' neighbors, Lisa Sowders, first met David at New Albany Elementary, where they were in the same class.

She remembers him as a handsome boy with a good personality, who largely kept to himself but had a distinct air of mystery.

"He'd come over to my house every now and then," she said. "But nobody was ever allowed to go over to David's house though. It sounded like his parents didn't want other kids over there."

3

First Love

At the age of 15, David Camm was an automobile fanatic with his heart set on owning a Jeep. To pay for it his Uncle Sam helped him get an after school job, working for the South Side Inn in New Albany, owned by one of Sam's ex-girlfriends. Every day after finishing school, and on Saturdays, the enthusiastic teenager would wash dishes and serve food at the canteen-style restaurant, which specialized in deep-fried chicken.

"Dave really wanted a car," said his sister, Julie. "Actually it was before he could even drive."

Eventually he had saved up enough money to buy an old secondhand Jeep, and immediately began renovating it. He enjoyed working on it so much that he enrolled for a high school course on auto body repair at the Prosser Vocational Center for a couple of semesters.

In spring 1982, David graduated from New Albany High with mediocre grades. His graduation picture, in the 1982 New Albany High School yearbook, *Vista*, shows him dressed in a tan jacket, a long-collared white shirt and a striped tie. With his full head of dark brown hair neatly parted in the middle and a knowing smile, David looks inscrutable and aloof.

After leaving school, David had little trouble turning his talent for fixing up old cars into a paying job. He found work with a local dealership called Kohl's Body Shop, but soon left for a better job with Carriage Ford in Clarksville, a few miles down the road.

"When he did bodywork he was a perfectionist," said his brother Donnie.

David, now six feet tall, was a grease monkey, coming home most days with his overalls spattered with spray paint from the cars he worked on.

"His hands were always rough and dingy from the spray paint that he used every day," recalls his sister, Julie. "He was pale and thin [weighing] all of one hundred and forty pounds."

According to his mother, at 18, David still secretly dreamed of following in the footsteps of his grandfather Amos and Uncle Leland: He wanted to become a minister. But all his hopes of a church career were dashed when he finally lost his virginity and got a local girl pregnant.

Tamara Lynn Zimmerman had just graduated Floyd Central High School when she first met David Camm through her brother. A month younger than David, she was a slip of a girl with red curly hair, looking far younger than eighteen. They got on well and soon slept together, resulting in her becoming pregnant.

When David confessed to his religious parents that his girlfriend was pregnant they were shocked. The Camms discussed this delicate matter with Tammy's parents, Donald and Donna Zimmerman. Although neither of the teenagers was ready for marriage, having an illegitimate baby in the early 1980s in rural Indiana would have been scandalous. So it was decided they should marry as quickly as possible to avoid any disgrace.

"You see, that was a big thing," explained Susie Camm. "Now he could never be a minister."

On October 22, 1982, the New Albany *Tribune* carried the official wedding announcement, headlined, "Miss Zimmerman to Wed David Camm," over a head-and-shoulders picture of the smiling bride, wearing a white floral V-necked blouse.

Mr. and Mrs. Donald Zimmerman of Rt. 1, Borden, announce the engagement and approaching marriage of their daughter Tamara Lynn to David Ray Camm, son of Mr. and Mrs. Donald Camm of New Albany. Miss Zimmerman is a 1982 graduate of Floyd Central High School and is employed by Warehouse of Groceries in New Albany. Formal invitations have been sent, but all friends and relatives are invited to attend.

At 4.00 p.m. on Saturday, November 13, David's Uncle Leland presided over the official marriage service at his Georgetown Community First Church of God. Tammy was four months pregnant when she walked down the aisle, but her wedding dress managed to conceal it.

"Well, everyone knew," said the groom's mother. "But she didn't really show. It was a really nice wedding with probably fifty or sixty people. Most of them were our family as her side didn't really have a big family."

Straight after the wedding, Tammy moved into David's room at his parents' house until the couple could afford their own place. Susie Camm began to prepare for the upcoming birth due in April.

But around Christmastime Tammy started bleeding, and the doctor ordered her to stay in bed until the baby was born. Every morning Susie would take Tammy her breakfast before going off to work. Then at night David would carry his new bride into the living room to eat dinner and watch television.

Soon after Tammy moved in, Susie Camm began to suspect her new daughter-in-law was still in close touch with an old boyfriend named Jimmy Lynch.

"It was a strange thing about the whole pregnancy," remarked Susie. "She was getting letters from a guy who was in the military in Germany. She told me he was just a friend."

While she was bedridden Tammy fell into a depression, and stopped contacting her family. Susie Camm was so worried about her daughter-in-law that she called Donna Zimmerman at work, suggesting she visit Tammy and cheer her up.

In January 1983, David's sister, Julie, temporarily moved back into the house, while her husband was in Florida at the police academy, to help look after Tammy. Julie thought Tammy was far too young to be a mother and too weak to bear a healthy child.

Then on February 9, 1983, as Susie Camm was doing laundry and preparing to go out to celebrate her twenty-seventh wedding anniversary that night, Tammy suddenly went into labor, two-and-a-half-months premature.

"My baby's coming!" she screamed, as Julie and her mother rushed into the bedroom to help.

Neither of them knew what to do, so Julie called 911, requesting an ambulance, as her mother comforted the panicking expectant mother.

"I was on the phone trying to get somebody to tell us what to do," remembered Julie. "We had no idea."

Eventually an ambulance arrived and brought Tammy to a hospital in Louisville, where she gave birth to a baby girl, later named Whitney Lane.

"So it was quite a scare," remembered Susie, who accompanied Tammy to the hospital. "Whitney was just a small little thing, but everybody loved her from the beginning."

For the first few months Susie Camm mostly looked after Whitney, as David and Tammy tried to settle down to married life. David was still working at Carriage Ford body repair, but realized he would need a better job to support his new family. So he decided to become a police officer, like his Uncle Nelson.

"I have several family members that have been police officers," he would later explain. "When I was young . . . I always looked up to them."

Camm joined the New Albany Police Department as a volunteer auxiliary policeman. It wasn't long before he surprised everyone, showing a natural talent for police work.

"He did a good job," remembers former New Albany Police Chief Randy D. Hubbard, who is now the sheriff of Floyd County. "David was a really good effective auxiliary police officer."

Chief Hubbard had known David Camm since he was at school and liked him. And during David's time as a volunteer, they would spend hours discussing their lives and police work. They'd also socialize outside the department, often going to NASCAR races together.

"He was very personable," said Hubbard. "We got pretty close and he would talk to me a lot about a career in law enforcement."

Chief Hubbard encouraged Camm, suggesting he apply to the Indiana State Police, as there was a two-year wait on new city police recruits. Camm took the chief's advice, enrolling for a part-time course in police administration at Indiana University Southeast, to qualify. He did this on top of his job at Carriage Ford and his shifts as a volunteer policeman.

"He had a great desire to be a law enforcement officer," said Chief Hubbard. "He liked policemen and was very much a motivated person."

David Camm would later explain he had wanted to become a police officer since he was 16, after being stopped for speeding two weekends in a row by an Indiana State Trooper.

"The second time I got pulled over he took me back to his car," said Camm. "He had a real nice brown-colored St. Regis and I was impressed by the car and the uniform. That's pretty much what got me headed in that direction."

As an unpaid volunteer auxiliary policeman, David Camm wore a uniform and had the same service training as a regular officer. He was then called in as back-up, working traffic, major events and crowd control.

Soon after joining the department Camm discussed Tammy and his new baby with Chief Hubbard. In confidence he admitted that he and his wife had little in common, and that he'd had no sexual experience prior to meeting her. Hubbard says that Camm told him he was interested in broadening his experience with other women.

"I think they were young," said Chief Hubbard. "They had the girl and then they grew apart. David was going around outside the family [and] had affairs, as it turned out, because he missed all that early on."

According to Susie Camm, Tammy was to blame and the marriage broke up after David became suspicious that she was in close touch with Jimmy Lynch, whom she would later marry.

"It broke his heart," explained Susie. Now if he had had a temper he would have hit her. [Instead] he hit his fists on the electric pole. That's the way he would express himself. He was really hurt over that."

Susie then asked Tammy to move out of the house with Whitney, as she was too tired working full-time and having to look after them too.

In April 1986, just over three years after they'd married, David and Tammy were divorced by the Circuit Court of Floyd County, sharing custody of Whitney.

"When [they] were divorced, Dave had Whitney full-time," said Julie.

Susie Camm then found herself taking care of her 3-year-old granddaughter, as David was unable to. Luckily Susie's boss at the furniture store was sympathetic and let her take time off.

But once again the stress proved too much for her and she got lupus, so Whitney found herself shuttled between her divorced parents over the next few years, until Tammy finally remarried and could take care of her full-time.

Over the next two years David Camm studied hard, determined to be accepted by the Indiana State Police. And towards the end of his course he applied to join several different departments, waiting patiently to see if he'd been accepted.

He was also seeking a new relationship. In early 1988 a friend of his set him up on a blind date with an attractive girl named Kimberly Renn. The night they met, they would later agree, it was love at first sight.

4

Kim

Ironically, Kimberly Star Renn had been one grade below David Camm at New Albany High School, but they had never met. Kim's parents, Frank and Janice, were born in New Albany, where they were both in Sheriff Randy Hubbard's class in high school.

"They went together in high school," Hubbard remembered, "and we were all pretty good friends."

Soon after they graduated in 1961, Frank and Janice were married and on March 14, 1964—just nine days before David Camm—Kim was born. She was a beautiful baby with a warm smile, and before long her parents realized she was extremely smart.

In 1966 the Renns had another daughter named Deborah, whom Kim would always be very close to.

"She was the big sister that I would always look to," explained Debbie. "We would keep little secrets together and play together."

One of Debbie's earliest memories is of them both being sent to their separate rooms by their mother as a punishment. They got around it by stretching across the hall between their rooms, so they could meet halfway and play cards, without getting in any further trouble.

As they grew older Kim would take Debbie into the bathroom, lock the door and give her makeovers.

"[She] would cut my hair," Debbie explained, "because she thought I needed some bangs."

Growing up, Kim was very quiet and reserved, never

causing her parents any trouble. From infancy she was a stunning-looking girl with thick brown hair, usually cut into a fringe, and dark piercing eyes. She always had friends, but was also very secretive, never discussing her problems with anyone, even her mother.

Years later her mother would describe her daughter as somewhat withdrawn.

"Kim was quiet [and] shy," Janice Renn said. "She kept her personal things to herself. She was just not an outspoken person."

Although Kim rarely complained, her mother could usually tell when something was bothering her. The quiet teenager would become "more withdrawn" and "look like she was tired or just not with it."

By the time she started New Albany High School, Kim began to shine academically. Her teachers knew she was going places.

"She was just always smart, very intelligent," her mother remembered. "Everything came easy to her."

With boundless energy, as a sophomore she became an enthusiastic junior varsity football cheerleader for the New Albany High School Bulldogs. Kim was pictured several times in the 1981 high school yearbook cheering on the team. Another photo shows the attractive brunette cheerleader posing in her miniskirted uniform with six of her friends, radiating smiles.

She also served on the student council and was pictured in a group shot including her best friend, Marcy Mahurin, who would remain close to Kim for the rest of her life.

In the 1982 *Vista*, Kim, then in her junior year, dominated with more mentions than almost anyone else, including a photo of the raven-haired 18-year-old studying in Mr. Fleshman's third period history class.

"She was what I would call a good student," remembered Fleshman, who is now retired. "She was a hard worker."

On another page she's pictured doing high kicks during a pep session, as a first year member of the newly inaugurated pom-pom squad. Kim and the rest of the twenty-four-member team practiced their complex dancing routines for six hours a week, successfully competing against teams from all over Indiana that summer. To pay for their smart uniforms, Kim and her other team members organized car washes and bake sales around the New Albany area.

She was also an active member of the school's Square Dance Club as well as the WNAS-FM Radio Club, although there is no record to indicate if she ever broadcast.

Somehow Kim also found time that summer to get a part-time job at Target to earn extra money. Already the teenager had developed a tough work ethic, apparently needing little time to relax.

In 1983 Kim graduated with honors and once again she totally dominated that year's *Vista* yearbook. Now in her senior year she had adopted a more sophisticated look, sporting a Farrah Fawcett–type hairstyle in her official Class of '83 photograph.

She looked stunning in a rented black lacy prom dress, as one of the candidates for that year's New Albany High School Prom Queen. But she failed to win, losing to her classmate Karen James.

After her last class on the final day of school, Kim and a group of her senior friends celebrated by taking a road trip to the Kings Island amusement park in Cincinnati.

"Seniors' Trip to Cincinnati Rounds Out A Year Full of Pondering, Playing, Partying," read the headline in *Vista* over a picture of the rowdy group trying to get as many seniors on a car hood as possible.

But "camera-shy Kim Renn" has her head turned away, as if deliberately removing herself from the stunt.

After graduating, Kim enrolled in an accounting course at Indiana University Southeast, in New Albany. There she may well have crossed paths with David Camm, who was also there, studying police administration.

Indiana University Southeast began awarding degrees in 1968 and its motto is "Excellence Close to Home." It proudly boasts of providing "high-quality education" on its beautiful 177-acre site in the "Knobs" part of southern Indiana.

Kim loved the university and after three years of studies she graduated with top grades in accounting. She immediately started applying for jobs to companies in Louisville and had little trouble finding employment.

On December 12, 1986, she began work as an intern at the accounting department at the Capital Holding Insurance Corporation. It would later be acquired in 1997 by the Aegon Insurance Company, one of the five largest insurance companies in the world.

The enthusiastic young woman so impressed her bosses that three months later she was put on the payroll full-time.

"Kim was an excellent employee," said Aegon's director of human resources, Sharon Long, who worked with her from the beginning. "She was very intelligent and hard-working."

Kim worked in the company's downtown Louisville offices, just a fifteen-minute drive across the Ohio River Bridge from her parents' home on Pamela Drive, in New Albany.

In January 1988, after working there thirteen months, Kim was given three months off to return to school to study for another accounting degree. After taking her exams she returned to work in March, where her professional future looked bright.

When 23-year-old Kim went on the blind date with David Camm, both were looking for love. On the surface they appeared to be very different. Kim was starting to make her way in the corporate world and dressed for success, whereas the painfully thin, six-foot-one-inch David Camm was pure blue-collar, his hands always covered in spray paint and grease.

Yet they found much in common, sharing a love for NASCAR and Indiana University basketball. Camm seemed especially fascinated with the petite, five-foot-three-inch Kim's regular monthly Bunco night with her girlfriends. He did his best to impress her, cooking elaborate romantic candlelit dinners on their early dates.

Although both were naturally shy and reserved, they immediately felt comfortable in each other's company. Later they would tell friends it had been love at first sight.

"She was very quiet, but Dave was even quieter," said his sister, Julie. "She was just a sweet, genuinely kind person—that almost sounds cliché, but it's very true."

And 24-year-old David Camm also impressed Kim's family with his good manners and single-minded ambition, verging on obsession, to become a state trooper.

"We all liked him," said Kim's younger sister, Debbie. "He was a polite guy—quiet, kind of shy. He made her happy."

Although Kim was far smarter and more academically inclined than he was, she supported him with his Police Administration studies at Indiana University Southeast.

When Camm proposed marriage, Kim immediately agreed to become his wife. She had already met 5-year-old Whitney and they got on well, although there would always be tension between her and David's ex-wife Tammy.

The May 3 edition of the New Albany *Tribune* carried a two-column wedding announcement, including a large picture of the happy couple, both smiling radiantly at the camera.

"If there's anybody who wanted to get married, have 2.5 kids and a white picket fence, that was Kim," her sister, Debbie, would tell CBS-TV's *48 Hours*. "Being a little sister, I thought he was nice and he was cute. And to me he seemed to bring Kim out more as a person."

Camm's extended family was delighted David had found a second wife with such good prospects. And a big May wedding was arranged at the First Church of God in New Albany, which could hold more guests than the Georgetown Community Church.

Once again David's Uncle Leland would be presiding over the service, the one problem being that Kim's family was Catholic. But her fiancé soon persuaded her to renounce her faith and become Protestant, much to the dismay of her parents.

In addition to his upcoming marriage, David Camm was also preoccupied with his imminent entrance exam for the Indiana State Police. He and Kim were planning a week's honeymoon to Florida to stay with his brother Donnie, and he worried it might clash with the interview.

On April 15, 1989, Kim helped him type a letter to a Lieutenant Johnson at the Indiana State Police headquarters in Indianapolis, explaining his predicament.

"I am writing in regards to my interview date," it began.

I understand that the interview dates will run from May 1st through May 26th. However, I will be getting married on Saturday, May 13th and will be out of state through Sunday, May 21. I understand that you have certain rules and regulations you must follow, but I would appreciate your cooperation in scheduling my interview date around this time period. Please advise me as soon as possible if this will be a problem.

Sincerely,
David R. Camm,
Trooper Applicant.

Within a week of his wedding he received a letter scheduling the interview at his convenience.

The stringent exam consisted of a written test, an oral

interview, a polygraph, and psychological evaluation. He also had to submit to a thorough background investigation as well as undergo a fitness examination.

It would be five months until he would hear the result, and know if he had achieved his dream of becoming one of Indiana's Finest.

David and Kim were married at 7:00 p.m. on Saturday, May 13, at the First Church of God in New Albany. Frank Renn led his beautiful 25-year-old daughter down the aisle, where the Reverend Leland Lockhart performed the ceremony. And if Kim's family were unhappy she had converted to Protestantism, they never showed it.

The bride looked beautiful in a snow-white wedding gown with a long flowing train and veil, a single string of pearls adorning her long neck. As she held a bouquet of her favorite white lilies, a big, broad grin lit up her face. The handsome groom wore a black tuxedo with a white silk shirt and white bowtie, sporting a boutonniere. Also in the wedding was David's daughter Whitney, dressed like a little bride in a long white dress and carrying a bouquet.

At the climax of Uncle Leland's moving ceremony, the bride and groom took lighted candles and symbolically lit one bigger candle on the altar, to symbolize their unity forever.

"It was a very sweet wedding," remembered Julie Hogue, who has a video of it. "It was a wonderful day."

After the ceremony all the guests went to the Redman Club for the official wedding reception. For the first time ever at a Lockhart family wedding, alcohol was served.

"Well, in our church you don't drink," explained Julie. "And so our wedding receptions have always consisted of cake and punch. Then you leave."

But as the Renn family were Catholic, there was alcohol, as well as a DJ playing music, and dancing.

"So we had a blast," said Julie. "People would probably

say that it was the most fun wedding reception our family had ever experienced."

The festivities went on late into the night and David's Uncle Sam personally interviewed all the guests for the official wedding video.

Best man Donnie Camm remembers it going off without a snag.

"It was a sizeable, big wedding," he said. "Everybody had tons of fun. Lots of people. Perfect."

After the wedding the bride and groom flew to Tampa to stay with Donnie, who had been living there with his wife since 1982. A week later they returned to New Albany to start their new life together.

5

The Indiana State Police

David and Kim moved into an apartment complex in New Albany, where they lived for the first few months of their marriage. And soon Camm received an official letter, informing him that the Indiana State Police (ISP) had accepted him, starting in November.

Delighted, he phoned his Uncle Nelson Lockhart, who had recently left the Kentucky State Police to become a captain in the Jefferson County Police Department.

"He told me," said Nelson, " 'The day some police department hires me I'll do a 360-degree dunk.' "

David Camm was officially sworn in as an Indiana State Trooper in November 1989, before being sent to the Police Academy for basic training. Then he was assigned to the Indiana State Police post in Scottsburg, Indiana, twenty-five miles north of New Albany on Route 65.

The newly married couple rented a nearby apartment and for the next few months Kim commuted thirty miles each way to her job, where she was making more than twice her husband's salary.

In early 1990 Trooper Camm was transferred to Sellersburg, which was much nearer New Albany than Scottsburg. So he and Kim rented a house at Dendal Court in Edwardsville, a couple of miles east of Georgetown, to be near his grandfather Amos and the rest of his family.

During his first few months as an Indiana State Trooper, David impressed his superiors with his hard work and dedication. He loved his job, driving out on duty in his smart new trooper uniform and wearing his gun belt low, like he'd seen in old Westerns. And he apparently enjoyed the admiring glances he was now receiving from the ladies.

"[His] ego got pretty puffed up," explained his sister, Julie. "[He had] all this pride in being a state trooper."

Julie, whose ex-husband was a law enforcement officer, believes it is deliberate ISP policy to flatter their troopers so they willingly accept low wages.

Soon the rookie trooper found himself being given special assignments, like escorting VIPs around town or acting as a press liaison on special occasions.

"When they needed a trooper [for someone] to ride around with, they would select Dave," said Julie. "He was doing very well."

It seemed that for the first time Camm felt valued and important, no longer struggling with low self-esteem and a lack of confidence.

"He discovered that he had some real gifts and talents," observed his sister. "And he was getting a lot of accolades."

In his first few months at Sellersburg Post 45, David Camm's whole personality changed. His nervous insecurity was replaced by arrogance.

"He got pretty pompous," admits Julie. "He went through a period where he got pretty confident and was really loving who he was."

His mentor, Chief Randy Hubbard, would frequently see Camm, either at the ISP post or at the New Albany police building, where they would discuss police business.

"He knew he was good," said Hubbard. "He was very cocky."

In his second year as a trooper, even Camm was surprised when he was handpicked for the elite Emergency Response Team, the ISP's version of a Special Weapons and Tactics team (SWAT).

He was now part of a ten-strong team of officers responsible for covering one-quarter of the State of Indiana.

And during the six years he served in the ERT, he worked murders, kidnappings and even a helicopter crash.

"He liked being in the ERT Team," said his brother Donnie. "It was fun and exciting."

Trooper Camm trained with the state-of-the-art Heckler & Koch MP5 Submachine Gun, and was considered an expert marksman. The powerful 9mm air-cooled, magazine-fed weapon can either be shouldered or hand fired.

An acronym for Machine Pistol 5, MP5s were first used by West German police and border patrols at the Berlin Wall. In the early 1970s, they were first imported into the U.S., soon becoming a favored special weapon for the military and law enforcement.

"[It's] like you would see on TV," Camm would later testify. "I'm a good shot. We had advanced training. More training than the average trooper."

The MP5 employed a high-tech red-dot laser aiming device to help troopers find their targets. And each month Camm and his team members were issued enough ammunition to last through training, as he would throughout his time with the State Police. Years later some of Camm's ammunition rations would be discovered in his basement, where he secretly hoarded them.

During his career with the Indiana State Police, David Camm would handle many weapons, including the infamous Beretta .380 semiautomatic handgun. But he would proudly say that he had never shot a weapon at anyone, although he would later boast that there had been opportunities.

"I probably should have [on one occasion], but didn't," he would later admit cryptically.

Trooper Camm still suffered from his "stinking headaches," that had started when he was in third grade. His doctor was now prescribing Imitrex, a strong medication to be taken at the onset of a migraine. Possible side effects listed were dizziness, weakness, nausea and stiffness, which could affect his performance on the Emergency Response Team.

Camm could go weeks without an attack and then have migraines daily until they passed again.

"He often had to go to the emergency room while he was working as a trooper," said his mother, Susie. "They got used to him coming there."

Camm was also prone to many allergies which could set off an attack of migraine anytime, making it difficult if he had one on duty.

"I have certain triggers that set them off as far as things that I eat," Camm explained. "They're numerous things. It also depends on my eating habits and sleeping habits."

Even so, Trooper Camm worked long hours and most weekends, and with Kim's busy schedule at the insurance company the young couple seldom saw each other. It wasn't long before David succumbed to temptation.

Undoubtedly his police uniform bolstered Camm's confidence with women. On highway patrol, often when he had occasion to pull over an attractive female, he would be flirtatious, and make suggestive comments. He also discovered the phenomenon of "badge bunnies"—women who enjoyed romancing troopers.

Easy sex appeared to be an unofficial perk at the Sellersburg post, where officers often boasted in the recreation room about their latest conquests.

"With the group that I ran with, it seemed to be part of the job description," Camm would later testify. "There were numerous individuals that I worked with that had the same things going on that I did."

Post 45's communications officer, Andrea Newland, often heard troopers' bawdy conversations about their badge bunny conquests during the three years she worked there.

"It's probably everywhere," she said. "My dad works for the sheriff's department and I've heard it [there]."

Donnie Camm, who often visited his brother at the post,

said troopers treated the badge bunnies as a competitive sport. "I'd be around the other troopers and they'd all be bragging about their conquests. And they were all married."

The Sellersburg troopers even had their own secluded lay-by on Route 64, where they brought available women for sex, usually in the back seats of their state police cars.

"That wasn't just Dave out there doing that," said Donnie. "That was a spot that all the police officers knew about [and] took their women. Look, they have badges, they have power, they have uniforms, sirens and lights, and certain women gravitate to them."

Some of the more promiscuous badge bunnies had slept with ten or more troopers, and the women's performances would later be rated back at the post.

"They would compare notes," Donnie said. "They would talk about them, saying, 'So-and-so did this, you ought to go and see this girl.'"

And there were also affairs between married Indiana State Troopers, which their superiors would conveniently turn a blind eye to.

In 1991 David Camm was promoted to the rank of Field Training Officer (FTO), along with several of his colleagues. He was now on the fast track, looking set to fulfill his ambition of a successful career in law enforcement.

"I'd only been on the department for two years," he explained. "Lord knows why they made me an FTO [but] I was picked and chosen."

As a field trainer Camm worked one-on-one with new recruits, supervising them at the beginning and end of a three-month training program. One of his first trainees was an attractive blonde rookie named Shelley Romero, who was in her early twenties. Before long they were having a passionate affair.

David would recall the affair beginning over lunch at

the KingFish Restaurant in Louisville. "I had her for three weeks as her field training officer," Camm would later testify. "We became friends, but the relationship progressed."

The two went from professional colleagues to sexual partners over a matter of weeks, and they would sleep together on and off for the next two years, according to Romero. Later David would claim the affair lasted just five or six weeks, but Trooper Romero, who still serves with the Indiana State Police, maintains it continued until June 1993, before becoming platonic.

"We would meet," said Camm. "See each other off and on, mainly during the course of of while we were working."

Kim Camm was apparently oblivious to the affair, and would never know the full extent of David's womanizing. By nature she was trusting, accepting his various excuses for not coming home. And although at this time he was involved with several women besides Trooper Romero, he appeared sincere about starting a family with Kim, and becoming a father.

But in the summer of 1992, as he and Kim planned to have a baby, David would meet a new woman who would almost break up his marriage.

Stephanie McCarty was a personal trainer in a New Albany gym called the Fitness Zone, which gave discounts to police officers. Soon after the health club opened in December 1991, Camm became a member, working out several times a week. Before long he had struck up a friendship with McCarty, sharing small talk and spotting each other on the equipment.

But at that time it never went further, as Stephanie was living with the gym's general manager, Mark Abbott.

"[Dave] was very friendly, nice," remembered McCarty, who had heard through friends he was married. " 'Hi. How are you doing?' Small talk."

One night, soon after they met, Stephanie found herself

sitting in front of David Camm and his wife at a local bodybuilding contest. Camm came over and introduced her to Kim and they had a short conversation.

Over the next few months Camm would pay the shapely dark-haired trainer more and more attention, and when her relationship with Abbott broke up, he was there immediately to offer a helping hand.

On a freezing Saturday morning in January 1992, Trooper David Camm was on duty when a call came in from two brothers who had discovered the naked, charred remains of a young girl on a lonely county road outside New Albany. When Camm arrived he was so traumatized at the sight of 12-year-old Shanda Sharer's butchered body, he burst into tears.

"It was such an emotional upset to [David]," said his Aunt Debbie TerVree, "that he went to his mother and broke down and cried like a baby."

The murdered 12-year-old, whose 16-year-old lesbian girlfriend Melinda Loveless and two female friends would later be found guilty of torturing and then killing Shanda, was the subject of a bestselling True Crime book by Aphrodite Jones.

"It really disturbed him," said his sister, Julie. "David had a habit of stumbling upon some pretty tragic things in his time as a trooper."

When Kim, at 28, discovered she was pregnant, her husband was delighted. For a while he made an effort to spend more time at home, as they began planning their future with a new baby. And right up to her due date in early 1993, Kim never let up in her busy schedule, working full-time at her accounting job.

Bradley Ray Camm was born on February 1, 1993, in New Albany. He was a beautiful, healthy blond baby and his father beamed with pride and joy, showing off his new son to his family.

"He was my little grandson," said Susie Camm. "Everybody just loved Brad because he had such a great personality."

Although, like his parents, Brad was quiet and reserved, right from infancy he loved dressing up and was unusually sensitive to other people's feelings.

"Brad was very soft-spoken," remembered his grandmother, who mostly looked after him as a baby, while his parents were at work. "He had a gentle way about him."

Camm's daughter Whitney, now 10 years old, fussed over her new half-brother and was always over at her father's house, playing with him. Brad worshipped her.

A few months after Brad's birth, Kim's company—recently taken over by the Provident Insurance Company—moved into an imposing new skyscraper, the National City Tower, in downtown Louisville. Situated on 5th Street and West Market, the gleaming 35-storey steel-fronted concrete-and-glass building totally dominated the skyline, and could be seen for miles.

Kim loved her accounting job. All her hard work and dedication had already ensured several promotions and increases in the six years she had been with the company. Somehow she managed to effortlessly juggle being a new mom with a demanding job, and her mother and David's would take turns looking after little Brad during the day.

Unfortunately the little boy's father was rarely at home, always complaining about an Indiana State Trooper's long hours and poor pay.

And although his rotation shifts meant he often worked nights and was on duty five weekends out of every eight, Camm still found time to pursue several young women during this period. Despite his later claims of being a good father, his affair with Trooper Shelley Romero continued until four months after Brad's birth, according to Romero's account.

In late 1992, Trooper Camm visited his childhood friend Sean Clemons at home. It was the first time the two young men had seen each other for a while, and after shaking hands Camm got to the point of why he'd come.

"[He] asked me to become a trooper," Clemons would recall. "He assisted me in the capacity of letting me know what the selection process entailed."

Camm told his friend what life was like in the Indiana State Police and Clemons decided it was a great opportunity and filled out an application to start the selection process.

Eventually, after he was accepted, Clemons worked alongside Camm at Sellersburg as a road trooper.

"We held the same rank," recalled Clemons. "He had more tenure than me, though."

6

Stephanie McCarty

In summer 1994, Stephanie McCarty walked out on her live-in boyfriend, Mark Abbott, generating much gossip at the Fitness Zone gym. On hearing the news David Camm offered a sympathetic ear, before making his move.

"There was just an attraction there," Stephanie would later explain. "We started talking a little more in the gym [and] got along really well."

Soon they were dating. Several nights a week they'd meet for dinner and then go on to a nightclub, and on their nights apart they would talk on the phone. Then occasionally on weekends, Camm would tell Kim he was on duty and take Stephanie to NASCAR races.

And surprisingly Camm never attempted to hide their relationship, often taking her out in public around the New Albany and Louisville areas. Stephanie would later claim their relationship didn't turn intimate for some months, as she knew he was married with two children.

On their dates Camm often spoke about problems in his marriage, saying he wanted to divorce Kim, as he was not happy. McCarty believed him, thinking their relationship might have a future.

"I was hoping that we would be together," she would later explain. "The two children didn't bother me. I'd known Whitney since she was little, since Dave started coming into the gym. And I really liked Brad. He was a very sweet little boy."

Soon after Camm started dating McCarty, Kim became pregnant again. She was overjoyed at the prospect of having another baby, apparently oblivious to her husband's unfaithfulness.

Then Camm began taking chances, almost as if he wanted his wife to find out about his adultery. He even invited Stephanie to the Sellersburg post, and it was common knowledge with the troopers he was cheating on Kim.

"I met him up there when he was on duty one night," remembered McCarty. "I was just up there hanging out with him."

But even if Kim was apparently the last to know, Camm's family began to suspect he was up to something as he became even more full of himself.

"Everybody knew something was going on with Dave," explained his sister, Julie. "He was just too cocky and just a little more aloof. He was just not the same old Dave."

Julie sensed that secretly he felt guilty about cheating on Kim, finding it increasingly difficult to be around his family. For he was only too well aware how strongly they condemned adultery, which they considered a grievous sin.

One afternoon in November, David Camm invited his girlfriend to visit his house, assuring her that they would be alone, as Kim was at work. The trooper was becoming increasingly frustrated that they still hadn't had sex, and was planning to seduce her. Stephanie agreed to come over and, after getting directions to his house, drove there in her blue Firebird.

"I just wanted to go out and spend some time with him," she would later explain, "but I didn't have a lot of time that day." As she was due to start her shift at the gym at 3:30 p.m., she planned to spend an hour with him first.

After parking in the driveway at the front of the house, David Camm brought her down to the basement, where there was a comfortable couch. A few minutes later as they were kissing they suddenly heard the garage door opening.

"That's Kim," hissed an exasperated Camm, as he got up and rushed to the window. Alarmed at the prospect of being caught, Stephanie dashed out the door, ran up some stairs and exited through some rear sliding glass doors.

Then to her horror she realized she had left her car keys in the house.

"I wasn't sure how I was gonna get out of there," she said. "I had no car."

But Camm, staying cool, had picked up her keys and managed to sneak out of the house without Kim seeing him. He drove her to a neighboring yard and Stephanie vaulted over a fence to join him.

"We were both very startled," she remembered. "We were surprised."

Camm then drove McCarty's car to a nearby gas station, calling another trooper en route on his cell phone to pick him up. As he drove off with the trooper, McCarty went to the gym for her afternoon shift.

"I was just relieved to be out of there," she would later testify. "I was nervous."

Later that day, Kim asked her husband about the blue Firebird parked in her driveway. Without missing a beat, Camm told her it was an undercover state police vehicle he had been using on duty.

Sounding angry that Kim had spoiled his long-planned seduction, David Camm called Stephanie's cell phone a few hours later that night, informing her Kim was five weeks pregnant. Camm emotionlessly explained that her pregnancy was "bad timing," as they had been having problems. He claimed he had only just found out, as Kim had waited a few weeks to tell him.

But if he thought the bombshell news would bring him closer to Stephanie he was wrong.

"The thought of another baby, and his wife being pregnant just really got to me," she said. "But it made me doubt any relationship with him at that point."

Upset, Stephanie told him their relationship was over and they should stay friends. She also informed him that she wouldn't be joining him and his brother Donnie for a long-anticipated trip to Atlanta they'd planned for the following weekend, for the NAPA 500 NASCAR race.

The Camm brothers rented a car anyway and drove to Atlanta for the race, where they were joined by Indiana State Trooper Mark Slaughter and a couple of other officers. They took several hotel rooms near the racetrack, with David and Donnie sharing one of them.

But Camm started missing Stephanie and on Friday night, soon after they had checked in to their hotel, he telephoned, begging her to fly to Atlanta and join him.

"I told him I didn't know if I could get out of there that soon," she said.

In the end Camm was so persuasive, she took up his offer to buy her a plane ticket, managing to get on a last-minute flight.

"I just wanted to see him," she said. "Plus I really wanted to go to the race."

At Atlanta Airport, Stephanie was met by David, who took her to his hotel on the shuttle bus and straight to the room he was sharing with Donnie, who had made himself scarce that night.

"She was a dark-haired bombshell," Donnie would later remember. "She was very pretty. But I really didn't know her very well."

McCarty spent the night in the Camm brothers' room, falling asleep before Donnie returned. Then on Saturday they all went to the Atlanta Speedway to see the NAPA 500 race. Although Stephanie would later say she and David acted like a couple that weekend, Donnie Camm says he had no idea they were romantically involved until far later.

After the race the three of them went out for dinner and on to some clubs. Then David Camm drove them back to New Albany in the early morning hours.

After his romantic weekend in Atlanta, David Camm threw caution to the wind and soon even Kim, now five months pregnant, suspected something was up. She had noticed how her husband had distanced himself from her and been acting strangely lately. So one night in late November she confronted him about her suspicions in their living room.

"I was sitting on the couch and she was sitting on a chair facing me," Camm would later testify. "She said, 'David, what is going on? What is wrong? I know something's not right.' And that's when I told her."

Kim's eyes went blank in disbelief as he coldly told her about his affair with McCarty, and how he'd met her in the gym.

"Kim, in her wisdom didn't ask a whole lot of questions," explained Camm, "as far as who, what, where, when, why. But I told her what I was doing."

Camm then told his visibly pregnant wife that he no longer wanted to be married to her and was in love with somebody else.

Devastated, Kim burst into tears and picked up their 20-month-old son Brad, telling Camm it was *she* who was leaving. Half an hour later Kim arrived at her parents' house in New Albany with baby Brad, sobbing that David was having an affair.

"She was carrying Brad and crying," remembered Kim's mother, Janice Renn. "[She] mostly just cried and was upset."

Tearfully, Kim told her mother how she had known something was wrong, as David was not acting normal.

"So she confronted him," said Janice. "He said he just didn't want to be married anymore," said Janice.

That night Kim and Brad temporarily moved into her parents' house, staying in a spare bedroom. Just two months shy of her thirtieth birthday, with an infant son and another on the way, Kim Camm's life lay in tatters. But she knew she had to stay strong for Brad and her new baby, and would have to rise above the situation to survive.

Early the next morning Kim returned to their Edwardsville house, asking her husband to leave. She then went to work, saying she would stay with her family until he had moved his belongings out.

Camm telephoned his mother and informed her he was divorcing Kim, asking if he could move back until he could find somewhere permanent. But Susie Camm was furious at David's adultery. For the very first time ever she told him no, refusing to let him move back home.

"I said, 'No, you're not going to come back here,' " said his mother. " 'You can't do this to her. You're wrong and I'm not going to support you.' And that was the one time he ever got mad at me."

When his mother refused to let him move home Camm went berserk, and started smashing up his house, completely wrecking the kitchen. He broke one of the kitchen chairs and then repeatedly slammed it against the roof of the dining area, puncturing the ceiling in several places.

His mother was so alarmed by his violent outburst she put down the phone, immediately calling the Sellersburg post, requesting urgent help.

Trooper Hugh Couch took her distressed call and tried to calm her down, as she explained how her son had become extremely emotional after his wife had left him.

"She said he was tearing up the inside [of his house]," Trooper Couch would later testify. "She asked if we could send someone over to calm him down."

Trooper Couch promised to send an officer over to Camm's house, immediately informing his superior, Lieutenant Monty McKee, as it involved another police officer.

As post commander, McKee had been in charge of David Camm since he had first become a trooper five years earlier. So he and Trooper Dale Traughber personally drove to the Camm house to take care of matters themselves.

"David was embarrassed," Lieutenant McKee would later remember. "He had lost his temper and torn his kitchen up, so to speak."

Camm stressed he had not tried to injure his wife, accusing his mother of overreacting. He admitted having had an affair, telling them he was "mad" at himself and all the trouble was "over this issue of another woman."

After spending an hour with Camm, they left, satisfied that he didn't pose a threat to anyone. A few hours later Julie Hogue telephoned her brother to find out what was going on. Then he broke down on the phone, admitting his affair with Stephanie McCarty and saying he wanted to be with her.

"I told him, 'Davie, you need to think about what you're doing,'" said Julie. "And of course he was confused."

Julie would also accuse her mother of overreacting with her call to the police, maintaining that her brother was merely being theatrical and not endangering himself or anyone else.

"Emotionally he was a bit of a wreck," she would explain. "Dave was in a bad spot and didn't know what to do. Basically he was broken, distraught and emotionally really screwed up."

No official report from the Indiana State Police was

even filed on the incident and there would be no follow-up investigation. Trooper Camm's record remained spotless and everyone would forget about his uncharacteristic fit of rage for another six years.

7

A Vision From God

A few days later, David Camm met Kim to discuss their future. Reluctantly she agreed the marriage was over and their house should be sold immediately. Camm said Kim and Brad could remain there until it was sold, while he searched for his own apartment.

On Monday, November 21, 1994, David Camm applied for a $300-a-month rental at the Lochwood Apartments on Slate Run Road in New Albany. He paid a $300 deposit to secure the one-bedroom apartment, taking advantage of the police discount he was entitled to. On his application form he stated he earned $24,000 a year as a state trooper and owned two cars. The following day his application was approved, without a credit check being run. Eight days later David Camm moved into his apartment in downtown New Albany to resume his bachelor life.

And in the first week of December, Stephanie McCarty moved into an apartment next door, with a friend named Mary-Beth Conley.

That same week Kim also found an apartment near her parents on Slate Creek in New Albany, moving in with Brad. She was now six months pregnant and found herself having to rely on the good will of David's family to care for her son while she was at work.

"The family pretty much took Kim's side," said Donnie Camm. "Nobody took David's side. My mom had more than one discussion with David about being wrong, and he shouldn't be doing that. That just wasn't the way we were raised."

Soon after she separated from David, Kim called her best friend, Marcy McLeod, formerly Mahurin, with whom she had stayed in close touch since they were in New Albany High School together. Since they'd graduated, Marcy had married, moving to Florida but regularly visiting Kim at Christmas or Harvest Homecoming.

In all the years they had known each other Marcy had never heard Kim so distraught, as she broke down on the phone saying David was having an affair and no longer loved her.

"It's probably one of the first times I've ever heard her really cry," said Marcy.

Kim's mother, Janice, was also very worried about her daughter, and tried to broker a reconciliation with David, before their new baby was born.

"I knew she never really discussed her personal feelings with me," said Janice. "But I told her she really needed to talk to somebody."

Kim finally agreed to let her mother call David's Uncle Leland Lockhart, pastor of the Georgetown Community Church, who had performed their marriage ceremony.

"So I called him and he came over," Janice said. "[Kim was] still upset."

Tearfully Kim told Pastor Lockhart how David didn't want to be married anymore. The kindly preacher sympathized with her plight, promising to talk to his nephew as soon as possible.

As Christmas approached there didn't seem to be much for the Lockharts to celebrate. The whole family was pressuring David to leave McCarty and return to his wife and son. But he refused point-blank, saying that for the first time in his life he was really in love.

Most nights when he wasn't on duty Stephanie stayed

overnight in Camm's new apartment, and they were planning to spend the holidays together with her family.

On Christmas Day, after finishing his shift, David Camm was still in uniform when he drove to Stephanie's father's house in Clarksville to join in her family celebrations.

"He stopped by while we were opening presents," remembered McCarty, adding that her father was aware of their relationship.

And it would be the first Christmas that David didn't spend with his parents and family, who went to the Renns' house to provide emotional support for Kim.

"Davy was too embarrassed to come around here," said his mother. "I had told him I didn't approve of what he had done. I mean, Kim was like my daughter."

In the weeks leading up to Kim giving birth, she spent more and more time at her in-laws'. Most nights after finishing work she drove back to New Albany, picked up Brad from his babysitter, and ate dinner with Susie and Don Camm. Then her father-in-law would drive Kim and Brad back to her apartment and stay and help bathe Brad before putting him to bed.

Debbie Karem said her sister absolutely refused to discuss her marital breakup, as she was so upset.

"She was very, very quiet about that," said Debbie. "We were worried about the baby. But she didn't talk about it, and we didn't press the issue."

On February 28, 1995, Kim gave birth to a baby girl she named Jill. Her parents and in-laws were there at the hospital but the new father kept a low profile. A few days after the birth, Kim's best friend, Marcy McLeod—formerly Mahurin—flew in from Florida to visit and see the new baby.

She met Kim in her small apartment, where she was

nursing Jill, as well as looking after 2-year-old Brad, who was still in diapers.

On the other side of New Albany, David Camm and Stephanie McCarty were virtually living together. But after Jill was born, Stephanie began to feel increasingly uncomfortable with the situation, and was considering breaking up with Camm.

One night in early March, she went over to her old boyfriend Mark Abbott's house on Fenwick Drive in New Albany, to give him some tickets and discuss their future. She arrived at about 10:30 p.m. and when she hadn't returned to the Lochwood Apartments by midnight David Camm started to panic.

"[Mark and I] were discussing how we were going to work together, and remain friends," she remembered. "So I was over there really late."

At 4:30 a.m. Abbott went to open up the gym, leaving McCarty at his house. About an hour later the telephone rang and it was David, who'd tracked her down to the house, less than five minutes' drive away from Lochwood.

"Good morning," he said coldly. "You need to meet me back at the apartment."

McCarty drove her blue Firebird straight to the Lochwood Apartments. As she pulled into the parking lot she saw David Camm, waiting for her on a public landing at the side of the building, wearing a denim jacket.

"He asked me why I was there at Mark's so long," McCarty would later testify. "I explained that we were just talking . . . about the relationship."

Then to her horror David pulled his black 9mm service revolver from his jacket, and pointed it at his own chest.

"What were you doing over there?" he asked again, shaking with emotion. "Well, I'll just end it right here."

McCarty told him to put the gun away so they could

talk it out, but Camm refused, saying he could "end it right here."

Once again, she asked him to be rational and put the gun away. This time he put down the gun and they went into his apartment, where he dropped the weapon on the way to the bedroom.

"I wasn't scared he was going to do anything," she later explained. "I just wanted to get him off that landing so we weren't outside in public."

Then Stephanie told him it was best if they didn't see each other anymore, as she felt uncomfortable with Kim's pregnancy. Later she would say that him pulling the gun that night had been the last straw.

"He was upset," McCarty said. "He said that Kim still loved him and that he could go back to her if he wanted to. I told him that was the best thing to do."

Then without another word, she gathered up her night-gown and a toothbrush and walked towards the front door, which Camm was holding open. As she walked out he slammed the door behind her. It would be the last time she would see him for almost five years.

A few hours later David Camm phoned his estranged wife, asking her to meet with him to discuss their futures. Kim told her mother about the meeting and then called back a little later to announce they had reconciled.

"She said she wanted to give it another try," remembered Janice Renn. "She still loved him and she wanted to make it work."

Janice told her daughter she would "stand behind her," but warned her never to take on more than she could handle.

Even Camm's family were surprised at how forgiving Kim had been, after what he had put her through during her pregnancy.

"Kim was more patient than a lot of women would have been," said Julie. "She didn't overreact. She didn't get overly emotional."

"I think Kim's ability to forgive was pretty huge," said Donnie Camm. "Kim being pregnant with Jill was probably the catalyst for them getting back."

In fact David Camm never told his family that Stephanie McCarty had broken up with him, failing to ever mention that he had pulled a gun and threatened suicide. Instead he told Julie and his parents that his grandfather Amos' prayers had been answered for him to have a vision from God, ordering him back to the family fold.

"I know this might sound crazy," said Julie. "He dreamed that the baby was born and then he woke up, thinking, 'What am I doing here? I've got a baby on the way. I've got Brad, I've got Kim—What am I thinking!'"

Seven years later David Camm would explain how he had seen a vision from God, telling him to return to his family. But by that time he had received so many other divine visions that some would wonder if it wasn't a little too convenient.

After David Camm returned to his family, his grandfather encouraged him to build a new house, directly opposite his own in rural Georgetown. The land around Lockhart Road had once comprised Amos' farm, before he had developed it into a family compound of just seven houses.

David and Kim willingly accepted his offer, hiring builders to construct the house next door to his Uncle Leland's and in front of his Aunt Debbie's.

"Davy was crazy about his Pappaw," said his mother Susie. "My parents were getting old, so Dave wanted to be there to look after them and mow the lawn and things like that."

During the eight months it took to build the house, Kim

and her two children moved into David's two-bedroom unit in the Lochwood Apartments.

But David Camm's claims of divine intervention bringing him back to the path of righteousness were short-lived. And soon he would once again fall prey to temptation.

8

Hero

After moving back with Kim, David seemed contrite, going to great lengths to pay her extra attention. His behavior over the next few months convinced her family he had mended his ways and the marriage was back on track.

For a while he spent more time at home with Brad and Jill, taking special interest in the little boy, who followed him everywhere. And when he came home at night he spent time fussing over Jill.

On August 13, 1995, David Camm became a bona fide hero when he risked his life attempting to save a drowning man at the bottom of a swimming pool. It was 2:00 in the morning, and Trooper Camm had just dropped a prisoner off at Floyd County Jail. He was driving home when a distress call from the New Albany Police Department came over his cruiser scanner, the dispatcher summoning help to the View Pointe Apartment Homes for a possible drowning.

David Camm was the first on the scene, just seconds before New Albany Police Officer Dan Dickey. He walked in to find a small crowd standing around the pool, helplessly pointing at the body of a man lying at the bottom of the ten-foot-deep end. Stripping off his uniform, Camm dived into the pool to try to rescue him. Missing the first time, he came out and immediately dove in again. This time he successfully dragged the body up to the surface, where Officer Dickey helped Camm pull the man out and lay him out by the side of the pool.

Camm administered CPR but it was too late to save the

man, who had been drinking and died without regaining consciousness.

"I thought, 'Holy mackerel,' " Camm later told New Albany *Tribune* reporter Les Reynold for a front-page story. "Talk about an adrenaline rush."

The following day Trooper Camm personally visited the dead man's family, who thanked him for his bravery.

"It was awfully emotional," Camm told the reporter. "I was so hands-on."

New Albany Police Chief Randy Hubbard had also been at the pool, witnessing Camm's heroics. He later wrote to Indiana State Police Superintendent Lloyd Jennings, requesting that his auxiliary officer receive a special commendation.

So in January 1996, the Indiana State Police Board awarded David Camm the Bronze Star for Valor, making him only the thirty-second officer in department history to receive it.

In fall 1995, David and Kim's new house at 7534 Lockhart Road, Georgetown, was finally completed, and they moved in. After almost six months living in David's cramped two-bedroom apartment, Kim was glad for the extra space for her two young children.

The large cream-colored ranch-style house with a big double garage was on the Lockhart family's own private street. At the entrance of the gravel road was a forbidding sign reading, "Private Property—Keep Out."

It was just a three-minute drive to Pastor Leland Lockhart's Georgetown Community Church, and the Camms soon became regulars, with Kim becoming church treasurer.

Ten miles northwest of Louisville, Georgetown has a population of just over two thousand people, who are served by a dozen churches. Religion plays a key role in this mainly farming community and almost everyone is a regular churchgoer.

To their neighbors the Camms appeared a devoted couple. David made a special effort to look after Pappaw Amos, now in his eighties and suffering from Parkinson's disease. Whenever David had some free time he would walk across Lockhart Road to his grandparents' house for a chat, or to do odd jobs like mowing their lawn.

Despite the demands of two young children, Kim was doing well at work and had just been promoted to senior accountant. Every morning she would get up early and make breakfast, before taking Brad and Jill to their grandmother Janice's house, where they would spend the day.

"[Brad] liked to watch some of the cartoon movies and things," said his grandfather Frank Renn. "He'd pretend he was the character in the play [and] we thought he'd be an actor some day."

Kim would collect them after she finished work and bring them home for dinner, before doing the washing and pressing David's uniform so he'd look his best the next day.

Since he was a state trooper, David Camm's hours were unpredictable. He worked a rotating shift system, so he was often on duty all night. He expected Kim to clean the house, do the laundry and look after the children, as well as working her full-time job.

Kim never complained about her growing workload, which would get even bigger as her children got older. But there was some relief in having so many close relatives living nearby, who also had children the same age as Brad and Jill.

David's Aunt Debbie TerVree lived right behind the Camm house with her ex-policeman husband, Bob, and their daughter, Hannah, who was one year older than Brad.

Hannah was delighted when Brad moved next door and they bonded immediately.

"They were inseparable," said Debbie. "And they played together almost every day at my house, so they had two homes."

During the day Brad and Hannah would play with little Jill under Debbie's watchful eye, and then when Kim came home from work they would all spend the evening together.

"She was like my sister," said Debbie. "She was a sweetheart. Very quiet [and] did things for herself mostly."

After Jill was born, Kim started suffering from headaches and indigestion, but rarely complained.

"I could tell when she had a migraine or when her stomach was bothering her," said TerVree. "Sometimes she'd be laying on the couch and I would go over. I could just tell."

Kim was determined that her new house would be perfect, personally selecting all the kitchen appliances, house fittings and wallpaper. She loved to leaf through interior decorating magazines, often going to Sears or J. C. Penney on shopping expeditions.

Several times a week, after putting their children to bed, Kim and Debbie would hang out, relaxing and talking.

"We had nights," said TerVree. "We would share things. She had domestication magazines and we would sit here and look."

Kim enjoyed dispensing decorating tips, and was always suggesting little ideas to improve Debbie's house.

"And then we'd discuss our children if we were having problems," she said. "Discipline, what should we do? This one's having this problem—so what do you think? That's how we were every day."

In May 1996, the Indiana State Police assigned David Camm to its newly setup Problem-Oriented Policing Squad (P.O.P.) He was now a troubleshooter for the Sellersburg post, in charge of identifying problems facing troopers, and then suggesting creative solutions. The previous year the state police had received a grant to set up the P.O.P. force, and Trooper Camm was in one of five squads set up around Indiana to solve common police problems.

He was delighted, considering it a promotion and a pat on the back from his superiors that they considered him detective material. In the one year he served in the Indiana P.O.P. work force, it received national recognition for its work in fighting a powerful new amphetamine called methcathinone.

Popularly known as "Cat," "Goob," or "Jeff," the highly addictive drug was easily made by mixing Drano and battery acid with over-the-counter asthma medication. Trooper Camm and his P.O.P. colleagues identified a bunch of illegal laboratories around the Bloomington area and made many arrests.

And in 1997, the Indiana State Police officially submitted its work on methcathinone for a national award for excellence.

Trooper David Camm was also still coaching new recruits at the Indiana State Police Academy. And in December 1996 an attractive young trooper named Lori Rumph arrived at Sellersburg to start training. Her firearms instructor was David Camm, who taught her basic tactical firearms training.

After completing her training and becoming a trooper, she would often work with Camm on the road as his subordinate. Off duty they regularly socialized and one night she went out drinking with some troopers to a bar called Coyote's in Louisville. Soon after they arrived David Camm walked in, joining Lori and the other troopers.

"I did two or three beers, probably, that evening," she remembered. "I was not driving."

At one point she and Camm left Coyote's and went to another bar next door, where there was music and dancing. After getting a round of drinks, Lori and Camm began dancing, and then to her surprise the married father of two tried to kiss her on the lips.

"He made advances towards me," she would later recall. "It was a fast song playing, so we weren't dancing close by any means. But he got closer to me and kissed me."

Lori, who knew his domestic situation, pulled away and ordered him to stop, saying she wished to keep their relationship professional. Then Camm stopped kissing her and stepped back, looking dejected. When he asked if he could take her home, she refused.

Observing Camm's unsuccessful attempts to seduce his subordinate was the Sellersburg post's communications officer Andrea Newland, who said it soon became a hot topic of gossip among troopers. The pretty civilian employee was no stranger to Camm's flirtatious behavior, later estimating that he'd come on to her at least twenty times in the years they worked together.

"[He'd] just wink at you," she remembered, "or rubbed my leg under the table in the squad room. Things like that."

Newland, now an elementary schoolteacher, said flirting was just part of life at the Indiana State Police post and no big deal.

And although things never went further, Camm kept tabs on Lori after she left the state police to begin teaching, and did not give up pursuing her.

By the start of 1997, David Camm was living a double life. On one hand he was a respectable family man, who doted on his two young children, and on the other he was a womanizer who would chase almost anything in a skirt.

In late February, David, Kim and the children joined the rest of the Lockhart family in Fort Lauderdale, where they attended his brother Daniel's wedding. The youngest Camm brother had been living in Florida since 1987, working in a variety of jobs, including bar catering, financial services and finally insurance.

A year or so after the wedding, Daniel helped his brother and sister-in-law purchase life insurance as a college education fund for Brad and Jill in the form of a $30,000 life insurance policy on Kim and a $20,000 child term rider policy for the children. The policy was taken in

Kim's name because it cost less than it would have for David to buy the policy, as he was a bit older and a male.

"This policy was primarily set up for college planning and college funding," Daniel Camm would later explain. "It was more of a planning tool."

The Camms also had additional insurance, including insurance David Camm received as an employee of the state police and another policy for Kim and the children.

And over the next few years Daniel Camm would continue to help fill his brother's family's insurance needs.

9

Indiana's Finest

David Camm had first met Michelle Voyles seven years earlier, after she graduated from Floyd Central High School. He had pulled the attractive teenager over at a traffic stop for a defective brake light. Then after a brief lecture he let her go with a warning.

In June 1997, they met again when the uniformed trooper was buying gas at Gas & Stuff in Georgetown. He spotted Michelle standing in line and came over to compliment her on being "very cute."

They agreed to meet the following week at the annual Georgetown Rod Run for pre-1949 vehicles, where Camm would be on duty.

"[It was] just a little conversation," she remembered. "It didn't amount to very much."

After the Rod Run, when the cars gathered outside Gas & Stuff, Trooper Camm was waiting for her in full uniform in the ISP official flag car.

"When I arrived there that night, he was there," she said. "We just walked around together through the Rod Run."

Then Camm invited Michelle for a ride in his state trooper cruiser, and she willingly accepted. During the drive he asked if she had a boyfriend and they discussed some mutual friends who had been at the Rod Run.

When she asked if he was married, he held up an empty ring finger, saying he wasn't anymore although he had three children he adored. He then proudly took out photographs of Brad and Jill from his wallet to show her.

Later the handsome state trooper dropped her back at Gas & Stuff and, after exchanging phone numbers, told her he'd call soon.

Later Voyles would admit she was interested in "a little bit of a relationship," but if she'd known he was married she wouldn't have pursued it.

About three weeks later Camm called, inviting her out on a date. They arranged to meet that night at 11:00 p.m. at a church parking lot behind the Marathon gas station, off Route 64. It was a cool night and she arrived to find Trooper Camm waiting in full uniform in his police cruiser.

With a boyish grin he greeted her, opening the passenger door for her to get in, and began driving out onto Route 64 eastbound, to a wooded rest area past the Georgetown exit. Then, seeing a car broken down by the side of the road, he made a U-turn to pick up the stranded motorist, whom he dropped off at the next intersection.

"He put his hat on when he got out of the vehicle," Michelle remembered. "That was something we had spoken about. Anytime he exits the vehicle he must have his hat on."

Camm drove her back to the same rest area and pulled up, turning off the engine. He got out of the car and walked around to the trunk, taking out a large blanket and laying it on the ground.

Then he came over and started to kiss her and Michelle responded, stroking his uniform. As they started taking their clothes off they moved into the police cruiser, as it was getting cold outside.

"We had sexual intercourse," Michelle later testified. "It started outside the vehicle and resumed on the inside."

After they finished, Camm straightened up his uniform and put on his hat, and they drove around for a while talking, before he dropped her back in the church parking lot where she'd left her car.

Over the next six months they would meet two or three times a week, and he'd often take her riding in his police car. Sometimes they'd have sex at the same rest area on Route 64, or just chat. Once he took her out for a Chinese meal and another time they rented a movie and went back to her apartment to watch it.

"I would ride with him a lot of times when he was on duty," she said. "If he was on nights."

Michelle never viewed it as a dating relationship, as she had no expectations for things to develop any further. Camm often told her how devoted he was to his children, breaking several dates to look after them. But he never mentioned exactly who the mother of his children was and Michelle never asked.

She says that on one occasion David Camm had a particularly unusual request, asking her to shave off her pubic hair. Michelle says she agreed and claims he even assisted her, using a safety razor. Then, as they were about to make love, Camm looked at her shaved pubic area, declaring, "Now, if I can do this without thinking I'm fucking a six-year-old . . ."

Later Camm tried to explain the alleged comment, saying that this was not something he would find appealing.

The relationship finally ended in early 1998 when Michelle discovered Camm was married, after he gave her Gas & Stuff cashier friend Judy Sarles a check with Kim's name on it.

"She broke it off not long after that," said Judy. "[Then] he stopped in and asked me if I could get Michelle's phone number for him."

Judy told him she would have to ask Michelle first and Camm left. Later that night Judy told Michelle her trooper friend wanted her phone number. But Michelle said not to give it out until they knew what he wanted.

"A couple of days later he came in and I wouldn't give

him the number," said Sarles. "And he got mad and called us bitches. He was mad that night."

Furious, David Camm stormed out of the gas station, slamming the door hard.

During David Camm's affair with Michelle Voyles, he was also pursuing a beautiful real estate broker named Lisa Korfhage. They had first met in late June 1997, on a Friday afternoon, when he'd flagged her down in front of her mother's realty office in Greenville because the tags of her fiancé's car had expired. His cruiser lights were flashing, as he slowly got out of his cruiser, put on his state trooper's hat and ordered Lisa out of her vehicle.

"I was really embarrassed," Lisa would later remember. "I asked him if he could turn his lights off, as I was going to get in trouble for being pulled over in front of work."

Camm obliged, turning off his lights before asking to see Lisa's driver's license and writing down her phone numbers. Then he let her go with a warning.

That evening Lisa was at home with her 1-year-old daughter when she received a collect call. When it came time for the caller to state a name, a male voice said, "I'll see you Monday," before putting down the phone.

Initially she thought it was a wrong number but later that evening, there was another call. This time the mystery caller whispered, "I'll see you Monday, Lisa," before putting down the phone.

"At that point," she said, "I realized that it was for me."

Over the next few hours she received a further ten increasingly bizarre calls. One told her, "I'll have a surprise for you on Monday." Another said, "You'll see my dick."

Feeling threatened, a tearful Lisa called the telephone company, but was told that collect calls were untraceable. Then she called her fiancé, Peter Carter (not his real name), who was a fireman, asking what she should do.

One of the other firemen suggested she call the state police and report it, so she did. Within a few minutes Trooper David Camm arrived at her front door to investigate.

"I was hysterical, crying and very nervous," she remembered. "He was very comforting and told me to calm down."

After getting Lisa to take a few deep breaths to relax, Camm interviewed her about the calls, writing up a report. She told Camm that she had seen someone on the road that day whom she hadn't seen in a couple of years and thought that he might have been the caller. After taking the report, Camm offered to stay and keep her company, as she was so nervous. Lisa thanked him, saying she would spend the night at a friend's house.

He then handed her one of his official white Indiana State Police cards, promising that there would be an investigation. He also showed her how to set up her answering machine to record any future calls, instructing her to call him immediately if there were any.

There were no more calls that night, but Lisa was too scared to stay in her house alone with her baby. And as her car was parked outside the garage, she'd have to walk across her yard. So she called David Camm, asking him to come over and see her safely to her car. The gallant trooper said he'd be straight over and then gave her a police escort halfway to her friend's house.

On Saturday morning, Lisa returned home to receive another intimidating collect call, but this time she recorded it. Somehow the caller knew that he'd upset her the previous night and apologized, making Lisa wonder how he could possibly have known that.

Later she played the tape of the call to her fiancé, who told her to call Trooper Camm and give it to him, which she did.

On Monday, Lisa went to work scared that her phone stalker might keep his word and surprise her as promised.

When she happened to mention the calls at work, one of her colleagues remarked that another agent had also received strange calls on Friday.

"She had got phone calls that said, 'I have a big surprise for your daughter on Monday,'" said Lisa. "I asked her if she would talk to Officer Camm and let him know."

Later that morning Camm telephoned Lisa and said he'd come to her house that night to pick up the phone recording, as well as interview her friend about her calls.

And when Camm came over, Lisa introduced him to her fireman fiancé and the two off them immediately hit it off, soon becoming close friends.

They discovered much in common, comparing the state police to the fire department, and agreed to exchange their department tee-shirts the next time they met.

A couple of days later, Camm turned up at Lisa's home with Kim and his children. He proudly introduced his family and then he and Carter exchanged tee-shirts and shook hands on the deal.

Over the next couple of years the Camms would regularly socialize with Lisa and her fiancé.

However, Lisa seems never to have considered the distinct possibility that Trooper Camm had made the calls himself. For who else would have known she'd been so hysterical that Friday night.

One night, soon after introducing his family to Lisa, Trooper Camm arrived at her house without warning.

"We talked a little bit," Lisa remembered. "He asked me if he could kiss me. I said yes."

Lisa says there was a strong attraction between them, but nothing further happened that time and Camm left, promising to call soon. Over the next month they were in daily contact, either by phone or in person. And cunningly, Camm researched her fiancé's shifts at the firehouse, and would arrive at Lisa's house when he was on duty.

"He would always compliment me and tell me I was beautiful," she said. "One time he just put a message on my pager that said, 'I love you —Dave.' I just blew it off."

About a month after their first kiss, Camm drove all the way back from Indianapolis just to see her. He turned up in a friend's unmarked car, as Lisa did not want neighbors spotting his police cruiser in her driveway.

"[That] night we had intercourse," she would later testify. "He stayed half an hour."

But almost as soon as they'd finished, Lisa felt guilty, telling Camm that they should never have sex again, as she loved her fiancé and Camm was a married man.

"This was a stupid fling," she said. "I was getting married. I said that, 'This is never going to lead anywhere.' And he said, 'That's fine, I'm married too.'"

Over the next couple of years David Camm and Kim became close friends with Lisa Korfhage and Peter Carter, who had since married. But neither Kim nor Carter had any idea their spouses had once been sexually involved.

They would all meet up regularly to socialize, sometimes with Brad and Jill, who got on well with Lisa's daughter. Once the two couples went to a car show together and another time they went out to dinner in Louisville, ending up in a blues bar, where they all danced together.

Lisa and Kim had much in common, becoming friends during the time they spent together.

"[She] was very sweet," Lisa remembered. "Very quiet."

One afternoon Camm brought Kim and the children over to Lisa's house for a cook-out, and she observed that he didn't seem to do much with the children.

"Kim was basically caring for the kids," she observed. "I think they may have even had words about it."

Over the course of their friendship David Camm would occasionally boast about his cavalier exploits, and how he was always out on the town.

"I said . . . 'Shouldn't you be at home with your wife?' "
Lisa remembered. "It's just, 'Yeah.' "

On another occasion Kim even allowed Brad, then 4,
and Jill, 2, to spend the night at Lisa's, as she and David
were going out somewhere.

It gave Lisa an opportunity to see Brad and Jill close up,
as they played dress-up. Brad had recently been diagnosed
as suffering from asthma and used an inhaler when he became short of breath. But Lisa was somewhat surprised to
see him play with her daughter and Jill, trying on dresses
and playing with dolls.

"He had some feminine qualities," said Lisa. "I just
kind of figured it was the age, and I know some little boys
do that."

She also noticed how "very talkative" little Jill was, almost the complete opposite of her older brother, who was
far quieter and more reserved.

The next morning Dave and Kim turned up earlier than
expected, and Brad rushed up to them wearing a girl's
dress.

"I could tell that it bothered David a little bit," said Lisa.

Throughout their friendship, Camm continually flirted
with Lisa. He would ask her when they were going "to
hook up again." But she would laugh, telling him she was a
married woman and there would be no more "flings."

Eventually they grew apart and stopped seeing each
other regularly.

But Lisa's realty company was still renting two run-
down rental properties the Camms owned, occasionally
phoning if there was a prospective renter.

That summer the state trooper lothario was also pursuing a
Sellersburg post dispatcher named Beth Ann Minnicus.
The attractive Indiana Police employee was going through
a divorce, often finding herself working the midnight shift
with Trooper David Camm.

A couple of times a week Camm would stop by her desk for a chat, and before long they were flirting with each other.

"We said some things that we probably shouldn't have," said Beth. "But it wasn't meant to be serious."

Sometimes he would confide problems he was having at home with Kim. One night Minnicus remembers him coming into the post after an argument, bitterly complaining that Kim wanted him to quit the police "and get a real job."

"He [was] angry," Minnicus would later testify. "They had been arguing about his salary ... occasionally he would call her names [like] *bitch*," a claim he would later refute.

When Beth asked him why he didn't divorce Kim, Camm replied he couldn't afford to, as she made more money than he did.

Late one night in August 1997, Camm showed up at Beth's apartment in Old Town Village, without warning. When she asked what he wanted, he said he wanted to talk, so she let him in.

Soon after he arrived they were sitting on the couch "just chit-chatting" when he suddenly reached over and placed his hands on her breasts.

"He put his hands on me and made some comments like, 'I know that you want me,'" she remembered. "And I said, 'No, David, no, I don't.'"

He pushed her down on the couch, attempting to kiss her. Beth fought him off, pushing him away, and he suddenly stopped, got up and walked out of her apartment.

Soon after that incident, Minnicus was transferred to the Lafayette post. But before she left she was having a cigarette one morning in the garage of the Sellersburg post, when she heard the door open. Although her back was towards the door, she immediately recognized David Camm's voice.

"Once again he placed his hands on my breasts," she

remembered, "turned around and kissed me. I told him to knock it off. He said it was my goodbye kiss, because I was leaving."

Then without saying another word he turned around and walked out of the garage, like a dejected child who'd been denied candy by his parents.

10

Flirting With Disaster

By now Trooper David Camm was chasing girls all over the place. Apparently without a thought for Kim or his children, he would be out all hours preying on women, many of whom he had met while on police duty around the New Albany area.

Floyd Memorial Hospital Emergency Room Technician Jamie Spurgeon was first stopped by the lascivious trooper in spring 1995, when he gave her a ticket. Then he had acted like a total professional, but six months later, when she ran into him again at the hospital, he was different.

Camm was on night duty, escorting a DUI prisoner to the emergency room, where Spurgeon happened to be on duty.

"We joked about [the ticket]," she remembered. "He said he could take care of it for me. But it was too late, I had already paid it."

It was another year before she next saw David Camm. This time he had pulled a driver over for a traffic violation early one evening, just a block away from her New Albany house. As Jamie drove by on her way to work, he flagged her down, and she pulled alongside his cruiser.

He put on his hat and walked over, asking where she was going, and she told him she was heading to her night shift at Floyd Memorial. Then he asked if she was working all night and she said she was, in the emergency room.

"Well, I'll stop by later and I'll chat with you," he said. "I said, 'OK,' and drove away."

At three o'clock the next morning he arrived at the emergency room in full uniform, finding Jamie. He told her he was still on duty, "working various strange third shifts."

"We joked around," said Spurgeon, who had noted he was not wearing a wedding band. "We talked about his job and going out in the future socially."

Camm gave her his Indiana State Police business card with his cell phone number. Spurgeon encouraged him to call her, believing that it could be "a potential relationship."

The following night she called Camm from the emergency room and they had what she'd later call "a casual, social conversation," flirting with each other. Because both of them were working nights for the foreseeable future, no date was arranged.

But when she heard from two separate sources that David Camm was married, Jamie immediately broke off contact with him, not wishing to become involved with a married man.

Jamie saw him one last time at a car wash next to Floyd Memorial Hospital on her night off. She had just arrived to wash her car at about 2:00 a.m. when Camm pulled in behind her, making her wonder if he'd been following her.

"He was at work in his uniform and in his police car," she remembered. "He got out of his car and started to speak to me casually."

Camm lecherously peered into her car, running his eyes slowly over the skimpy tank top and shorts she was wearing.

"Nice outfit," he said.

Then he asked her to meet him at a quiet, secluded park nearby, saying he wanted to talk. Jamie told him they could talk just as well at the car wash, as no one else was there. Camm insisted the park would be better. When she refused a second time he reacted angrily.

"I don't know who you think you're dealing with!" she

says he yelled. "I am a grown man and I'm not gonna play this game with you."

Then he jumped into his police cruiser and drove off, without even saying goodbye.

"It was a little creepy," Jamie explained. "I was a little intimidated."

In spite of his extra-curricular activities, David Camm found plenty of time for police work, and was still an active member of the Emergency Response Team. Once, in the late 1990s, he almost died in a highly dangerous assault practice.

"He was involved in a helicopter crash in Seymour, Indiana," said his brother Donnie. "He was on the outside of a chopper ready to make an assault."

The helicopter was three or four feet off the ground when a gust of wind caused it to tilt, throwing Camm and another team member to the ground.

"Dave was thrown clean and got bruised and banged up," said Donnie. "But the other guy was injured pretty badly. That led him to decide to get out of the ERT team because of the danger."

According to his sister, Julie, Camm had an "epiphany," later delivering a moving sermon about his "death kind of experience" to the congregation at the Georgetown Community Church.

"It was another little awakening for him," she explained. "'Cause he thought there was a message there about life and a commitment to God. A commitment to doing the right thing."

David's family had no idea of the extent of his womanizing over this period. They were convinced he was a reformed family man, and later when they found out about his dissembling they would find it hard to accept.

"I guess there was a part of him that maybe at times was

torn," rationalized Julie. "Dave knew what a good husband should do and he knew he had a good wife—because Kim was a good wife. Sometimes he wasn't strong. He struggled with that and he made some poor choices."

His sister knew nothing of her brother's affairs and says she was "disgusted" when she finally learned about them. And Donnie too maintains he never saw signs of David's adulterous behavior.

By this time Donnie had moved back to Louisville from Florida, with his wife, Brenda, and two daughters, Kara and Lauren. They soon became close to Kim, Brad and Jill.

"The four of us did things together all the time," remembered Donnie. "We went to NASCAR races in Indianapolis, Charlotte and Tennessee."

At the time, Donnie's marriage was breaking up, and Kim was highly supportive. She helped him through the difficult divorce, in which he retained custody of his daughters.

"We would go out to eat and have a lot of cook-outs," Donnie remembered. "So the kids could just run and play out there and have a good time together.

"Kara and Brad were about six months apart, as were Jill and Lauren. So they grew up together their whole lives."

In 1998, Brad and Kara started kindergarten together at Graceland Christian School on Kamer Miller Road in New Albany. Two years later, Jill and Lauren would also start there.

According to its Web site, Graceland combines the best of home, school and church to give children a "Bible-based, God-centered" education.

The school's principal, Kevin Wilson, considered the Camms a strict religious family.

"[They] saw the value of Christian education and its importance for their children," he said.

Principal Wilson's daughter also began kindergarten

with Brad and thought him far nicer than the other boys, who were often mean to the girls.

"He was a kind little guy," said Wilson. "He treated girls like they were regular people."

Unfortunately Brad's father did not possess his 5-year-old son's respect for the opposite sex.

One night while he was on duty, Trooper Camm stopped Miss Kentucky for speeding on I-64, on her way back from the Miss America Pageant. The stunning beauty queen was with her boyfriend on the way to a public appearance at a gentlemen's club.

Camm was so overawed to be in the presence of a famous beauty queen, he said he wouldn't be giving them a ticket. Instead he accepted a signed photograph of her in a swimsuit, and an invitation to dinner at her boyfriend's restaurant in Lexington.

"I did try and hook up with her for a dinner date," he would later boast. "But that just didn't work out."

Several years later, when Indiana police searched his basement, they would find dozens of traffic violation tickets that he had never bothered to turn in.

"Well I made a lot of mistakes," he would explain. "I probably wasn't as good as a policeman as everybody thought I was."

If Kim Camm was frustrated that her husband wasn't earning enough as an Indiana State Trooper, she kept it very quiet. As a senior accountant she was making more than twice his salary, as well as hefty annual performance bonuses. And in 1997, the Providian corporation insurance company had been bought by the Dutch-based Aegon Corporation, which based its financial services division in Louisville. The Kentucky division was one of the largest employers in the state, with 650 people on staff.

Kim's position remained unaffected by the takeover,

and she still reported to the same bosses as before. And as a senior accountant in the investments division, she was part of a team responsible for managing about $90 billion of Aegon's investments.

On March 23, 1998, David Camm celebrated his thirty-fourth birthday and Kim bought him a 1966 Mustang Coupe, out of money from her annual bonus.

"Originally I had been looking to buy one myself," he later explained. "I had been looking through the *Bargain Mart* and Kim had just gotten her bonus check. She bought me that for my birthday."

According to Camm, he wanted to rebuild the sports car for 5-year-old Brad to use as his first car when he turned 16. Even at his young age, Brad had loved speed, and had the reputation locally as a daredevil bicyclist, who raced down the steepest hills in the neighborhood.

Later Camm would boast that his young son was already so knowledgeable about cars, he'd even selected the specialist parts he wanted for his Mustang.

"He knew what kind of shifter knob he wanted in it," said Camm proudly. "He picked out which seat he wanted to go in the car . . . told me how loud he wanted it. He wanted the white GT stripes on the bottom of it. I mean, that was gonna be his car."

For the next couple of years David Camm would work on the Mustang and his Corvette in his workshop, alongside the double garage next to his house. It was his private den, full of specialist welding tools and equipment. And when he came home after finishing a police shift, he would spend hours restoring the cars. It was perhaps the only time he would find any real peace of mind.

Some nights when he was home alone he would go on the Internet, checking the stock market and at least occasionally going on America Online chat rooms to meet women.

"I can think of two individuals that I talked to," Camm

later testified. "I'm trying to think of the particular chat room that I was in."

He would later claim that he spent "ninety-five percent" of his time trading bonds and stocks over the Internet, only ever visiting "normal" chat rooms. Later, when police seized his computer, they found no evidence to the contrary.

A sexual opportunist, Trooper David Camm would flirt with and come on to almost every woman he met. Sometimes it was innocent enough, but he was always looking for the next romantic adventure.

One woman he had an eye on was Suzanne Proffit, the New Albany police dispatcher. Whenever he went into police headquarters to drop off a citation, or see his old friend Chief Randy Hubbard, she says he flirted with her. In the summer of 1998 they made tentative plans to meet for drinks one night, but Proffit cancelled at the last minute to work an extra shift.

The trooper then gave her his Indiana State Police business card, with his personal cell phone number. But it would be another two years before he would call again and sexually proposition her.

11

Disillusionment

In January 1999, David Camm and two other troopers were involved in a high-speed chase with a 19-year-old motorist. Camm had initially clocked the vehicle, and then two other troopers gave chase in their cruiser. When they forced the car to a stop, a video camera in Camm's police car filmed another state trooper viciously pulling the teenager out of the vehicle, and brutally kicking him on the ground.

Soon afterwards the victim found a lawyer and sued David Camm and two other troopers for assault. The local Louisville television station somehow got hold of the sensational police footage of the beating, and aired it over the next few days, until the story died down.

"[It] was shown repeatedly on TV," Camm later complained. "And my name kept popping up with that."

A subsequent internal police investigation would later fully exonerate Trooper Camm, but he was furious with the Indiana State Police, who he felt had not been supportive.

For the next six months, Trooper Camm lived under a cloud of suspicion, before officially being cleared of any wrongdoing. Ultimately his two colleagues were found guilty of assault, and were suspended without pay.

From then on Camm would harbor a deep grudge against the Indiana State Police, believing his superiors had betrayed him.

"I don't know how to describe it other than just hell

hanging over your head," he said. "[It] left a bad taste in my mouth."

At this low point Camm considered leaving the department, after ten years of exemplary service. He had an unblemished record, but was making just $38,000 a year, compared with Kim, who earned almost $70,000 and had just received an $11,500 performance bonus from Aegon.

Later he would claim Kim influenced his decision, as she now wanted to stop working, to be a full-time mom to Brad and Jill.

Over the next few months he became increasingly disillusioned, constantly complaining to his family. "I had a lot of disagreements with brass as far as [how] the department was being run," said Camm. "Things had changed a lot. Not just over the ten years I had been on the department, but over the last twenty to twenty-five years."

Camm believed that the Indiana State Police internal investigations department had "specialized themselves out of business," citing his own problems as an example and privately making frequent suggestions as to how things could be improved.

Soon after he was cleared of involvement in the beating incident, he applied to become a detective. But he was devastated when he was turned down in favor of his boyhood friend Sean Clemons, who had a college degree.

"Dave had trained Sean," said Julie Hogue. "He felt very let down."

The final straw came in late 1999, when his superiors wanted to transfer him to work security at Caesars Riverboat Casino. Billed as the world's largest such vessel, and moored in Elizabeth, Indiana—directly across the Ohio River from Louisville—the riverboat is owned by the Las Vegas–based Caesars Palace organization. With a capacity for 5,324 people, it boasts four themed decks, one of which features a performance of "the burning of Rome" every hour.

The Indiana State Police routinely assigned eight troopers and a sergeant to the riverboat, but David Camm had no intention of joining them.

"It's not a real desirable job," he explained. "All you do is sit in a room and look at TV monitors. I joined the department to be out on the road to assist people and help people in need—to be a public servant. Not to sit on some gambling boat and look at TV monitors all day."

The disgruntled trooper felt this was a demotion, and that he was being punished for making waves. He told his commanding officer he didn't want to go, as being on the boat would exacerbate his migraine headaches.

"He also didn't want to put himself in a situation where there's drinking and women," said his mother. "He just didn't want to set himself up for anything like that."

With his once promising police career now on the decline, David Camm threw caution to the wind. It was as if he needed to prove something to compensate for his flagging career and the fact that Kim was more financially secure than he was.

One Saturday night in September 1999, he attended the annual Lanesville Heritage Festival, about ten miles southwest of New Albany. He went with some friends and was drinking in the festival's beer garden when he ran into Toby Asher, a former state trooper friend, who was there with his attractive wife, Anita. Camm immediately came over to chat with Anita before rejoining his friends.

Later that night Toby and Anita's group left to go to the Hog's Tavern in Lanesville, and David Camm followed them.

Outside the bar he approached Anita and smiled, asking where her husband was. She said he had gone to the bar but had not come back.

Camm gallantly offered to help her find him, walking her out into the street towards Kim's black Ford Bronco.

"We ended up at his vehicle," she would later remember. "He was parked down the street."

They then got into the front seat of the Bronco and had a conversation.

"Then he started coming on to me," said Anita, who admits to drinking heavily that night. "Kissing me."

She responded and soon they were engaged in heavily petting each other. A few minutes later a friend of his knocked on the window. Camm immediately stopped kissing Anita, opened the door and whispered something to his friend.

Then Camm told Anita his buddy was going to drive them around a little to look for her husband, suggesting they move into the back seat of the Bronco, where it would be more comfortable.

"Things," said Anita, "got a little carried away."

Later she said they engaged in "sexual activities" in the back seat, while Camm's friend drove them around Lanesville.

Eventually they dropped Anita back at Hog's Tavern, where she later found her husband nearby.

In October 1999, David Camm was officially designated a firearms expert by the Indiana State Police. Under test conditions on an ISP shooting range he scored a ninety-eight and a ninety-four, out of a possible one hundred maximum.

Ironically his boyhood friend Sean Clemons scored even higher, with a ninety-six and a perfect score.

"That puts me in the expert range," Camm would later declare. "It would have given me an average of ninety-six."

Soon after his firearms test, the trooper visited the Powder Keg gun store in Greenville in his uniform. While there he noticed an attractive blonde woman named Tammy

Rogers, who was buying a shotgun. Rogers, who had recently been laid off from her job, wanted the shotgun so she could go hunting with her dad and her brothers, but she knew nothing about firearms.

Trooper Camm strolled over, asking what gun she was buying. And on learning she was a beginner, started dispensing his expert advice.

After she bought a gun and left the store he followed her outside, continuing the conversation, proudly showing her his gleaming Indiana State Police cruiser.

"He asked if I would like him to show me how to use the shotgun," she remembered. "Since I've never used a shotgun before, I said, 'Sure.'"

The trooper then handed her his white police business card, asking for her home phone number. A couple of days later Camm telephoned, inviting her to meet him at the Henryville Forestry Shooting Range, where he'd give her a lesson. She agreed and they met up a few days later.

While he was demonstrating how to fire his black, semiautomatic handgun, he asked Tammy her age. When she told him she was twenty-nine, he looked surprised.

"Oh, I thought you were seventeen or eighteen-years-old," she says he told her.

Tammy, who was then separated from her husband, thought it strange that a man over thirty would be "interested in meeting" a teenager, and asked him his age.

"Well, older then you," the trooper replied obliquely.

Then she asked if he was married and Camm said he and his wife had been separated for a year.

At one point on the shooting range, Camm put his arm around her shoulder protectively.

"I remember feeling uncomfortable," she said. "I was thinking, 'He put his arm around me.'"

Over the next few weeks they talked several times but then she left a message on his answering machine, saying she didn't want a relationship with him and telling him not to call again.

While her husband continued his secret double life, Kim Camm appeared completely unaware of his activities. And her busy schedule left little time for analyzing the state of her marriage, as she was too busy looking after Brad, now 6, and Jill, 4.

"She was wrapped up in her children, totally," said Sam Lockhart. "Her whole focus basically was on the kids."

Often, after working a long day at Aegon, Kim would collect Brad and Jill from Graceland School and take them to her mother's house for the night. Then she would drive to Georgetown Community Church for a finance committee meeting, which could run until midnight.

She was becoming more and more involved in the running of the Georgetown Community Church, sitting on several committees, as well as being treasurer. But the shy former Catholic maintained a low profile, always underplaying all the volunteer work she did for the church.

At one particular meeting the church council was struggling to resolve a problem involving the construction of a new family life center and gymnasium. Kim sat there patiently for two hours without saying a word, but listening closely to everything that was said.

"Suddenly," said Steve Bobo, "She spoke up and boiled the whole discussion down to two sentences."

Everyone agreed with her advice on how to pursue the project, and the chairman moved on to the next subject on the evening's agenda.

"She was a very intelligent person and a hard worker," said Sam Lockhart. "She was willing to do things for you and was very helpful."

That Thanksgiving was a traditional one in the Camm household. Early in the morning David drove Kim and the children to her parents' home in New Albany, for breakfast and to open their presents. Then they returned home, to host the extended Lockhart family Thanksgiving dinner.

Kim Camm was in a difficult position at holiday time, as her husband would expect his family to take priority over hers. Janice and Frank Renn would have their own family festivities, where Kim and their grandchildren would stop briefly, before moving on to David's family celebrations.

"Kim came to ours," observed Julie Hogue, who was by that time separated from her policeman husband, with a grown-up daughter of her own. "They would go to [her family] and make the obligatory stop to eat the meal, but they came to our gatherings to have fun."

When David Camm was growing up, the Lockhart family would take turns hosting Thanksgiving and Christmas festivities. But in the 1990s, as Amos and Daisy Lockhart became too old to organize them, they began to go to David and Kim's house, as it was just across the road from his grandparents.

"Often there could be eighty-something people and that's just Mom's siblings and first cousins," said Julie. "That's what we call immediate family."

As a new generation of Lockhart children had grown up, each part of the family would have its own celebrations, before converging on Dave and Kim's house to pay their respects to the family patriarch, Amos, who would soon celebrate his ninety-second birthday.

Everybody would bring food to the Camm house for the Thanksgiving dinner, where the adults ate on tables set up in the Camms' front room and the children retreated to the basement for their meal.

The highlight of the Thanksgiving festivities came when Amos and Daisy Lockhart, known to everyone as

"Mummylock" and "Pappaw," would come over to David and Kim's house to see their children, grandchildren and great-grandchildren.

"That last year my grandma was really feeble," said Julie. "So it was a handy way for her to be able to come over and see everybody and then go back home. So people could spend more time with Mummylock and Pappaw, if they wanted to."

At Christmas, as there were so many Lockhart relatives, there was an agreement that only the immediate family would exchange gifts.

"I'd buy presents for Brad and Jill," remembered Donnie Camm. "And Kim and Dave would buy presents for my kids because there were just too many to buy for everybody."

There were always a lot of games at Lockhart family gatherings, and one of David's favorites was a word game called "Balderdash." The players split into teams and obscure, unusual words were called out, with each team writing down what they thought they meant. Then the opposite team would vote on whether it was the true meaning or not.

They also played the game "Scattergories," at which David became a family legend after coining the word "cigling" during one notable Thanksgiving.

"Dave's definition of that word," explained Julie, "was the smell in the bathroom after Dad's been in there. He would smoke in there, so it was this mixture of smoke and [whatever]."

Later someone made a large sign with the word "cigling," and hung it on Don Camm's bathroom mirror, where it stayed up for years.

On Thanksgiving 1999, David Camm's former lover Stephanie McCarty became engaged. A couple of days later, Camm called the Fitness Zone to congratulate her.

But she was unsure whether he was genuinely pleased or still bitter that she had once broken off their relationship.

"[He] was matter-of-fact," she remembered. "He didn't sound real excited, mad or anything like that. It was kind of normal."

12

A Fresh Start

In January 2000, Sam Lockhart offered his nephew a job, as a part-time salesman in his thriving business, United Dynamics, Inc. (UDI). Sam and the rest of the family were concerned David was floundering in his police career, and wanted to help him find a more secure, higher-paying job.

As a teenager, David had worked for his uncle's New Albany–based foundation repair company to earn extra money, impressing him with his dedication and hard work.

"So he knew our company," said Lockhart, "and he knew how it operated."

Incorporated in 1989, UDI repaired foundations in homes while its sister company Perma Dry specialized in waterproofing. The two companies employ about thirty people, including many Lockhart family members. David's father, Don Camm, works there as a general mechanic, and Sam Lockhart's nephew Jeff is a part owner, his son Philip and son-in-law Eric Minzenberger are both employees, and many other family members work part-time.

So on February 1, David Camm started moonlighting as a part-time salesman, while he was still working as a state trooper.

"I felt it was kinda like fate," he would later say. "Just kinda fell on my lap."

From the beginning, Camm loved working for the company and his Uncle Sam thought him a talented salesman. Unlike his schedule with the Indiana State Police, the hours were regular, and he had weekends off. And on Fridays all the Lockhart employees would spend the day on the golf course.

So straight after his thirty-sixth birthday, with Kim's full support and encouragement, David decided to leave the Indiana State Police and go full-time with United Dynamics. Although it would mean sacrificing his valuable police pension, Kim had agreed to have Aegon cover medical and dental insurance for the family, including her stepdaughter Whitney.

Soon after making his decision, Camm strolled into the New Albany Police Department to tell his friend and mentor Chief Randy Hubbard that he was leaving law enforcement.

"He was going to leave the state police because he didn't like the way they were treating him," remembered Chief Hubbard. "He thought they were out to get him."

Camm then went through the list of his grievances against the Indiana State Police, as Chief Hubbard just sat there shaking his head.

"I disagreed and didn't think that was the case," said the chief. "I told him he shouldn't leave. He'd got over ten years invested in his career and you just don't throw that away."

Camm then explained that his Uncle Sam had offered him "a pretty good deal" with United Dynamics, where he could make a lot more money than he ever would with the state police.

"And I told him money's not the object here, or we wouldn't be doing it," said Chief Hubbard. "I said, 'David, I know you well enough, or at least I think I do, that you want to be a policeman. You're not going to be happy out there.'

"He told me he was going to go ahead and resign. And he did."

At the end of February, David Camm gave three months' notice to the Indiana State Police, to start full-time with United Dynamics. His uncle initially brought him in to manage the waterproofing division. But he also had Camm develop a new gutter protection system, and he would prove instrumental in getting that off the ground.

Sam Lockhart was a generous boss. He paid David $600 a week plus a 10 percent commission, giving him the opportunity to earn a six-figure salary if he worked hard. There was also the chance of buying into the Perma Dry company once he'd proven his worth.

"He was excited about it," said Lockhart. "He had put everything in his background with the state police and was now trying to move beyond that. Also there were regular shift hours, so he could be home with his family. He didn't have to work midnight or weekends [anymore]."

Although he was still obligated to finish working almost three months with the ISP, he managed to get out of most of it by taking comp time and vacation entitlements.

"I was kinda double-dipping there for a while," he would later explain. "[I was] getting paid by the state police and working for UDI at the same time."

In mid-April, on one of his final shifts as a state trooper, he was assigned to security at the annual Thunder Over Louisville festival, which officially opens the two-week-long Kentucky Derby celebrations. During the evening pyrotechnics display, Camm's former lover Trooper Shelley Romero turned up to relieve officers who needed to go to the bathroom or get a snack.

As she walked past Camm, who was sitting at the police security post, he hit his radio three-way button to get her attention, saying, "Hello, snob."

Romero came back to where he was sitting and asked if he wanted to go and get something to eat. Camm said he'd eaten but invited her to sit down anyway for a chat.

"We hadn't talked in a while," remembered Trooper Romero. "Dave and I were good enough friends . . . we'd sit and talk when we had the chance and just shooting the bull, catching up on life."

Romero confided she was having problems in her marriage and things weren't going well at home. Then, when she asked how he and Kim were doing, Camm tried to proposition her for sex.

"[It was a] kind of running thing," she remembered. "Have you changed your mind yet . . . about having sex? Would you want to get back together with me?"

Romero declined his offer, but claims he continued doggedly pursuing her for sex for the next five months.

Later Camm would claim it was the pretty blonde trooper who had a crush on him.

"Shelly has always looked up to me," he would explain. "She's always come to me for advice."

In spring 2000, David Camm started frequenting PT's Show Club, in a rough area of downtown Louisville. He would go there so often over the next few months that he knew most of the strippers by name.

The pressures of his life-changing decision to leave the Indiana State Police had apparently taken their toll on his sex life, and a doctor had prescribed him Viagra, for erectile dysfunction.

"I was going through a problem," he would later admit. "But I don't have to have it."

On one of his last shifts, Camm came to the rescue of Emily Shepherd, a gorgeous exotic dancer who later worked at PT's. Emily was driving through New Albany on her way to a bar in Louisville, when her hood flew open and she pulled over on Route 62 to fix it.

As she was readjusting her hood, she noticed a police car pull in behind her and turn its lights on. Then David Camm got out, donned his hat, and strolled over.

"Are you OK?" he asked. "Do you need help?"

Shepherd, who was wearing a sexy tank top and Capri pants, explained how her hood was loose and kept flying up. Camm smiled, telling her to wait a minute while he got something out of the back of his car. When he returned he was holding a towel, which he then ripped into four strips to secure her hood.

Shepherd thanked him for his help but then the gallant trooper surprised her, asking where she was going "dressed like that," and if she needed a ride.

"I said, 'I'm going to a bar in Louisville,'" she would later testify. "Then he asked me if I had a boyfriend. When I said [I hadn't] he said, 'You're too sexy not to have a boyfriend. You're so pretty, why don't you have a boyfriend?'"

Camm told her he had to make an urgent call on his radio, inviting her to sit in his cruiser. After he made his call he asked her how old she was, and when she said she was 23, he lied, shaving two years off his own age.

"I asked him if he was married," she said. "He said no and he didn't have a ring on, because I looked and made sure. And I thought he was pretty nice, you know."

Then the trooper made his move in the police car and Emily responded.

"We kissed for a minute and he stopped and leaned back in his chair," she remembered. "He said, 'I feel weird doing this because I have a daughter your age.'"

Shepherd asked how old his daughter was and Camm told her she was 16.

"Well I'm not sixteen," she told him. "I'm twenty-three."

After they talked some more and began kissing again, Camm started feeling her breast under the tank top. Then he asked if she was wearing a bra and Emily said she was not.

"He was like, 'Well, show me,'" she said. "And I just kind of flashed him real quick."

They resumed kissing and Camm tried to touch her between her legs. When she pushed his hand away, Camm said he got off duty in an hour and a half, inviting her to "hang out" with him.

She told him she was meeting friends in Louisville and they exchanged numbers. Then he asked if she needed a ride anywhere and when she declined, he once again suggested they meet later that night. Emily said she couldn't but promised to call him.

"He called me the next day," she said. "But I never returned his call. He just sounded too desperate."

On May 8, 2000, David Camm officially left the Indiana State Police, turning in his cruiser and equipment. Earlier he had tried to buy his .38-caliber service weapon at cost, claiming he wanted it as a "memento." But ultimately he decided not to, as the department refused to give him a discount.

Several years later, Floyd County Police Officer Frank Loop would swear under oath that Camm told him he owned a .38-caliber weapon, after leaving the department.

Soon after failing to persuade his friend not to leave the ISP, Sheriff Randy Hubbard recruited David as a reserve officer. But when David Camm came into the Floyd County police building to officially sign up, Sheriff Hubbard was out sick with a back injury, so Officer Loop briefed him and helped him fill out the forms needed to get an ID card.

"I told him all he needed to do was tell me when he was ready," said Loop. "I could get the ID card signed by the sheriff."

Camm asked what weapons he would be using as a reserve officer, saying he had to save up to buy a gun, as he did not have one.

"That struck me as odd," said Officer Loop. "I said, 'What do you mean, you don't have one? You just spent ten years on the state police, you're a SWAT guy, you don't have any weapons?'"

Loop maintains that Camm said that the only firearm he now possessed was a .38 gun. But the officer told him it was too small and would look "kinda silly" in the holster. Camm was eager to know where he could get his reserves uniform, and Loop promised to get him one.

A few days later Officer Loop ran into Camm again at a SWAT training session and told him that his ID card had been signed, and he just needed to collect it.

"He said he still hadn't bought a gun yet," said Loop. "He never did pick up the card."

Later, Camm unequivocally denied owning a handgun after leaving the police department. "Anyone that says different is a liar."

At his exit interview on May 8, David Camm critiqued the Indiana State Police, telling his superior officers what he considered wrong and even making suggestions on how to improve efficiency. Bursting with confidence, he told his commander that troopers underperformed, as they were expected to do too many things in areas where they were inadequately trained. He advised the state police to delegate some of their work to the sheriff's department or local police.

But even if Camm had little influence on the Indiana State Police, he would make quite an impression on United Dynamics over the next six months.

As manager of the company's waterproofing division, Camm was responsible for sales and scheduling, and monitoring jobs through to completion. He was expected to be at his desk every morning to begin work by 7:30 a.m., but other than that there was no set schedule.

"You don't punch a time clock in Dave's position," said his new boss, Sam Lockhart. "There's no actual set hours and sometimes you'd work on Saturdays, because you couldn't get people during the week."

And Camm soon adjusted his schedule to fit his own personal needs. Normally he worked a four-day week and would have most Fridays off.

"We'd play golf a lot of times on Friday," he explained. "Our work crews would be off on Friday."

His migraines were also under control. His doctor had prescribed him a hundred milligrams a day of a powerful new drug called Topamax, a long-established epilepsy medication now used for severe headaches.

"It's an anti-convulsant," said the knowledgeable patient, "for someone who has a lot of seizures, and they don't have to test your liver."

But if David Camm's new job gave him plenty of leisure time, Kim's was more punishing than ever: now Brad and Jill were both attending Graceland School. On a typical morning she'd get up at 5:45 a.m., shower and then wake David up so he could wash, while she dried her hair.

Then, as he was taking a shower at around 6:30 a.m., Kim would get Brad and Jill up and start preparing their breakfast.

At about 7:00 a.m. Camm would leave to go to United Dynamics, but Kim would have to drop off the children at school, before driving through busy rush-hour traffic to Louisville, to be at her desk at 8:30 a.m.

Most weeknights, after a hard day's work, Kim would have to collect the children from Graceland School. Three times a week she took Brad to swimming practice, and Jill also had her regular dance and tap classes.

Every Wednesday night Kim went to the Georgetown Community Church, for her weekly committee meetings and to do the books, while Brad and Jill attended Bible class.

Then after all the various activities, a weary Kim would either take the kids to McDonald's for dinner, or get a take-out meal to eat at home.

Usually when they got home David would already be there, watching television or checking his stocks on the computer. He'd help Kim give Brad and Jill their baths at about 8:30 p.m., before getting them ready for bed an hour later.

"Sometimes if I was really tired [at] 9:45 p.m.," said Camm, "I'd say, 'Come on, you guys, you can both pile in bed with me.'"

But after everyone else had gone to bed, Kim would usually still be up, working hard to make sure her husband looked his best for work the next day.

"She generally would stay up later," he explained. "Because she did all the laundry. A lot of my work shirts and stuff. She'd press my pants for me. Made sure I had the clothes I needed for work and the kids had clothes to wear to school.

"It wasn't unusual for her to stay up until 11:00 p.m. or 11:30 p.m., washing clothes, ironing or starching my shirts."

And if both Brad and Jill were asleep with their father, Kim would sometimes just crawl into one of their single beds or the living room couch to sleep.

That May, 5-year-old Jill gave a public performance with her class at the Becky Seiler Dance Studio. Afterwards Kim brought her back to her mother's house to shower and change. That was when Kim told Janice Renn that little Jill had been complaining of soreness in her vaginal area.

"So she took her in the bedroom," Janice later testified. "And then she called me in later to look and see what I thought it was. She was just really red. I can only describe it like a bad case of diaper rash."

Then Janice asked Kim if she'd recently changed brands of soap, toilet paper or laundry detergent, in case her granddaughter was allergic to any of them.

"Nothing had changed," said Janice. "I advised her to put Diaperene or something on it and if it didn't clear up in a day or so, have the doctor check it out.

A few weeks later, Jill's dance class gave another recital in its auditorium, celebrating the start of the summer season. After the performance, Kim left to pick up Brad from his swimming class, asking Helen Schroeder, whose daughter Amber was also in the class, to keep an eye on Jill until she returned.

Schroeder was waiting off-stage when dance instructor Becky Seiler brought Jill over, still wearing her tights and leotard.

"Jill was crying," Schroeder would tell a jury. "She was holding herself."

When Schroeder offered to take her to the bathroom and make sure no one else came in, Jill refused, saying she wanted her mommy. Schroeder would later testify that she became concerned about Jill, who wouldn't stop crying, and kept holding her crotch as if in great pain.

Becky Seiler returned and took the sobbing girl to the practice room. Schroeder peeked in and saw Jill sitting in her chair, still crying, as Seiler tried to comfort her.

Soon after that, Kim walked in with Brad, and Seiler took her to one side to talk. Then they all left the studio, leaving Schroeder puzzled as to what exactly was wrong with little Jill Camm.

In June 2000, Kim Camm telephoned her old school friend Marcy Mahurin McLeod to discuss bringing Brad and Jill to Florida for a visit. Kim explained that David's change of careers had been "stressful" on the family, and she and the kids were badly in need of a summer vacation.

Kim had also begun worrying about Brad and Jill's safety after seeing the movie *The Deep End of the Ocean*, starring Michelle Pfeiffer. The emotional movie, which had just been released on video, is about a parent's worst nightmare—a 3-year-old boy is kidnapped in broad daylight in the crowded lobby of a hotel. The boy is finally found nine years later, unable to remember his parents, who have since split up under the pressures.

It deeply affected Kim, making her feel insecure and even more determined to leave Aegon so she could spend more time with Brad and Jill.

During the phone call, Marcy claims she complained that she never had any time for herself, and David was not pulling his weight with the children.

"We talked about how busy she was," said Marcie. "She was working full-time and going home and taking the kids everywhere. She said that she was the one running all the time and that he didn't do a lot, because of his job."

Marcy told her to pick out a weekend to visit, but when she next heard from Kim a couple of months later, things were even worse.

13

"History Is Repeating Itself"

Soon after starting full-time at United Dynamics, David Camm strolled into the Fitness Zone to give Stephanie McCarty one of his new business cards. He was in good spirits and chatty, talking of his ambitious plans for the future and boasting that he would soon own a piece of his uncle's company.

He also reestablished contact at this time with another of his ex-lovers, Lisa Korfhage.

"He would call me periodically," said Korfhage, who was now happily married with two children. "I was in real estate, so I could refer customers to him."

On June 16, 2000, Lisa and her husband, Peter, were out with a group of friends, celebrating a friend's birthday at Jillian's bar in Louisville. At around midnight the party moved on to PT's Show Club, where they bumped into David Camm.

"He said he had been at the track all day," recalled Lisa. I thought he was talking about Churchill Downs so I was talking about horses. But he said no, he was at the NASCAR track."

Camm told Lisa he was at PT's with his cousins and some friends. Soon afterwards David said he was leaving, telling Lisa he'd be in touch.

The following day he left a message on her home answering machine, suggesting they meet up for lunch while Peter was on fire duty.

"I really didn't want to call him back," she said, "when my husband was not going to be there."

On July 1, on the advice of David Camm's brother Daniel, the Camms took out a new life insurance policy, using an insurance agent named Robert Barber, who was assisted by Daniel Camm, now living in Clearwater, Florida. The policy was for $150,000 for Kim with a $10,000 rider for each of the children, an increased coverage of $50,000 on Kim's previous policy and a $5,000 increase for each of the children. The primary beneficiary of the policy was David R. Camm, just as he had been on the prior policy. He used his brother Dan's home address in Odessa, Florida, so the sale could be made under Florida state law. In the application process Nationwide Insurance was told that David Camm and his family would soon be relocating to Florida.

Barber says he personally called Kim in Indiana, to go through the details of the policy. According to him, Kim explained she wanted to increase her husband's coverage, as he was receiving fewer benefits from UDI than he had from the ISP.

"Usually [the] husband and wife both get involved," said the agent. "[Kim] pretty much seemed like she was the one that handled those financial decisions." Daniel Camm also noted that it was always Kim who handled her family's insurance matters.

Kim Camm signed the letter, requesting the Western Reserve Life Assurance Company, a company owned by her employer Aegon, transfer her old $100,000 policy to Nationwide. Dan Camm then hand-carried the policy to Georgetown, where he witnessed Kim signing it on July 1, 2000, purportedly in Tampa, Florida.

In a separate policy David Camm increased his life insurance from $80,000 to $350,000, naming Kim as his primary beneficiary. Under the terms of both policies, if something happened to both David and Kim, Dan Camm would receive full payment, the idea apparently being that he would become the children's guardian and this money would go for their financial support.

Two weeks later, Sam Lockhart offered $315,000 to buy twenty-eight acres of land in Clarksville, Indiana, intending to relocate his United Dynamics business there, if he could get it commercially zoned.

"I liked the property," said Lockhart, "but it was zoned residential."

The land had only just been bought by a Jefferson, Indiana, Realtor named Douglas Toland, who intended to start a horse farm. But soon after buying it Toland received a call from another agent named Pat Harrison, asking if he wanted to sell it.

"She told me she had got a buy," Toland would later testify. "A contract from United Dynamics."

Then Harrison gave him Sam Lockhart's phone number asking him to handle it from there and pay her a finder's fee, if the sale went ahead. That evening Toland called Lockhart, saying he didn't foresee any problem having it zoned commercial.

"He asked me to call his nephew David," Toland would claim, although Lockhart would later strenuously deny ever doing so, "because he said he was the one that handled that."

The next day Toland claims he called UDI and spoke to David Camm, explaining the situation.

"I told him exactly what I told Mr. Lockhart," said Toland. "The zoning change wouldn't be a problem."

He also told him that UDI would have to file the application in the courthouse and that, once approved, it could not be reversed.

David Camm said he'd take care of it.

One way or the other, Camm was certainly taking care of business at United Dynamics. During the six months he worked there he proved himself a talented salesman, generating a lot of new business.

"He was excellent," said his direct boss and first cousin, Jeff Lockhart. "He was running that end of the business very well."

Virtually overnight he more than doubled his old salary as an Indiana State Trooper, and was on target to earn more than $70,000 in his first year. And he wasn't shy about blowing his own horn whenever he met his old police colleagues for lunch at Frank's Steak House in Jeffersonville.

Over a steak and beer, and wearing his United Dynamics golf shirt, he would enthusiastically discuss how his life had improved since he'd left the department. He boasted about how Kim would soon be able to leave Aegon, and live off his salary.

That summer David socialized a lot with his cousin Jeff. They were both the same age and had been close as children, before drifting apart when Camm became a state trooper.

"Then when he started working for us again," remembered Lockhart, "we were pretty close."

They played golf together on Fridays and weekends, as well as the occasional Thursday night basketball game. They also went gambling at Caesars Riverboat Casino, where Camm now regularly played the tables.

"I lost about $1,000 there over the summer," he would later admit. "But that's just play money."

He had also started playing the stock market, signing up with the online brokerage company TD Waterhouse. He invested $1,300, mainly buying and selling penny stocks.

On several occasions he took Jeff—whose father Leland Lockhart is the pastor of Georgetown Community Church—for nights on the town, ending up in Louisville strip clubs like PT's and Déjà Vu. They usually stayed about forty-five minutes, sipping beer at a table while watching the all-nude strippers dance for dollar bills.

Camm also became close to his other first cousin Phillip, who worked part-time for his father, Sam Lockhart. Phillip, who was still at Purdue University, would join United Dynamics after he graduated in Construction Management the following year.

"When I was in high school we weren't all that close," said Phillip, who is almost fifteen years younger than Camm. "We [went] to family events and would hang out and stuff."

Phillip shared Camm's passion for NASCAR and they would go to races together, as well as playing golf and basketball.

In August, David took his young cousin gambling at Caesars and then on to several strip clubs around Louisville, where he introduced him to several of the strippers.

At one club a stripper winked at David, prompting him to boast, "I think she recognizes me from the last time I was here."

The two cousins also regularly ate lunch together across the bridge in Louisville at Tedesco's or Mark's Feed Store Barbecue. One day at lunch Phillip asked his older cousin about handguns and where he'd kept his service weapon when he left the Indiana State Police. Phillip had noticed an ammunition cabinet in the Camm basement when he'd been over there the previous Thanksgiving.

"I just asked him if he owned a gun," said Lockhart. "He said he didn't own one. I didn't ask him anything about the ammo."

During the long summer vacation Brad and Jill shuttled between relatives, who would look after them during the day. They especially loved spending the day with their doting grandmother Susie Camm, who let them dress in old clothes.

"They wanted to play wedding one day," she said. "Jill loved performing. She was the one that just talked while [Brad] was off in the corner dancing."

Her maternal grandmother, Janice Renn, said Jill was a tomboy and wanted to do everything the boys did. And like Brad, "she loved to get fancied up," said Janice. "she loved every sport that came along."

Kim's sister Debbie Karem said her little niece was "fearless," and had boundless energy.

"She was a pistol," said Jill's Aunt Debbie. "A wild child with a lot of energy."

Although both children adored their older half-sister Whitney, the Camm grandparents say the teenager, who was now working at Floyd Memorial Hospital with her mother, Tammy, didn't spend much time with them.

"Well she didn't come visit them," said Susie Camm. "One day they came and said, 'Whitney's coming today.' They were both so excited."

"Oh they loved Whitney," said their grandfather Donald Camm.

Brad and Jill would also spend a lot of time at their Aunt Debbie TerVree's house, just a few yards down the path behind their own. They'd arrive with their pet chocolate Labrador, Rusty, her favorite stick between her teeth, and spend hours playing with their cousin Hannah, who was especially close to Brad.

One of their favorite games was bringing out their aunt's combs, brushes and bobby pins to fix each other's hair. Brad also loved playing checkers and the good-natured boy would even feel guilty whenever he won, as he usually did.

On hot summer nights Brad and Jill would sometimes play T-ball in a team, coached by their parents.

"Things were about as good as they could possibly be," David Camm would later say. "The best way I can describe it is *perfect*."

A year earlier, Sam Lockhart had been the force behind a new building to house the expanding Georgetown

Community Church, across the parking lot from the original. The gleaming new Family Life Center and gymnasium had opened in spring 2000, and was also used at night for basketball and for meetings of the Georgetown chapter of Alcoholics Anonymous.

Ever since it opened, Sam Lockhart had talked about starting a weekly Thursday basketball night for family and friends, but no one had followed through. Eventually in early August, Jeff Lockhart started calling around his friends and relatives and inaugurated the first Thursday night pick-up game.

David Camm was one of the first to sign up for the informal games, which began in early August. Every week Camm, his cousins Jeff and Phillip, their friends and assorted United Dynamics employees would meet in the church hall at around 7:00 p.m. and split into teams. Then they would play games to twenty points, the winner having to beat the other team by a margin of four.

They would usually finish by 9:00 p.m., when David would take up a collection to pay for electricity, which he would later give to Kim. The pick-up games soon became popular, and over the summer and fall there was no shortage of players who wanted to join in.

Janice Renn had always known when her older daughter Kim was upset. And by mid-August she noticed that Kim seemed totally preoccupied with something, but characteristically refused to discuss what was wrong.

"She wasn't acting her normal self," Janice would later testify. "Her mood was just different."

Over the previous few weeks Kim had seemed generally run-down, suffering several severe migraines and stomachaches. And on top of her busy schedule she'd taken on a new project, redesigning her and David's bedroom, and had already redecorated and ordered new sheets and curtains from Sears.

Other projects currently on Kim's back burner that summer were finishing off the basement and putting a swimming pool in the back garden for the children.

One day in early September, Kim telephoned her best friend Marcy McLeod in Florida, saying she needed to talk. It was the first time they had spoken since Kim had discussed bringing Brad and Jill for a visit.

"She was very preoccupied," McLeod would later tell a jury "Just down, depressed."

In all the years they had known each other, Marcy had never heard Kim so desperate and needy.

"She didn't want to get off the phone [and] kept hanging on," Marcy said. "We were on there for quite some time compared to our normal conversations, and she just kept making conversation, which is really unlike Kim."

At one point Marcy was so concerned about her friend, she asked if there were any problems with David.

According to Marcy, Kim said sadly, "History is repeating itself," refusing to elaborate further.

Then she promised to tell Marcy more when she saw her in Florida soon. Kim said she'd tell David that night she was taking the kids to Florida, and then book airfare for an upcoming weekend. She put down the phone, saying she'd call back the next day with flight information.

After the call, Marcy was so concerned she called a mutual friend to see if she knew what was wrong. It seemed strange Kim would consider taking Brad and Jill out of class at the beginning of the school year to go on a Florida vacation. It just didn't add up, and Marcy felt there had to be a more pressing reason for the trip.

Later, as she remembered Kim's enigmatic phrase, "History is repeating itself," she became convinced that her friend was trying to tell her David was having another affair, just as he had six years earlier with Stephanie McCarty.

A couple of days later when Kim still hadn't called,

Marcy started calling her at home and work, leaving several messages.

"I thought it was weird that I didn't hear from her," she said. "But after a week or so you get busy with the kids."

Kim never did call back. It would be the last time that Marcy would ever speak to her best friend.

In mid-September, Indiana State Trooper Shelley Romero was talking to Sellersburg post dispatcher Julie Richmer, when David Camm suddenly came on the line. It had been the first time Shelley had spoken to him since he had left the department, and she was curious to know how he was doing.

"I was just always kind of afraid that maybe he didn't make a good decision leaving," she would later explain. "Because a lot of people tend to regret it."

Romero asked him what life was like outside the department, and Camm said it was really good.

"I said, 'So you're happy?' And he said, 'Yes, very happy.'"

Then Camm changed the subject, asking if she had changed her mind yet about having sex with him again.

"It was a given he was going to hit on you," the trooper would later explain. "He was going to propose an innocent kind of liaison or something like that."

14

The Playhouse

Saturday, September 23, 2000, was a big day for the Lockhart family. Sam Lockhart had built a smart new playhouse for the children in his father's front yard, and invited the whole family to an afternoon ribbon-cutting ceremony.

David Camm and his cousins had all grown up playing in a rickety old red playhouse their grandfather Amos had built decades ago. But recently the family patriarch had decided the new generation of Lockhart children needed something a little more modern. He also wanted to erect a memorial to his beloved wife, Daisy, who had died that spring, after almost seventy years of marriage.

"Pappaw always had a playhouse for his kids," explained his granddaughter Julie Hogue, "even going back to when we were little. He just said it was something that the kids needed."

Sam Lockhart put up the money, drafting a team of his United Dynamics employees to design and construct it.

"We built that in honor of my mom, who loved kids," he proudly explained.

The two-story cream-and-blue wooden structure was a miniature colonial house, with stairs leading up to a second-floor porch. It was right across the road from Brad and Jill's house, and they were so excited, they had already invited all their friends over for a tea party the following week.

Before the early afternoon ceremony, David drove Kim and the children to New Albany to watch Whitney compete in a band contest. Afterwards they returned to Lockhart Road, where the family was already starting to gather for the 3:00 dedication.

Donnie Camm came with his daughters, Lauren and Kara, as well as little Hannah TerVree, who had given her cousin Jill one of her favorite white-and-blue–striped shirts to wear for this special occasion.

Then the grown-ups and kids assembled in front of the playhouse to await the arrival of 92-year-old Amos Lockhart, who would say a few words. The aged patriarch of the family had wanted the project completed before his death, and was beaming with satisfaction as he was helped across the yard to the playhouse.

His son Sam videotaped the frail old man's moving speech to five generations of Lockharts, stressing the importance of playing for children's later development. Then, to a round of applause, he cut the ribbon, declaring the playhouse open.

"That was a big day for us," remembered Julie.

After the ceremony Brad and Jill played with their cousins in their new playhouse, while their father planted chrysanthemum seeds in front. At one point Jill slipped over and fell, bawling her eyes out.

"She cried a lot, which is unusual for Jill," David would later remember. "But it didn't last a lengthy period of time. She was a tough little girl and after a few minutes she was back out playing again."

Indeed, family video and pictures taken later that afternoon show Jill smiling and having a great time, while her brother, Brad, looks on admiringly.

There were several Lockhart babies at the family gathering that afternoon. Later a couple of relatives would claim Kim had told them she and David were planning to have another baby.

"I think one of the goals was to get Dave's income to a

level where Kim actually would quit working," explained Donnie. "She'd take care of the family, have another kid and maybe even buy a home. So things were never brighter for them."

On Sunday morning David drove Kim and the kids to the Georgetown Community Church, where Pastor Leland Lockhart based his sermon around the playhouse. Then Kim drove into New Albany to go shopping at her brother-in-law's store, Karem's Meats on State Street.

Janice Renn was working behind the counter that day, and Kim asked if Janice could babysit Brad and Jill that night, as she and David wanted to go to a movie. Janice agreed and Kim said she'd call later to finalize arrangements.

After returning from church, Brad and Jill went next door to their Aunt Debbie's house to play with their cousin Hannah.

"Jill wanted some corn bread," remembered Debbie TerVree. "Then I let them go and fix my hair. That was so sweet."

The three children and a neighbor's boy named Troy spent the afternoon playing golf outside in the yard, with Rusty the dog happily retrieving balls.

"The kids had their own little set of clubs," said their Aunt Julie. "Dave was teaching them how to play."

Later Kim called her parents to say she'd drop off the kids at 6:00. When they arrived Janice and Frank Renn were waiting.

"They were playing with their grandfather while I was fixing supper," Janice would remember. "Then we ate and then they played with him some more while I did dishes and stuff."

She then prepared Brad and Jill for a bath, promising to make them popcorn when they'd finished. Brad took a shower while his sister had a bath.

"I washed her back," said Janice, "but then she wanted to do the rest, so she kind of played."

Janice left Jill alone for a few minutes, before returning to help her out of the bath and dry her.

"When I dried her between her legs she said it hurt," her grandmother would later testify. "She was, like, chapped. It was just really [badly] chapped. Reddish. I told her she had to be sure to wipe herself better. I put some Vaseline on it. That's all I had at the time."

Across the river, before seeing the movie *The Perfect Storm* at the Tinseltown USA Movie Theater on Towne Center Drive in Louisville, David and Kim had visited a bookstore for coffee and cookies. After the film, which David thought "unrealistic," they drove back to the Renns' house to collect Brad and Jill.

Janice told Kim that Jill's vagina was hurting and that she had put medicine on it. Later David would deny ever knowing anything about it.

"No, I never heard about it," he'd say. "Never heard it mentioned."

That night after putting Brad and Jill to bed, David Camm says he and Kim made love for the final time, hoping that she might get pregnant.

On Wednesday, David Camm met his brother Donnie for lunch at Frank's Steak House in Jeffersonville. While they were eating, several state troopers whom Camm had remained friendly with came over to join them.

Indiana State Police Press Officer Sergeant Marvin Jenkins said Camm had stayed in close touch with many of his old colleagues after leaving in May.

"A couple of us saw him at lunch," he said.

After lunch Camm returned to work at United Dynamics, where he received a call from Douglas Toland, who wanted to know what was happening with the sale of his land in Clarksville to Sam Lockhart, who was considering it as the new base for United Dynamics.

"[David] said he was waiting for an appraisal back," said Toland. "He said he'd been out the day before and walked the property."

A few days later, Lockhart pulled out of the land deal after his appraisers valued it at $245,000, far less than the $315,000 asking price. Later prosecutors would suggest that Camm had taken too personal an interest in the land to impress his uncle, driving out there on Wednesday afternoon to see it for himself.

"I just pulled up and looked around a little bit," he would explain later. "Outside of that I had no involvement whatsoever."

That night David telephoned a realtor named Susan Lottie, regarding a property he'd seen in a realty magazine Kim had brought home.

"I liked the picture," he would later explain.

According to Camm, he and Kim had discussed moving closer to Graceland School, so it would be easier to take the kids. Camm favored the "perfect house," preferably one with a swimming pool, but Kim did not like the location.

On Wednesday evening, after working a full day at Aegon, Kim had picked up Brad and Jill to take them to a new children's Bible night at Georgetown Community Church. On the way there she met her husband at a three-way stop sign near their house. They spoke for a few minutes and then Camm returned home, saying he'd see Kim and the kids later.

It was a busy Wednesday night at the Life Center and Debbie and Hannah TerVree were also there.

At dinner Kim sat next to the chairman of the church council, Steve Bobo, and proudly discussed her children.

"She said Bradley had gone through a growth spurt," he remembered, "and was getting too tall for all his pants."

After dinner Kim and her children said goodbye to everyone and then went home to watch the Olympic gymnastics on television.

"All three were normal and happy, with their sweet, smiling faces," said Debbie. "That's the last time we saw them."

15

Thursday

On the last morning of her life Kim Camm overslept, exhausted from the night before. David Camm finally woke her, and they were running a few minutes late when they roused Brad and Jill to get ready for school. After showering, Camm drove to a local store to buy some Hostess cupcakes for breakfast.

At about 7:10 a.m. he left for work, telling Kim he was playing basketball that night at the church.

"It was the normal routine," he would testify. "I kissed her goodbye and told Brad and Jill, 'Bye, and have a good day.'"

Although Kim was running late, she took Brad and Jill to Graceland School, officially signing them in at the day care center, as she did every school day. Then she drove to her mother's to drop off Brad's bag with his swimming trunks and a towel. Later, as it was Thursday, Janice would pick Brad up from school and take him to his allergist for his weekly asthma shot.

Kim stayed for a couple of minutes, as her mom wrapped her up a piece of coffee cake to eat at work. Then, shortly after 8:00 a.m. she kissed Janice goodbye, driving through the rush-hour traffic into downtown Louisville.

Camm had a busy morning at United Dynamics, organizing work crews and cold-calling prospective new clients, scribbling notes in his day planner.

"I made tons of calls that day," he said. "Probably in the neighborhood of twenty to thirty, I would guess."

It was a stressful time for the new UDI salesman, who was juggling two major projects. And he was under deadline to finish a waterproofing job that night, as his crews had Friday off.

"I had to make sure it was completed," he remembered. "I was communicating back and forth between my crew leaders."

"I had been extremely busy that day," he explained.

Kim Renn was preparing to leave her desk at Aegon Insurance at 3:55 p.m. when Johnna Bailey, her colleague in the real estate division, came into her office, and they had a short conversation.

Kim got into her black Ford Bronco to drive across the bridge to collect Jill from Graceland School for her Thursday jazz and tap dance class.

When they arrived at 4:35 p.m. the class was already under way, so Kim helped Jill change into her tap dancing shoes and she went into the studio to join the girls.

Then Kim sat down on a bench outside with several other parents to wait for Jill, who was due to finish at 5:30 p.m.

"We talked the entire time," said Cindy Mattingly, whose 5-year-old daughter Leah was in the same class, and also went to kindergarten with Jill. "Basically I was just starting to get to know her."

The two mothers had recently discovered they had much in common, as Cindy had once roomed with one of David Camm's cousins.

"I know the Lockhart family really well," she said. "The week before, we had talked a lot about who we knew and how we knew them. I thought that was kind of neat."

The working mothers also discussed their hectic schedules and the tough logistics of ferrying their children from one practice to another.

"We talked about working the day," said Mattingly, "and then having to get off work and go straight into taking the kids to the dance and soccer—you name it.

"And we talked about how our husbands played into that, with helping us out and that kind of thing. I said my husband was going to be home later on that evening, she stated that [David] was going to be home between 7:00 p.m. and 7:30 p.m. She was expecting him."

After the class finished, Kim collected her daughter and they walked towards the parking lot to her SUV. Cindy was walking a few yards behind when her daughter Leah suddenly began running towards her friend.

"She ran up and she hugged Jill," recalled Mattingly. "She said, 'I'll see you tomorrow.'"

At about 3:50 p.m., Janice Renn picked up Brad from Graceland School. After signing him out on the register she drove him to the doctor for his weekly asthma injection.

"He would always want to sign in himself," Janice remembered. "He would always double-check with me what time it was, because he couldn't really tell time yet."

Janice told him the time and Brad proudly filled out the form and signed it. When he had first started having his shots, his grandmother would make him wait half an hour before leaving, in case he had a bad reaction. But he had been having the medication for so long that she had now cut down the wait to fifteen or twenty minutes.

That night Brad had swim practice as he did three nights a week. He loved swimming and had been riveted to the television over the last week watching the Olympics swimming competition. His grandmother drove him back to her house to change into his costume.

"He wanted something to eat," she remembered. "So I fixed him a snack. He had a bowl of ice cream and Oreo cookies."

Then she helped him with his homework before he went off to watch television.

A little after 5:30 p.m. Kim arrived at her mom's house with Jill, to collect Brad for swim practice. The bubbly blonde 5-year-old was still wearing her tights and leotard from dance class.

"Kim was in a good mood," said her mother. "I didn't see anything different than normal."

Kim was in a hurry to get Brad to the swimming pool on time, so Janice got Jill some cookies, while Kim helped her change out of her clothes. Then she changed out of her executive business suit into a more casual blue-ribbed sweater and slacks.

As she said goodbye, Kim took some crackers out of the kitchen cabinet and snacked on a few.

"I asked her if she wanted some too in a bag," said Janice. "She said, no, that's all she wanted."

At about 5:45 p.m., Kim and her children left for Hazelwood Junior High School in New Albany, where Brad had his swim practice.

Janice would later recall watching Kim pull out of the driveway and both her grandchildren flashing the peace sign, which they'd recently learned, saying, "Peace, Grandma."

And she says that last poignant image of Brad and Jill laughing in the back seat of the Bronco will remain "in my mind and in my heart" forever.

By 6:00 p.m., little Brad Camm was poolside, waiting for the previous class to finish, so he and the other thirty-three members of the Silver Developmental Group could start its one-hour practice.

"He was one of the better swimmers in that group," said his swim coach, Catheryn Collings. "For the few weeks that we had run the program, he had been there almost every night that practice was available."

Collings knew Brad and his parents from the many occasions they brought him to the pool. And she would remember David Camm occasionally coming to collect Brad, wearing his distinctive United Dynamics golf shirt.

While Brad was in the pool swimming, Jill walked next door to a volleyball game, where a team from Graceland was competing against another school. Kim stood by herself in the hallway between the pool and the ball court, so she could keep a watchful eye on both of her children.

Other parents there that night remember her being restless and preoccupied. At one point she came over to sit in the bleachers by the deep end diving board. Then, looking concerned, she returned to check up on Jill at the volleyball game.

"She was bouncing back and forth," remembered Lisa Bristol, whose two sons Kelsey and Pete were on Brad's swim team. "[I was] sitting next to her probably ten minutes, fifteen minutes max."

Then Kim left to talk to another parent named Debbie Sue Aven, about an upcoming Saturday swimming competition. For the rest of the practice Kim and Debbie Sue alternated between the pool and the volleyball court.

The two mothers had both met eighteen months earlier at the parking lot at Graceland School, which Aven's three children also attended. As they both lived in Georgetown, they regularly crossed paths driving to and from school, striking up a casual acquaintance over time.

"In passing we'd say, 'Hi, how are you doing?'" said Debbie Sue, who recalls Kim introducing her to her husband Dave one night at a Graceland open house. "She was kind of quiet and shy."

Debbie Sue says that when she arrived at the practice, she saw Kim sitting in the top bleachers, and sat down next to her. Uncharacteristically, Kim seemed eager to talk, as if there was something worrying her.

"We talked about living out in Georgetown and making that commute every day," she recalled. "Her and David had considered moving [closer] at one point, but they liked where they lived. And she felt safe in Georgetown."

Then they discussed a television documentary they had both seen recently, about children being kidnapped and taken out of America as slaves.

During the conversation, Kim told her about the movie *The Deep End of the Ocean*, which had so unnerved her.

"And I remember Kim asked me, 'Do you think they're safe in there?'" said Debbie Sue. "And I said, 'Yeah,' because there were a lot of Graceland parents and things that we knew. We talked about cleaning the house and that it's good just to leave the dishes in the sink and play with the kids, because life is too short."

Just after 7:00 p.m. Kim led Brad and Jill out to the parking lot and helped them into the back of the black Bronco, making sure they were buckled up before closing the door. Then she got into the driver's seat and slowly pulled out of the Hazelwood parking lot for the twenty-five-minute drive home.

It would be the last time any of them would be seen alive.

David Camm left United Dynamics for the day just before 5:00 p.m., and drove his company van west on I-64 towards Georgetown. When he got to the junction at I-150 near Duncan, where he knew he'd get a strong cell phone reception, he pulled into an emergency lay-by to make some business calls.

"I was waiting on two different calls from two different crew leaders," he later testified. "I just pulled off to the side and was waiting for them to return my calls."

He spoke to Lisa Brown, a client who was having tile work done in her basement. A few days earlier while inspecting it, he had expressed interest in buying an oak pool table she was selling, saying he had to speak to Kim first.

"That's not the kind of purchase that I would make without Kim first having looked at it," he would later explain, "because our intentions were to finish the basement."

At about 5:20 p.m. Camm finished his calls and drove back to Georgetown, arriving at Lockhart Road about ten minutes later.

As he parked the van outside his double garage by the

side of the house, he saw his Uncle Nelson coming down the driveway. It was Nelson Lockhart's night to look after the increasingly frail Amos Lockhart and keep him company.

David walked over and chatted with his uncle for a few minutes, and then went to his house.

"I had a pretty hectic day," Camm remembered, "and [I had] a pretty bad headache when I got home."

He then went into the kitchen and took out a little plastic dispenser of his migraine drug Imitrex, which he kept in a drawer in the counter.

"I gave myself a shot," he would recall, "and then laid down for a little while and turned on the television. It takes about twenty minutes."

After the drug took effect and his headache abated, he logged on to the computer to check his stocks, and see how the market was doing. He took off his work clothes, throwing on some old blue shorts that he'd had since his earliest days as a state trooper.

At 6:19 p.m. Camm telephoned a client in Louisville named Roland Dean Miller, who had leaks in his basement. Eight days earlier he had spent almost three hours at Miller's house, doing an estimate. The two men had started talking and Miller, who is an estimator for a paint contractor, was most impressed with Camm.

"He's probably the best salesman [I've seen]," Miller would later say. "And I've been in the business for fifty years."

Getting no answer from Miller, Camm picked up an apple from the kitchen and returned to his computer. At about 6:30 p.m. he heard a truck pull up outside his house. It was the Schwan's food delivery man making his twice-monthly calls.

The Schwan driver, Robert Steier, usually dealt with Kim Camm and had only seen her husband a couple of times. Camm invited him in and then sat down to scan the catalogue, ordering deluxe ham and cheese omelets, and jalapeño peppers.

"I'd purchased [the stuffed jalapeño peppers] before and Kim ate the majority," he said. "She really liked those."

Steier punched up the items on his handheld PDA and they came to $17.98. Then Camm walked out to his truck to fetch his checkbook to pay, while the deliveryman collected the order from the back of his van.

"As I was getting ready to leave," said Steier, "he said he had to be at the church to play ball at seven o'clock."

Calling the Georgetown Community Church an "underground" one, Camm explained how they had just installed a gym and he and his family played Thursday nights.

After Steier left at 6:45 p.m. Camm placed the frozen food in the freezer and threw on a gray, oversized Indiana State Trooper tee-shirt and sneakers.

A little before 7:00 p.m.—as Kim and the children were leaving swim practice to return home—David Camm set out for his weekly basketball game. He locked the front door and walked into the yard, where his pet Labrador, Rusty, ran out to greet him with a stick in her mouth. Then he got in his United Dynamics van to drive the three miles to Georgetown Community Church.

16

Massacre

When Jeff Lockhart arrived with the keys to the church, his cousin David was already there, waiting in the parking lot, chatting to Jeremy Little and Tony Ferguson, who were also there to play. Jeff unlocked the front doors to let them in and they began shooting baskets to warm up, waiting for the other players to arrive.

Over the next ten minutes the remaining players drifted in, and after Sam Lockhart arrived they split into two teams of five to begin.

"We played old guys versus younger guys," said Eric Minzenberger, a relative of David Camm by marriage who also worked at UDI. "Sometimes the older guys didn't want to run full court so we played half court."

The first 20-point game took about fifteen minutes, and then they took a short break to get a drink of water, before returning to the court for a second game.

Later when Indiana State Police investigators closely questioned each player about what had happened over the next two hours, there would be many discrepancies as memories fade. But no one would remember David Camm ever leaving the church gymnasium for a short period after the first game, as detectives are convinced he did.

At 7:35 p.m. Debbie TerVree and her daughter, Hannah, were returning from a doctor's appointment in Clarksville. As she stopped by her nephew's house to turn into her driveway, Hannah asked if Brad and Jill were home so she could play with them.

The sun was setting and it was fast getting dark on Lockhart Road, an unseasonably cool night with temperatures in the mid-50s. Debbie noticed that no lights were on in the Camm house and both garage doors were down.

"That was unusual," she explained. "Normally they would have a light on, and when Kim came home the doors were up."

Hannah said they were probably running late because Brad had swim practice on Thursday, so they continued on home.

Debbie's husband, Bob, was in the yard, tidying up from a bad storm a couple of days earlier, so she and Hannah stopped to chat with him for a couple of minutes.

"Rusty the dog was out there," she recalled, "carrying a stick in her mouth. Then we came in the house."

At about 7:35 p.m. another neighbor would later tell police she saw Kim's black Bronco arriving home.

"Kim must have come in five minutes after I did," said Debbie. "The way I think, [someone] was there waiting."

After the first game ended at about 7:30 p.m. detectives think Camm sneaked out of the Life Center, walked across the parking lot to his truck and drove the 2.4 miles to 7534 Lockhart Road, arriving at 7:35 p.m., soon after Kim and the children.

Floyd County prosecutor Stan Faith believes that sometime between when Kim had collected Jill from Graceland School and arriving home, her daughter had revealed she had been sexually molested by her father, as recently as in the last twenty-four hours. So when he unexpectedly arrived home, Kim confronted him in the garage and it soon turned murderously violent.

"There is evidence of a scuffle," said Faith. "Or he might have been planning this cold-heartedly . . . I don't know."

According to the prosecution's theory, the ex-trooper suddenly lost all control as his angry wife got out of the Bronco, pulling out a .38-caliber gun and shooting her at point-blank range, through the left side of her head above the ear. The bullet passed straight through her brain, exiting on the right side. As Kim slumped to the side of the SUV, microscopic particles of her blood ricocheted off the concrete onto Camm's sneakers. She may have lived for up to five minutes after being shot.

Sitting in the back seat next to his little sister, the theory continues, Brad saw his father shoot his mother, and screamed, desperately unlocking his seat belt and trying to escape over the back seat into the trunk storage area. Then the highly trained marksman pointed his gun straight at his young son and fired, sending a bullet ripping through his left shoulder, passing through his left clavicle and first rib, before exiting.

Then Camm turned his attention to his daughter. Jill was still strapped into the back seat, cowering in fear with her head bent down, as if she were trying to black out what was happening. Camm's third bullet lashed through the right side of her forehead, entering her brain and exiting just behind her left ear. It was such a clean shot that the first detectives on the scene couldn't even see the fatal bullet wound through Jill's thick, wavy brown hair. Jill's massive head injuries also did not kill her immediately, and it's impossible to know how long she might have lived. But invisible to the naked eye, an aerosol spray of blood from her fatal wound spattered onto the front of her father's Indiana State Trooper tee-shirt.

Later, pathologists found that Brad may have lived a full five minutes after he was shot, and would have been conscious for much of that time. And as his young life ebbed away he would have witnessed his sister's murder by their father.

Detectives contend that using all his training and

expertise from his years in the Emergency Response Team, the ex-trooper could have wiped out his family execution-style in less than a couple of minutes.

They believe that after slaughtering his whole family, David Camm calmly walked out of the garage, past Rusty the dog—apparently the only witness—leaving one door of the double garage open. He then retraced his steps back to the church recreation center in his distinctive UDI truck, somehow getting rid of the murder weapon on the way. Then, without the other ten players noticing his absence, he cooly rejoined his team to continue the game, as if nothing had happened.

Later Sam Lockhart would claim David wanted to sit out a game at about 8:10 p.m., as his muscles were sore, inviting him to take his place.

"I went ahead and played," said Lockhart. "And Dave started stretching on the side. Eric, my son-in-law, was making fun of him, having to sit it out. 'You're getting older,' he told him. It was teasing back and forth like guys do."

Ten minutes later an old friend of Lockhart's named Tom Jolly arrived to watch the game, sitting down in some chairs by the bathroom. He saw Camm doing stretching exercises on the elevated walkway above the court, preparing to run laps.

"He walked over to talk to me," Jolly would later testify, adding that he'd known Camm since he was a young boy. "[We talked for] ten or fifteen minutes, probably."

Camm seemed relaxed as he asked Jolly how his two sons were doing.

After the game finished, Camm left Jolly and walked back onto the court to rejoin his team. They played two more quick games before taking a lengthy break at about 8:45 p.m.

Then Sam Lockhart had an informal United Dynamics

meeting on the sideline, to discuss what everybody was doing tomorrow.

"I was talking to Dave, along with my other nephew, Jeff Lockhart, and my son, Phillip Lockhart," said Sam. "Some of us were going to play golf and some of us were going to come up and do some charity work at the church."

Then Camm took one of his crew members, Martin Dickey, to one side, asking if he could work Friday on the church.

"I had given him and the rest of the crew the day off," said Camm. "He said, 'Yeah, no problem.'"

A few players had already started leaving about 8:55 p.m. and those remaining played one last four-a-side half-court match, with the old guys' team squarely beating the young guys.

At 9:15 p.m. they called it a night. Camm took up a collection of a few dollars to cover electricity, for Kim to deposit in the general church account. He reportedly joked that Kim would probably kill him for coming home so late.

Then Jeff Lockhart walked around the church, checking that it was secure, before locking the front door and setting the alarm at 9:22 p.m.

Everyone got in their cars and Camm and Phillip Lockhart drag-raced out of the rear parking lot, before heading off in different directions along State Road 64. Camm turned onto Oakes Road, leading to Frank Ott Road where he turned right into Alonzo Smith Road, taking him to Lockhart and home.

Investigators believe that David Camm returned home at around 9:25 p.m., and parked his truck in the driveway before going into the garage to clean up and stage an elaborate murder scene. Almost two hours after the slayings, blood from Kim's gushing head wound had already seeped about thirty feet out of the garage, and began to coagulate and separate into a clear liquid.

They theorize that Camm then took off his dead wife's shoes, placing them on top of the Bronco and well out of her normal five-foot-three-inch reach. Then he removed her pants, leaving them alongside her body to make it look like a sex crime had occurred. Some of her hairs would later be found caught around one of the buttons.

Then, prosecutors think, Camm heard a noise and went over to his little son's bloody body.

"When he came back he moved Brad's body out," says prosecutor Stan Faith. "He was checking to see if Brad was still alive."

Satisfied that the boy was dead, investigators think, despite evidence to the contrary, that Camm began cleaning up the bloody scene using a mop and strong bleach.

After surveying the garage, and convinced he had removed all incriminating evidence, he went through the back of the garage into the house to alert his friends at the Indiana State Police.

17

"Get Everybody Here Right Now!"

David Camm's hysterical call to the ISP Sellersburg post dispatcher came in at exactly 9:30 p.m. He would later explain that he'd called Post 45, more than three times the distance of the New Albany Police Department, because he considered it more professional.

> Dispatcher: Indiana State Police radio control. This is Patrice, may I help you?
> Camm: Patrice, this is Dave Camm, let me talk to post command right now.
> Dispatcher: OK, he's on the other line.
> Camm: Right now! Let me talk to him right now.
> Dispatcher: OK, hold on.
> Post commander (Andrew Lee): Dave?
> Camm: Get everybody out here to my house now!
> Post commander: OK. All right.
> Camm: My wife and my kids are dead! Get everybody out here to my house!
> Dispatcher: (Go to Dave Camm's house now.) OK, David, we've got people on the way, OK?
> Camm: Get everybody out here!
> Post commander: Calm down. Everything's going to be OK, all right. We're going to get . . .
> Camm: Everything's not OK, get everybody out here!
> Post commander: They're coming. (Go to Dave Camm's house now.)
> Camm: [unintelligible]

Post commander: Do you know what happened, David?

Camm: No! God— I just got home from playing basketball. Oh my God, what am I gonna do? [unintelligible]

Post commander: Listen, I'm going to let you talk to Patrice, while I get people coming.

Camm: I've got to go across the street, I've got to get some help!

Post commander: OK, David, do you need an ambulance?

Camm: I've got to go across to my parents' house!

Post commander: Do you need an ambulance?

Camm: Get everybody out here!

Post commander: I am. Do you need an ambulance?

Camm: I've got to go!

Patrice: Dave? [ringing sound] He hung up.

Commander Andrew Lee then radioed a Signal Ten—the highest priority call—to all units in the area, ordering troopers to turn on their lights and sirens and rush to the scene.

Detective Sean Clemons and Trooper Roger Halbert were returning from the Washington County Sheriff's Department, where they had been troubleshooting a faulty computer system, when they heard the priority call, ordering them to their former ISP colleague's home.

Exactly fifteen minutes after Camm's call to the post, the two troopers drew up in front of 7534 Lockhart Road. The experienced officers would be tortured for the rest of their lives by the horror they saw.

A few hours later, when David Camm had calmed down somewhat, he would tearfully recount his version of events after he left the basketball game. In the first of several interviews with ISP investigators, he claimed he had arrived home that night to find Kim had left the garage door open, which was highly unusual.

"She usually shuts it behind her and mine was down,"

he began. "And as I rounded the corner I pushed the button to raise it and I saw something lying there."

He said it was so dark in the garage, he had first mistaken Kim's bloody body for his daughter Jill's.

"She'd had pants or skirt on," he sobbed. "They'd been ripped off. But I first saw her there with that black, whatever she had on— It looked like Jill's dancing outfit.

"And I could see all the blood run out of the garage, but I mean, it happened so fast. As I'm going in I thought she had fallen and slipped, had fallen and hit her head. [That's] what I thought. And I went up, of course. I've seen a lot of dead people and as soon as I looked at her I was like, 'This ain't good!' So I immediately thought, 'Brad and Jill! Brad and Jill!' And I looked inside and I couldn't see them at first, but because of where they were positioned in the car I knew that they were trying to get away.

"I know they were trying to hide because they were both ducked down in corners. And then I saw them and I checked Jill and she was gone. And then Brad was still fairly kind of warm and somewhat limber, and I thought, 'Maybe he's got a chance.' And I pulled his butt out of there and tried to do CPR on him. I take that back. In between, before I pulled Brad out— You know, the funny thing about it is, guys, I was thinking so clear. I didn't get rattled, I didn't go nuts. I was thinking so definite 'cause I knew I needed to call somebody.

"I ran in, picked up the phone, thought about dialing 911, didn't want to call the sheriff's department, figured I'd get some stupid ding-y dispatcher."

After alerting the ISP post, he told the detectives, he'd gone back into the dark garage and pulled Brad out of the Bronco to try to revive him with CPR.

"And from then I didn't know what to do," said Camm, who, in spite of his heroic Bronze Star rescue several years earlier at a swimming pool, said he was in too much shock to remember what to do.

"And I knew my Uncle Nelson was staying with my grandpa across the road [so] I ran over there, yelling, 'Somebody's killed my wife and kids!' "

That Thursday night it was Nelson Lockhart's turn to look after his aging father, Amos, and make sure he took his medication for Parkinson's. The retired 61-year-old Kentucky State Trooper had arrived at 4:45 p.m. and they'd sat in the living room, watching two episodes of Amos' favorite TV program, *The Andy Griffith Show*, before switching over to the Olympics.

Just after 8:00 p.m., Nelson's older brother, Carlin, called from his home in Indianapolis, saying he would visit their father for a few days in October. Carlin gave Nelson the dates he was coming, so whoever would be on duty could be told not to come.

Nelson called his younger brother, Sam, informing him Carlin would be relieving him next month, but his wife, Carol, answered, explaining he was playing basketball at the church.

"We had a conversation about [Sam's] foot," remembered Nelson. "That he shouldn't be playing basketball because he's got a real bad foot."

Then Nelson called his sister Gloria, the other person who needed to be notified about Carlin's upcoming visit, but she wasn't in either.

Just before 9:30 p.m. Sam Lockhart called back and Nelson told him about their brother's visit.

As they were talking about a project Nelson was doing for UDI, there was loud bang on the kitchen door. Then it sprang open, revealing a hysterical David Camm with tears pouring down his face.

"Nelson, come quick" yelled his nephew. "Someone killed my family! They're all dead!"

Stunned momentarily, Nelson dropped the phone receiver and Sam heard a "loud screaming noise" and then
the sound of the phone hitting the wall.

"I kept yelling, 'Nelson, Nelson, what's wrong? What's
wrong?' " Sam would recall. Finally Nelson picked up the
phone receiver: "Sam, something bad has happened at
Dave's house," he said anxiously. "Get over here quick.
Something's happened to Dave's kids."

Nelson rushed out of his father's house barefoot, running across Lockhart Road, following David into his
garage, barely lit by his van headlights. But he could clearly
see a flow of colorless fluid, coming from the garage and
onto the driveway.

Once inside the garage he found David kneeling over
Brad's body.

"I didn't know if he was performing CPR on him or
what," said Nelson. "But he was down over him and
yelling, 'Breathe, Brad!' at the top of his voice."

Then Nelson looked around and took in the full chilling
horror of the bloody murder scene. And nothing in his
thirty-six-year career in law enforcement had prepared
him for the shock of seeing three close members of his
family gunned down so heartlessly.

"These people are real dear to me," he would explain,
on the verge of tears. "Kim was lying by the car on her
back, with a pool of blood around her head."

Then David asked his uncle to check on Jill, saying she
was still in the back of the Bronco. Nelson walked past
Kim's body, where a stream of blood already extended
from her head to the garage door. He skirted the front of
the Bronco, until he came to the driver's door, which he
opened. From the corner of his eye he noticed a spider web
pattern in the windshield just above the steering wheel,
about ten inches across.

"It looked as if a bullet had hit the windshield," he would
remember. "It was dim inside the truck . . . but I remember

partially entering the Bronco and I saw the shadow of Jill in the back seat. She seemed to be slumped over. I could not make out her little face. I called her name two or three times."

Then he bent down and held her arm and her hand, but they felt "cool to my touch." Her dancing shoes lay beside her in a little green bag.

Nelson told his nephew he thought they were all gone.

"Why didn't I go with them?" wailed David Camm, breaking down in tears. "I shouldn't have played basketball."

As an experienced state trooper, Nelson knew they had to get out of the garage at all costs, to avoid contaminating the crime scene. But when he told his nephew they must leave it for the detectives, David didn't want to go.

"I may have had to push him out," said Nelson. "Then Rusty showed up with a stick in her mouth."

Nelson only realized the family Labrador was there when the stick hit his leg. Usually gentle and overfriendly to strangers, Rusty now seemed highly agitated, as if something terrible had spooked her. Her whole personality changed after that night.

Nelson grabbed Rusty to try to keep her from getting in the garage and contaminating it. He dragged her outside toward another small detached garage, which Camm used to repair his cars. Throwing the stick inside, Nelson slammed the door shut, but the dog ran straight out through an adjoining door. Once again he grabbed her, chucking the stick back, but Rusty was too quick for him.

"I said, 'Dave, we got to get Rusty out of this scene,'" said Nelson. "So we both grabbed her, shoved her in there and slammed the door."

While his uncle had been trying to stop Rusty wrecking the murder scene, David Camm had been calling his brother Donnie on his cell phone, to give him the news.

Across the river in Louisville, Donnie and his two young daughters, Lauren and Kara, had just finished watching an episode from the first season of *Survivor* when he got the frantic call.

"Dave was so distraught I couldn't really understand what he was saying," remembered Donnie. "He kept saying over and over, 'Someone has killed my family!'

"I'm like, 'What are you saying, Dave?' Then he goes, 'You've got to get out here. Go tell Mom and Dad. You've got to get out here! Someone has killed Kim and Brad and Jill.'"

Julie Hogue was getting ready for bed when her brother Donnie called with the tragic news.

"Julie, Kim and the kids have been shot," he said breathlessly. "Somebody broke into Dave's house."

At first Julie didn't understand what he was saying, and kept asking her brother what he meant.

"Really, they're dead," Donnie told her. "Kim and the kids are dead."

As the terrible realization hit her, Julie hung up the phone and headed out of her house. As if in a trance, she drove to her parents' house to comfort them.

"It was surreal," she later explained, grasping for words to describe that horrific night. "You know, I can picture it. I can remember how I felt. You don't have the capacity to comprehend what's happening as it's happening. And then it just gets worse and worse and worse. I just went to find Dave and help him."

After a long, successful career running his own business, Sam Lockhart, 57, keeps cool under most circumstances, but after his phone call to Nelson he was shaken. He had been in the middle of changing his basketball clothes in his upstairs bedroom, and was still wearing gym shorts. Pulling on some jeans and a pair of flip-flops, he ran down the stairs as fast as he could.

His wife, Carol, met him at the landing, asking what was

up. He quickly told her something "wrong" had happened at Dave's house, and he had to get over there immediately.

At that moment his son, Phillip, arrived home from basketball, and Sam told him about the call. They both jumped in Sam's Tahoe SUV to drive to 7534 Lockhart Road and find out exactly what was going on.

"I drove as quickly as that vehicle would take me without flipping over," he said. "I passed people on the wrong side, going through emergency lanes. I did all those things."

They arrived at Lockhart Road at about 9:35 p.m., before the police, and as Sam pulled into his father's drive, Phillip pointed over the road and said, "Dad, it's over here," and ran across the road.

Backing his truck out of the drive, Sam pulled up to the left of his nephew's UDI truck outside the double garage. He climbed down from his truck to see the back of Kim's Bronco in the garage.

"I wanted to help," he would later testify, close to tears. "I ran up towards the garage door, wanting to know what's wrong. I [saw] little Bradley lying there. I wanted to pick him up and see if there's anything wrong with him."

Suddenly his brother Nelson yelled at him to stay out of the garage, as it was a crime scene.

"I could see Bradley pretty plainly," he said. "Then I looked up and saw another body over there, who turned out to be Kim. I first thought it was Jill laying over there.

"That's when [Nelson] pointed at Kim. I don't know how to describe it, other than it's like flashes of strobe lights . . . like back in the seventies. You could see people moving."

Nelson screamed and had to physically restrain his brother from going in to touch Brad. When Sam walked out of the garage he saw David Camm kneeling on the asphalt driveway, just rocking back and forth behind his UDI truck.

At that moment Indiana State Trooper Josh Banet arrived in his cruiser. As he pulled in, his red lights flashing,

David Camm let out a piercing, tortured scream, hitting the back of his van three times with his bare hands, as hard as he could.

"It was a scream that I've never heard before and I've never heard since," recalled Sam. "All I heard was Dave screaming and I heard sirens, as officers were responding to the call. [Dave] was hitting the back of his tailgate. That's where he was at. Then he went down on his knees and just laid down on the ground and started wailing."

18

"Do It Right!"

At 9:45 p.m. Detective Sean Clemons and Trooper Roger Halbert arrived at 7534 Lockhart Road, only seconds behind Trooper Josh Banet. They parked by the corner of the garage and saw Sam, Nelson and Phillip Lockhart in a huddle, talking. Next to them Dave Camm was on his knees, his hands gripping the tailgate of his monogrammed UDI van.

"[Our] headlights hit the fluid flow coming out of the garage," said Trooper Halbert. "And I remember seeing it, thinking, 'Oh my God, I hope that's not what I think it is.'"

As Clemons got out of his cruiser he looked his boyhood friend in the eye, gesturing as if to ask what was going on.

"He kind of nodded at me," said the detective, "and told me to go into the garage."

Clemons entered the garage, followed by the two troopers. To their horror they saw a gruesome tableau of the blood-soaked bodies of Kim and Brad, dimly lit by the headlights of the van outside.

Trooper Banet walked over to Brad's body, bending down to check for any signs of life. Then Halbert checked Kim for a pulse. At that point the troopers had not even noticed Jill's slumped body, still strapped into the back seat of the Bronco.

Detective Clemons—who, under ISP protocol, then became lead investigator, by virtue of being the first detective on the scene—led the other two troopers to the back of the garage, up some stairs to a breezeway and into the kitchen. There they were joined by Trooper Dave Miller, who helped sweep the house, searching for any more possible victims or even the killer or killers.

Holding flashlights, their guns drawn, the four troopers walked through an unlocked door into the kitchen, around the island and past some double French doors leading into the dining room. There Clemons made a mental note that the doors were locked, not appearing to have been disturbed.

There was a chilling silence as they continued into a small hallway, leading into a small utility room. Then Clemons turned right, into the laundry room, stepping over a pile of dirty clothes on the floor. He then continued to the next doorway on his left, checking a large walk-in closet.

"I was looking for any other persons that could be injured," Detective Clemons would later explain. "A suspect or whatever the situation."

They slowly continued their sweep through the rest of the ranch-style house, checking the en suite master bedroom, taking particular interest in the shower and toilet.

David Camm's computer was still switched on, Clemons noted.

By this time more troopers had arrived at the house, so they all returned to the kitchen, checking the front door on the way, noting it was locked and not tampered with.

"I then began to secure the crime scene," said Clemons. I called the post to request additional personnel be sent to the scene."

As the troopers began descending on Lockhart Road, Nelson Lockhart left to make sure his father was all right, and tell him about the murders.

"My dad was almost 93 years old at the time," he explained. "I knew he was wondering what was going on. We can't leave him alone because he tends to fall down. [So] I told him what was going on."

Then Nelson started calling other family members to tell them the tragic news, before they saw it on television.

"The first person I called was my brother Leland because he's our minister," he said. "I wanted him to know so he could start telling people that needed to know."

Shocked, Pastor Lockhart said he was coming straight over. Then Nelson called his wife, Karen, who burst into tears when she heard Kim and the children had been killed.

After his brother Nelson left to check on their father, Sam Lockhart suddenly noticed there were no lights on at his sister Debbie's house.

"I started telling the police officers, 'You need to get somebody over there,'" said Lockhart. "Someone may have killed them too."

Then Sam Lockhart and a couple of troopers went to check on them, finding them safe but completely oblivious to what had been happening less than fifty yards away.

Neither Debbie nor Bob TerVree had heard anything until about 9:30 p.m., when she'd seen car headlights coming up her nephew's drive and stopping.

"I thought, 'Kim and the kids are already home,'" said David's aunt. "They'd taken their baths and gone to bed, so it must be Dave coming home from basketball. But the lights stayed on and that's when I heard the noise."

Later she would learn it was David Camm, beating his clenched fists on the back of his truck in a fit of emotion, but initially she thought it might be her husband, Bob.

"I thought my husband was banging on the computer or the desk," said Debbie. "I walked in and said, 'Bob, are you hitting the computer?' It sounded as if someone was hitting the end of my house, pounding on it."

Her husband told her it wasn't him. And as Debbie went back to the living room her brother Sam and the troopers arrived, and told her the terrible news.

"I screamed," she remembered. "I fell on the floor. It was like a nightmare, chaos."

Debbie says she thanked God that her 8-year-old daughter, Hannah, who was so close to Brad and Jill, had been asleep and was not awakened by all the commotion.

"When she went to bed that night everything was normal," said Debbie, "and I believe God kept her asleep so she would not know what was going on until the next day. And then we had to tell her."

Trooper Shelley Romero was heading south in her cruiser on I-65, returning from a weeklong K-9 training school, when she heard the ISP Signal Ten alarm call, for all units to go to Dave Camm's house. Although officially off duty and not in uniform, she immediately called the Sellersburg post dispatcher, saying she was on her way. Then she turned on her siren and lights and hit the accelerator.

About fifteen minutes later the attractive blonde trooper, now in her early thirties, arrived at 7534 Lockhart Road, while Detective Clemons was still sweeping the house. She parked in the yard and saw Camm standing by his van, outside the garage.

Romero got out of her cruiser, going up to another trooper to find out what had happened.

"One of them said, 'It ain't good,' " Romero would later testify. "And I said, 'Where's Dave?' and they said he was up there, and pointed. I just ran up and I grabbed Dave and I said, 'What the hell happened?' "

Then he just looked at his former lover with tears in his eyes.

"Someone just killed my family, Shelley," he sobbed. "Someone just killed my fucking family."

As Romero tried to comfort him, Camm seemed in a daze as he explained how he'd returned from playing basketball to find Kim's garage door open. He said he'd hit the garage door opener and seen the bodies.

"He thought Kim had been shot in the back of the head," said Trooper Romero. "I wondered how he would know something like that. He was still just in a kind of can't-believe-it's-happening mode. [But] he was still rather calm around me."

But when Sean Clemons came over to ask what had happened, Camm became upset.

"He got extremely agitated," remembered Romero, "to the point where he was walking around just kind of swinging his fists. Tensing up and flinching quite a lot."

Camm described finding his family's bodies, somehow determining that Kim and Jill were both dead, without touching them.

"He then turned his attention towards Bradley Camm," said Detective Clemons. "He told me it appeared as though Bradley was attempting to climb over the back seat into the storage area of the Bronco, in an effort to get away. That Bradley had the 'best chance' and that he pulled [him] out of the Bronco and laid him on the garage floor and began CPR."

Suddenly, Camm grabbed his old friend by his shirt and began to pound on his chest.

"[He] told me that he wanted this 'fucking done right,' " said the detective. "I assured him that it would be done correctly, and that we were going to do everything we could to figure out what had happened."

For the next few minutes Trooper Romero stayed with Camm, hugging him and trying to comfort him. By now there were more than a dozen state troopers milling around the yard, waiting for instructions. Then Romero spotted Roger Halbert coming out of the garage, and asked about Kim, Brad and Jill.

"Have you checked 'em?" she said.

"They're gone," Halbert said sadly.

"Are you sure? Check 'em again."

"Shelley, they're gone."

"Check 'em," Shelley told him.

At 10:17 p.m. Pastor Leland Lockhart arrived and went straight over to comfort his weeping nephew. A few minutes later David's father, Don, turned up too.

"I kind of handed [David] off to them," said Trooper Romero. "I walked up and I looked into the garage, but I didn't enter the crime scene."

There Romero observed a thirty-foot trail of clear fluid ebbing from Kim's head. It was slowly running down the driveway and had already passed the UDI van. She asked Josh Banet if the fluid was still moving, but he said he didn't know.

"And I don't know why I did it," she would later testify, "but I picked up a little rock in the driveway and I sat it down next to where the trail was at the time. That way, in case anyone asked later whether it was moving, I could look at it and say this is where it was at a certain time."

For the next few hours Romero stayed with David Camm, trying to console him. It was getting cold so she borrowed a state police jacket to put on top of his basketball tee-shirt to keep him warm. But she was also wearing her policewoman's hat, looking for any clues to who murdered Kim, Brad and Jill.

"We talked for hours that night, yeah," she remembered. At one point she asked David if he was having an affair with someone who might have committed the crime.

"He kind of looked me dead in the eye and he said, 'No, Shelley, that's the one good thing about all this. I haven't been seeing anybody. Things have been going great.' "

Sergeant Sammy Sarkasian, an Indiana State Police crime-scene investigator attached to the Sellersburg post, had known David Camm for years. At 9:35 p.m. on Thursday night he'd just returned to his home in Georgetown, after working a case with the New Albany Police Department, when he made a routine sign-off duty call to Post 45.

Post Commander Andrew Lee answered the phone, saying he'd just received a very disturbing call from David Camm.

"Sam, I'm glad you called in," Lee told him. "[Dave's] found his family dead in the garage."

"His family?" asked Sarkasian incredulously.

"Yeah, he's found his wife and two kids dead in the garage," repeated Lee.

Trooper Sarkasian agreed to make some calls and round up a technical team to perform the crime-scene investigation. In the meantime he asked Lee to alert Detective Sergeant Robert "Mickey" Neal, who was in charge of the Bureau of Criminal Investigations at the Sellersburg post.

After hanging up the phone, Sarkasian realized he would need outside help for a triple murder involving the family of an ex-trooper. So he put in a call to his CSI opposite number at the ISP's Jasper post, Sergeant Jeff Franklin. He said he would call his technician advisor, Sergeant Jim Niemeyer, to make the necessary arrangements, before meeting him at David Camm's house.

Sergeant Sarkasian left for Lockhart Road, arriving at about 9:50 p.m., where he was met by Sean Clemons. Ten minutes later, after briefing Sarkasian, Detective Clemons officially requested search warrants to be able to reenter the Camm garage and house and start the investigation. But it would take more than three hours before the Floyd County Prosecutor's Office provided the necessary paperwork.

While they were waiting, Clemons sent out troopers to canvass the neighborhood, looking for pertinent information. He requested that all detectives assigned to the District 45 area and three additional evidence technicians be sent to Lockhart Road.

Clemons asked Detectives Mickey Neal and Darrell Gibson to officially interview their close friend and ex-colleague David Camm later that night at the Sellersburg post. Clemons told them he felt compromised "based on our history and our old friendship." He also knew Kim

Camm well and had met Brad and Jill several times. But right from the beginning he had determined not to let his personal feelings enter into his investigation.

During the next three hours the perimeter around the Camm house was sealed off, as an active crime scene. A trooper sat at the entrance at all times for the next three days, logging the names and times of everyone going in and out.

A second staging area was set up across from the Camm house on Lockhart Road, to accommodate all the police officers, technicians and specialists that had been drafted in for the investigation. And a third area, at the junction of Lockhart and Alonzo Smith Roads, became a press center, catering to the scores of print reporters and TV crews that soon converged on the house.

As the garage with Kim and the children's bodies was strictly off-limits until a search warrant could be issued, Sergeant Sarkasian had to kneel by the doors, using a flashlight, to make his initial observations.

"I saw a white adult female lying with her feet toward the vehicle," he would testify. "And there was a white male child lying to the side of the female."

Sarkasian also noted the three-foot plume of blood emanating from Kim's body, leading to a long trail of clear fluid going out of the garage doors. From the waist down, he observed, Kim was only wearing black underwear. He then shone his flashlight inside the black Bronco, and saw Jill's body in the back passenger seat.

Later he would express surprise at how neat the whole crime scene was, as if it had been cleaned up.

"I didn't see a lot of footprints or tracking in the blood," he said. "I didn't see much disruption whatever of the scene."

Earlier, Detective Clemons had explained how Camm had gotten into the Bronco to remove Brad over the front seat, before trying to revive him with CPR. So Sarkasian was astonished that there were only one-and-a-half shoe prints by the boy's body. His experience as a criminal scene investigator had taught him that if someone gave aid at a crime scene, they usually left footprints behind.

"I didn't see footprints," said Sergeant Sarkasian, who immediately questioned David Camm's account of what had happened.

19

"I'm Hurting"

Floyd County Prosecutor Stan Faith arrived at 7534 Lock-hart Road at 10:32 p.m., for his first look at what would become the biggest case of his long, distinguished career. A huge, bulky man with a perfectly clipped gray Amish beard, Faith, 55, had been the Floyd County prosecutor since 1987 and was one of its most respected citizens.

Born in southern Indiana of Irish descent, Faith spent the first nine years of his life around the New Albany area, before his father, who was a teacher, moved the family to Indianapolis.

He went to Indiana University, earning a Bachelor of Science degree in 1966, before spending four years as a social sciences teacher. Then he changed careers and became a salesman, peddling textbooks school-to-school.

"I had the State of Indiana as my territory," he said proudly. "I enjoyed the salesman part of it, but I hated the desk job."

After briefly returning to teaching, he entered law school in 1979, determined to become a lawyer and change the world. An avowed Democrat and idealist, Faith was inspired by the assassinated civil rights champions Robert Kennedy and Martin Luther King Jr. In 1982 he passed his bar exams and was licensed to practice law in Indiana District Courts.

Faith interned as an investigator for Green County for two years, before moving to the Floyd County Prosecutor's

Office. A year later he was appointed chief deputy prosecuting attorney, and elected prosecutor in 1987.

During his twenty-three-year career Faith has tried sixty-six cases, losing just three. His most high-profile murder case up to this point had been successfully prosecuting Jonathan Whitesides, who was convicted of the 1992 killing of his best friend, Eric Humbert, although the body was never found.

On January 15, 1992, Humbert, from New Albany, had been reported missing by his wife. Two months later his blood-stained vehicle was found in a Louisville garage, launching a murder investigation. Police soon zeroed in on his friend Jonathan Whitesides, the last person to see him alive.

Whitesides admitted getting into a fight with Humbert over his wife, but claimed his friend had stabbed himself in the neck. He had then panicked, he told police, dumping Humbert's body into the Ohio River, before returning to clean up the murder scene.

As it was a circumstantial case with no body, it almost didn't go to trial. But then prosecutor Stan Faith remembered a blood spatter course he had taken several years earlier, at the National District Attorneys Association in San Francisco. On a hunch he contacted Rod Englert, the Portland, Oregon–based expert who'd conducted the course. The prosecutor then hired Englert as an expert witness, flying him to New Albany to reexamine Humbert's vehicle. The resulting blood spatter and tissue evidence would prove key in convicting Whitesides of murder one.

Since then Faith had remained in touch with Englert, who'd become nationally known as a crime-scene reconstructionist and expert on blood analysis. He'd worked on the O. J. Simpson and Bob Crane cases, as well as the Selena murder, and often appeared on television to discuss newsworthy crime-scene investigations.

That night, as he observed the bloody carnage at 7534

Lockhart Road, Stan Faith knew blood could hold the answer to who had murdered Kim, Brad and Jill Camm.

"It was the most emotional crime scene I've been to in twenty years," said Faith. "It was like two very nice-looking, wonderful individuals, laying there all alone. I mean, it was lonely at that crime scene.

"I didn't see Jill. I asked where she was and they said she was still in the back of the Bronco. And I certainly didn't want to go in any further and look. That was my first meeting with the Camm family."

As he walked out of the crime scene, already roped off with yellow tape, Faith met with Sean Clemons, to discuss what had to be done next.

"We talked about DNA evidence," remembered Faith, "and calling in blood spatter experts."

Twenty-seven minutes after first arriving at the crime scene, the prosecutor went home, determined to call Rod Englert the next morning.

At 10:56 p.m. David Camm's ex-wife, Tammy, and her new husband, Jimmy Lynch, arrived at Lockhart Road. An hour earlier Camm had telephoned her, breaking the news of the murders and asking her to tell their 17-year-old daughter Whitney.

"I need you to tell Whitney something for me," Camm had told her. "This is serious and I need you to do this."

After putting down the phone, Tammy and Jimmy drove to Georgetown, and were allowed into the driveway to see David. The first thing he asked was if Whitney had been told. When Tammy said she hadn't had the nerve, her ex-husband became even more upset.

"You've got to go back," he told her. "You've got to tell Whitney."

Reluctantly, Tammy agreed to go home and tell Whitney her two half-siblings had been murdered, along with Kim. She then promised to bring her straight back to see her father.

"Whitney is close with my kids," Camm later explained. "They go back and forth."

At 11:15 p.m. Donnie Camm and his sister, Julie, arrived, after spending an hour comforting their "devastated" mother. A helicopter with searchlights hovered overhead, as troopers directed them into their grandfather's yard, where they were logged into the crime-scene book.

"The police had the driveway blocked," remembered Donnie. "They were only letting family members in. A lot of my family were already there—aunts, uncles and my dad. And David was just standing out there numb. They wouldn't let me near him or even get close to the house."

Eventually Donnie and Julie were allowed to see their brother, who was weeping uncontrollably in his driveway.

"We mostly just hugged," remembered Julie. "The three of us just held each other for a long time. There wasn't a lot of conversation."

Donnie says they were so deeply shocked, no one knew what to say.

"It was the most surreal thing I think I've ever been through in my life," he explained. "Just the sheer gravity of it. You just couldn't make any sense out of this. And especially children."

At about 11:30 p.m. Frank and Janice Renn had just gone to bed, when their doorbell rang. They answered the door to find Pastor Leland and Sam Lockhart, accompanied by a state trooper, who took them inside and broke the devastating news that their daughter and grandchildren had been murdered.

After trying to console them, the Lockhart brothers left, so Frank could call their other daughter Debbie and grieve behind closed doors.

20

A Rollercoaster Ride

Around 11:45 p.m., Detectives Mickey Neal and Darrell Gibson asked David Camm to accompany them to the Sellersburg post, to be officially interviewed.

"I was reluctant to leave," Camm would later testify. "I just didn't want to leave my family. I wanted to wait until the bodies were removed."

Trooper Neal, who had partnered shifts with David Camm for years, explained that nothing further could be done until a search warrant had been granted, so a coroner could examine the bodies. Finally Camm agreed to have his friend Trooper Mark Slaughter drive him to Post 45 for the interview, while Neal and Gibson went separately.

"Mark and I are friends," explained Camm. "As soon as I saw him he just came up and he just gave me a big hug. And I just said, 'Mark, how am I gonna get through this? You're the only one that understands. I'm hurting.'"

But before leaving, he asked Donnie and Julie to pick up some medicine for him at New Albany Memorial Hospital, as he was getting a migraine.

David Camm arrived at the post in Sellersburg ten minutes after Neal and Gibson, who were already waiting in a small interview room. As the video equipment was broken, the interview was only recorded on audio.

At 12:21 a.m. on Friday, September 29, Trooper Neal turned on the tape recorder and began the interview. Both detectives felt highly uncomfortable interviewing their friend and ex-colleague so soon after his entire family had been wiped out.

"Darrell and I both talked about this on the way down here," began Detective Neal, pouring Camm a cup of coffee. "There's no way for us to know what you're going through. No way."

He told Camm that if he felt uncomfortable at any time, he could walk out of the interview and go home.

"You know as well as I do the reasons we're here," Neal continued. "We're going to try and find out what happened, so we can bring that person to justice."

"Just do it," replied Camm. "And do it right."

The troopers first asked him to describe the day, leading up to when he discovered Kim and his children dead.

"It was a pretty normal day," said Camm. "It's like clockwork. I went to work, did my thing all day long."

He then told the detectives about playing basketball at Georgetown Community Church, where his Uncle Leland was pastor.

"[It's] an underground church," he told them, referring to its unorthodoxy. "We just built a big gymnasium and we've been playing ball every Thursday from seven to nine."

Detective Neal then questioned Camm about Kim's movements that day and Brad's swim practice. Then Camm described how he had found Kim and his children, lying dead in the garage.

"It happened so fast," he began, explaining he had called the Indiana State Trooper post instead of some "ding-y dispatcher" at the New Albany Sheriff's Office.

Detective Gibson asked Camm if he had locked his front door when he went off to play ball.

"I didn't lock it," he replied. "We live on a private road. We're all related."

Camm told the detectives how he wished he'd gone to Brad's swim practice, instead of playing basketball.

Someone must have been "laying there waiting" for Kim and the children to come home, he theorized.

"What makes you think that?" asked Gibson.

"It's the only way I can explain it," said Camm. "I think it was somebody after me."

Asked if he had any enemies who might have done this, Camm mentioned a neighbor he had busted for drugs several years earlier.

"He knew who I was," said the ex-trooper. "And on the way to jail he was bitching and moaning. And I was like, 'Man, you're not going to come over and shoot my dog or anything like that, are you?' And I just blew it off."

Gibson asked if he had made enemies in his new job at United Dynamics.

"Well, maybe," replied Camm. "We've got a lot of Mexicans that work there. Some of them know where I live."

Suddenly David Camm stared at his hands, still covered in blood from moving Brad's body out of the Bronco.

"Look at all the blood on my fingers," he said, holding them out to show the detectives.

When Gibson asked if he had noticed anything unusual in his house when he'd run in to make the emergency call, his response was puzzling, considering the circumstances.

"No, damn it," he began. "My check is in an envelope, but I don't think it's been touched. It's lying right there. My paycheck. Not to make you guys jealous, for a week it's almost fourteen hundred dollars, I think. And it's laying right there. All you've got to do is pick it up and look."

The detectives looked at one another, wondering what he was getting at.

Then Camm complained about his "stinking headaches," saying his medicine was by his paycheck in the kitchen.

"Yeah," said Gibson, "I knew you had migraines."

When asked what valuables were kept in the house, Camm said there was nothing of much value, except a Folgers jar of loose change in the laundry room.

Suddenly Camm started referring to Kim impersonally. "She doesn't have that much nice jewelry," he told the detectives. "She's got some earrings that I bought her a couple of years ago. They were about three thousand dollars, and I don't know if she wore them. But they'll probably be on the dresser."

He admitted having a "few guns" in the basement for hunting deer. Downstairs was a little gun cabinet with an old muzzle loader and an ancient 410 shotgun, but Camm assured the detectives it was always locked.

"The one that's worth the most is a three hundred and fifty-six Lever Action Rifle with a scope and stuff," he said. "I've shot it two times and that's the one that I like the most that I shoot."

Gibson asked if he had purchased his ISP-issue 9mm or .357 firearms when he left the state police, as many retiring troopers do. Camm had no need for them, he said, but admitted having "a bunch of ammo" in his basement and "other state police stuff," that he should have turned in.

"We'll just look the other way," quipped Neal, but no one laughed.

"I mean, it just doesn't make any sense," Camm said. "Unless somebody was just after my wife, gonna rape her. But why in hell they had to kill my kids . . . You know, I can't figure that out."

Gibson then asked about Kim's job at Aegon, and whether she'd had any recent problems with co-workers, "flirting" or "stalking" her. Camm said she hadn't mentioned anything.

Neal wanted to know if Kim might have been having an affair, saying that he wasn't trying to "insult" him.

"Mickey," Camm replied, "I don't know she'd have time to. Her schedule is full. I've never suspected her of that. I mean, her days were full. Unless there would be something during the day that . . . you know. She'd have to be pretty good about it, 'cause there's no phone calls, no nothing. She's always there when I call."

Kim's life revolved around Brad and Jill, he told detectives, and she devoted every weeknight to them.

"It's like four courses now," he explained. "They have church stuff on Wednesdays, Brad has swimming three nights a week. I mean, it's always something. Jill has jazz classes, and weekends we generally do something."

Then Camm wondered out loud how the driver's-side door of the Bronco had been open, as Kim would always use the front passenger side door to let the kids out.

"That don't make sense," he said. "I can't figure out why . . . unless the guy came around [and] she was shot, or however it happened."

Gibson asked about Brad's position in the Bronco when Camm had carried him outside.

"I know he was trying to get away," Camm replied. "I couldn't find either one of the kids when I first looked in. They were both turned in the corners towards the back. I mean, they were trying to hide. Gosh, man, this is killing me!"

Then he started tearing up. Neal asked if he wanted to take a break, but he refused, saying he wanted to continue.

"I know that the kids saw things and they were probably trying to get away," he sobbed. "Probably saw things happen to their mom. And maybe they were yelling for me and I wasn't there. And how long did they lay there and bleed before they died? How long did they hurt? Those are things I just don't know if I can live with."

Detective Neal then attempted to comfort his friend and former partner, sensing his thoughts were turning to suicide.

"This is straight from the heart," said Neal. "I'm a Christian. I believe that there's a lot after this planet that we live on and that God takes kids to be with Jesus."

Then Camm asked how God could expect him to go through all this and carry on living.

"What kind of God puts a human being through so much?" he asked. "What lesson is he trying to teach me? I'm a little angry with God 'cause I swear to you . . . If I killed myself, I will probably end up in hell. That's the only thing that's keeping me from doing it."

Detective Neal urged him to look to the Bible for answers.

"Satan lives on this planet," said the detective. "He's very strong and that's my belief. It's not because God's testing, it's because Satan is alive and well.

"My suggestion to you, Dave, is that you talk to God, you pray a lot, you ask for strength. But you've got to lean on God. You've got to lean on Christ."

Then the detectives called a short break and turned the tape recorder off. Without the tape running, Gibson asked about his previous girlfriends. Camm readily admitted cheating on Kim, but said he didn't believe he'd upset any woman enough to resort to murdering his wife and children.

After the tape recorder was turned back on, Darrell Gibson leveled with Camm, telling him that as a spouse he was automatically a suspect and they wanted to clear him as fast as possible.

"As of now we're looking at anything," said Gibson. "We don't have a hell of a lot to go on."

Camm offered to make himself available whenever needed to help them find the murderer.

"Just right now I don't know how I'll feel tomorrow," he said. "I'm sure it's going to be a rollercoaster ride."

About an hour into the interview the detectives asked David Camm to take off his basketball clothes, which he was still wearing, so they could be forensically examined for DNA and blood.

"The reason we're taking your clothes and stuff is just to clear you," Detective Gibson assured him.

Camm agreed and some spare clothes were brought in for him to put on, after he was assured that he would not have to "sit around naked."

Gibson warned him to expect some "gossip" from people who might believe he was responsible, urging him to stay in control. He had to put any thoughts of suicide out of his mind, said the detective, so he could stay strong for his surviving daughter, Whitney, and his other relatives.

"You're going to be going through a hard time," said Detective Gibson. "And probably everything hasn't sunken in yet. You have lost the most important things in your life . . . but I want you to promise me that you're not going to do anything to yourself. Will you promise me that, Dave?"

Suddenly, for the first time in the interview, Camm became angry.

"Fuck, no," he sobbed. "I won't sit here and tell you that. We'll find out who the son of a bitch is that did it first."

Urging him to be rational, Detective Gibson told him that the murders affected a lot of other people as well.

"I don't know what the hell I would do in your situation," said Gibson. "But I know there's a lot of people out there that care for you."

"It's easy for you to sit there and say that, Darrell," he sobbed. "I don't know if I can handle it. It hurts."

Finally Gibson asked him to promise not to "do anything" until he was cleared of the murders, so he didn't look guilty.

"Darrell, I ain't making you no promises," said Camm. "But you guys have got to find out [who] did this first."

At the end of the interview, Donnie and Julie arrived with his anti-anxiety and migraine medicine, which they'd obtained from a twenty-four-hour Walgreens. They were immediately taken up to the interview room to see their brother.

As he took the medications, Camm began rambling, asking the detectives if somebody really did murder Kim, Brad and Jill or if he was having a nightmare.

"This just doesn't happen," he wept. "I live on a nice private road. There, nobody bothers me. I don't have any problems. I mean, somebody doesn't just pick out my house and kill my wife and kids. This just doesn't happen."

The detective told him there had to be "some kind of thread," tying it all together, and vowed to find it.

Then Mickey Neal asked if Camm had ever been involved in drugs or anything "under the table," during his ten years as a state trooper.

"The last time I smoked any marijuana I was about nineteen," he replied. "I've drunk beer about once a week. I've never taken any dope. I've never given anybody any dope. I've never taken anybody's money or taken any bribes."

As Gibson left the room to take contact numbers from Julie, Camm completely lost it, breaking down in front of Mickey Neal.

"I swear, Mick," he said. "I don't have a fucking clue. I don't have a fucking clue. I swear I don't. Unless there is something I just don't know about."

As Camm was about to leave with Donnie and Julie to spend the night at their parents' house, Detective Neal asked if he would be willing to take a polygraph test to eliminate him from their inquiries.

"My answer is yes," replied Camm. "Absolutely."

Ultimately, the prosecution never pursued his offer.

The search warrant finally arrived at 1:05 a.m., three-and-a-quarter hours after it had first been applied for. Immediately an army of state troopers and forensic specialists moved into the garage and the house, searching for evidence and clues.

The Indiana State Police had a seven-step crime-scene protocol, used for every criminal investigation. First the crime scene is defined and then secured, using police tape and personnel, to avoid any contamination.

Then a case officer is appointed, who is responsible for assigning the various tasks and then documenting the findings for a later trial. In the Camm case it would be his friend Sean Clemons who would head the investigation, as the first officer at the scene. The fourth step is to establish what resources and experts will be needed for the investigation, and whether any outside help would be needed.

Next is a primary walk-through, so officers can observe the crime scene objectively. This is followed by a secondary walk-through, documenting and photographing evidence and taking notes.

The seventh and final step is to collect and preserve evidence, by brown bagging and carefully marking before sealing.

This was the responsibility of Sergeant Sammy Sarkasian, as the ISP crime-scene specialist. And while he supervised state police technicians, videotaping and photographing every inch of the crime scene, Detective Clemons organized the search for the murder weapon, which involved more than fifty troopers over the next three days.

They looked in the Camms' septic tank, outbuildings and all the surrounding fields, but at no time did they ever search Amos Lockhart's house, where Camm had first gone to summon help.

At 1:21 a.m. Floyd County Deputy Coroner Becky Davis-Balmer arrived, to arrange the removal of the three bodies for autopsy. Four-and-a-half hours later her husband Greg, the Floyd County coroner, joined her to place the bodies in black-and-gray plastic body bags, before transporting them to the Kentucky Medical Examiners Office in Louisville. Under a long-standing arrangement the autopsies would be conducted by Kentucky's M.E., whose jurisdiction covers parts of southern Indiana.

The bodies of Kim, Brad and Jill were put in refrigerators overnight, until they could be autopsied the next day.

At 4:25 a.m. Detective Sean Clemons left the crime scene to grab a couple of hours' sleep. He knew that his job as lead detective on the first triple murder in local history had only just begun and would be particularly challenging, as it involved such a good friend.

And it would be made even harder as Clemons, and several other detectives, already considered their former brother-in-arms the prime suspect.

21

A Family Affair

It was almost 2:00 in the morning when David Camm left the Sellersburg post with Donnie and Julie, to spend the night at their parents' house.

"He was like a zombie," Julie remembers. "Bewildered and just empty. Mom and Dad were a wreck, so I stayed over there and helped Dave."

For the rest of the night the Camm family sat in the living room on couches in silent shock and disbelief. At one point Susie Camm became so hysterical, a doctor was called. He prescribed tranquilizers, which everybody ended up taking.

"[Dave] would sit there like he was in a hole," remembered Donnie. "And then he would cry and then dry up. And then he would cry some more."

Julie remembers the whole night as "surreal," with what little conversation there was skirting around the murders.

"We didn't even grasp what had happened," she said. "I don't know if we still do."

As it was getting light outside, Julie walked past her brother and noticed he still had blood on his left thumb, which he was tenderly caressing with his other hand. Julie thought it was upsetting him and told him he had blood on his hand.

"I know," he sobbed. "It's Brad's."

And when she offered to get him a cloth to wash it off,

he refused, saying that these few drops of blood were all he had left of his son.

At about 7:00 Friday morning, David Camm telephoned Aegon, on the advice of his sister. She thought it would be better to tell them about Kim before they read about it in the newspapers. He agreed, saying he'd just have to be a man and cope now. Julie looked up the number in the phone book and her brother dialed it.

Aegon's switchboard operator, Nancy Steward, took his call at about 7:15 a.m. She had already heard about the murders before she'd left for work, soon realizing the caller was Kim Camm's husband.

"He told me he wanted to speak to the head man," she would later testify. "I made two or three different phone calls but at that time of the day there is no one in the office."

Steward asked him if a supervisor would do, but Camm refused, saying it had to be the head man. So she dialed Aegon's CEO Rudy Gernert's extension, explaining the situation.

Gernert, having also heard about the murders on the radio, took David's call. He knew Kim by reputation, although he had never met her in person.

"He wanted to let me know that his wife would not be in to work that morning [as] she had been murdered the previous night," Gernert recalled, saying Camm appeared rational and subdued. "He asked that we save any information, particularly any e-mails or voice mails."

Explaining he was a former police officer, Camm said he thought investigators would be interested in reviewing them, so they should be saved at all costs.

Gernert commiserated about what had happened, saying he was a father himself. Aegon's human resources department would soon be in touch to wrap up her affairs at work, he assured him.

Then the issue came up about what to do about Kim's

benefits and life insurance policies, which would be estimated to be worth $681,000.

The CEO said he'd have the head of Human Resources get back to Camm on that, and Camm promised to keep the company apprised of funeral arrangements.

On Friday morning, news of the murders exploded through the normally quiet streets of New Albany and Georgetown. All three Louisville TV stations led off with it, and it was on the front page of the New Albany *Tribune*. One enterprising TV station even dug up old footage of David Camm's January 1999 high speed chase, running it as B-roll, during the ensuing coverage of Kim, Bradley and Jill's murders.

The story also went national, being reported on CNN. Indiana State Police Press Officer Marvin Jenkins was busy, fielding questions as best he could, refusing to speculate on the cause of death or any possible motive.

The Tribune trumpeted the headline, "Triple Murders" on its front page, informing readers how the ten-year state police veteran had come home to find his entire family massacred.

Floyd County Coroner Greg Balmer told the newspaper Kim and her children had all died from gunshot wounds, refusing to give any further details.

The Louisville *Courier-Journal* weighed in for its first of many stories on the murders with the headline: "Two children, mother are slain near Georgetown." A strap-line below read, "Ex-trooper finds his family's bodies in garage."

Next to headshots of David, Kim, Jill and Brad, the newspaper could barely contain itself, informing readers, "shock, grief grip small Indiana town."

Floyd County Sheriff Randy Hubbard told reporter Meghan Hoyer how he'd first encouraged a teenaged David Camm to become a state trooper.

"He's a friend of mine," declared Hubbard. "He's a good policeman."

As soon as Kevin Wilson, Principal of Graceland Christian School, heard the tragic news, he personally called all the parents of Jill and Brad's classmates, requesting they keep their children at home that day. He also organized grief counseling for pupils, to help them come to terms with the murders.

Donnie Camm's daughters, Lauren and Kara, who had grown up with Brad and Jill and were in their classes at Graceland, were inconsolable. They would spend months in counseling, to get over their fears that it could also happen to them.

They were like brother and sisters," said Donnie. "They'll never be the same. There's just a hole there and they miss them terribly."

And little Hannah TerVree, who had virtually lived with Brad and Jill, was also heartbroken when her mother finally told her she would never see them again.

At 9:40 a.m. Kentucky Medical Examiner Dr. Donna M. Hunsaker began Kim Camm's post mortem, at the Urban County Government Center on Barret Avenue in Louisville. She was assisted by Dr. Leigh Thorne and Dr. Angela Wetherton. Sergeant Sammy Sarkasian also attended as a witness for the Indiana State Police, and to officially document the autopsy findings.

"The body is received wearing a long-sleeved, dark blue ribbed sweater, a white bra and a pair of black brief panties," wrote Dr. Hunsaker in her official autopsy report.

Later she would testify that she observed Kim's sweater was blood-soaked and the waistband of her panties was rolled inward.

"In addition," said the doctor, "she had some white particulate powder-like substance to the pubic region of her panties."

There was rigor mortis in all the joints, showing Kim had been dead for a long time, although there was no medical way of knowing the exact time of death. The doctor removed the brown evidence bags, put on at the crime scene to protect Kim's hands and feet. She found the fingernails dirty and one of the nails of her right hand was ripped, as if she'd attempted to fight off her attacker. There were numerous scratches, abrasions, and bruises to her neck, chin, right elbow and left knee.

"The torn fingernail could be a defensive injury," explained the doctor. "[Kim] is trying to get away or trying to defend [herself] or others in an ongoing attack."

But the catastrophic through-and-through bullet wound to the head had proved fatal. Dr. Hunsaker found that the .380 bullet had entered the left side of Kim's skull, three-and-a-half inches from the top of her head, causing multiple fractures. Kim's thick hair had made it impossible to accurately determine how close the shooter had been when he fired. It had ripped through the left side of the brain with a slightly downward trajectory, exiting through the right-hand side, behind the ear.

"Kim died of a perforating gunshot wound to the head," said the doctor, who added that it was impossible to know exactly how quickly she died, as the brain stem was not severed.

"I can say she died quickly," said the doctor.

But even though Kim was medically brain-dead, her heart had continued to pump blood out of her horrific head wounds onto the cold concrete garage floor for five minutes or longer.

At 11:50 a.m., Kentucky's chief medical examiner, Dr. Tracey S. Corey, began to perform Brad and Jill's autopsies. Once again Sergeant Sarkasian was there as a witness and to collect evidence as needed at any future trial.

A nationally recognized expert on pediatric forensics, Dr. Corey, 42, also works as a consultant to the FBI in Quantico. Three times married, the attractive petite blonde forensic pathologist had been Kentucky's chief medical examiner since 1997.

"Bradley was a normally developed, apparently healthy little boy," Dr. Corey would later testify. "The first thing that I noticed, as far as injuries, were the gunshot wounds, both of entrance and exit."

Dr. Corey found that the bullet had entered the 7-year-old's left shoulder, tearing left to right through his clavicle, first rib and spinal cord, before exiting through his right back shoulder blade. There were numerous stippling tattoos all over the left side of his face, where burning gunshot residue had struck the skin.

"As a forensic pathologist this helps me estimate the range of fire," explained Dr. Corey. "This tells me the gun was somewhere around two feet or less close to Bradley when it was fired."

The position of the stippling also meant Bradley Camm was looking directly at his killer when he was shot.

"I would estimate his survival in minutes," she said. "When the bullet passed through his spinal cord he would lose the use of his legs and some of the use of his arms. There were no findings to indicate that he would immediately lose consciousness."

Dr. Corey found that Brad had died as a result of internal bleeding a few minutes after he was shot.

At 2:15 p.m. Dr. Corey moved on to little Jill Camm's body, still dressed in a striped blue-and-white shirt, dark blue leggings and white cotton panties with a floral design.

"Jill sustained a gunshot wound to the head," observed the chief medical examiner.

Jill's thick brown hair had all but obscured the tiny entrance wound, but after shaving part of her head, Dr. Corey saw a thin trickle of blood behind the ear, where the bullet had entered.

The fatal bullet had ripped straight into the right side of

Jill Camm's skull, passing through her brain and wiping out her motor skills. It exited through the left side of her head, behind her ear. Dr. Corey believes that, like her brother, Jill could have survived for several minutes after being shot.

The stippling marks to her face were in a tighter cluster than Brad's, meaning the shooter was even closer to Jill when the gun was fired.

As she continued the autopsy, Dr. Corey was shocked to discover evidence of blunt force trauma to Jill's external genitalia, consistent with sexual abuse, which could have been caused by a penis.

"That was very alarming and disconcerting," said Dr. Corey. "And that's what started the whole detailed examination. As soon as we began removing her panties we could see blood right there, which is obviously not something we usually find in five-year-olds."

In her autopsy report, Dr. Corey noted that Jill Camm, who weighed just 43 pounds, had a light abrasion and other small injuries to her genital area. But her hymen was intact, meaning she had not suffered penetrative sexual intercourse.

She also found an unusual pattern of broken capillaries, known as petechial hemorrhaging, on Jill's upper chest, arms and face. It showed that she had recently been forcibly held down, with something cutting off her circulation. The only time Dr. Corey had ever seen these kinds of injuries in a young child was in a Louisville rape case she'd once worked on.

The forensic pathologist also observed that the injuries were in a well-protected area of the genital region, and would have been painful, especially when urinating, and could easily have been mistaken for a rash.

Even more disturbing was the finding that Jill may have been sexually abused within twenty-four hours of her death, although Dr. Corey could not be more specific on the timing.

At the end of the autopsy, Dr. Corey tested Jill with a sexual assault kit and handed the results to Sergeant Sarkasian. He took them back to the ISP laboratory for analysis, along with Jill's little blood-soaked barrette.

After his call to Aegon, David Camm and his sister, Julie, started making funeral arrangements for Kim, Brad and Jill. They arranged a viewing for the bodies on Monday, October 2, from 11:00 a.m. to 8:00 p.m. at Graceland Baptist Church in New Albany, where the children had attended school, with services on Tuesday at 11:00 a.m. This would be followed by burial at Graceland Memorial Park. Mourners were advised that gifts should be sent to the Georgetown Community Church or the Graceland School's elementary education department.

They also wrote three almost identical obituaries for *The Tribune*, which would run in the local Sunday edition.

At 10:30 a.m. Aegon's director of human resources, Sharon Long, returned Camm's earlier call. When she'd arrived at work Rudy Gernert had summoned her into his office, asking her to secure Kim's desk and collect her voice mails and e-mails.

"I expressed sympathy on behalf of Aegon," remembered Long. "He gave me the visitation information and the burial arrangements for Kim, so we could share that with our employees."

Then Long, who had worked closely with Kim on several projects and thought her an "excellent" worker, asked Camm if she could do anything to help. She felt personally involved, as Kim had often spoken of Brad and Jill, proudly discussing all their school activities, like swimming and dancing.

"I understand that you're the person I need to talk with about benefits," Camm had said. "I will be getting in touch with you after this is over."

ABOVE LEFT: Julie, David, Donnie and baby Dan, all grew up as a very close family in their parents' house in New Albany. *Credit: The Camm Family*

ABOVE RIGHT: David Camm may have been a mediocre student at New Albany High School, but he was a talented car mechanic. He and Kim were inseparable in the days they were courting. *Credit: The Camm Family*

ABOVE LEFT: Amos and Daisy Lockhart (*front*) with their children in the 1970s. *Credit: The Camm Family*

ABOVE RIGHT: David's mother, Susie Camm, like the rest of the family, is convinced of his innocence. *Credit: John Glatt*

ABOVE LEFT: New Albany High School, which David and Kim both attended without knowing each other. *Credit: The Camm Family*

ABOVE RIGHT: Tammy Zimmerman married David after becoming pregnant with his baby. *Credit: The Camm Family*

ABOVE LEFT: Kim Renn as a teenager, a few years before she met David on a blind date. Although she was shy by nature, Kim was a leading member of New Albany High School cheerleading squad. *Credit: The Camm Family*

ABOVE RIGHT: The Aegon Center in downtown Louisville, where Kim worked as an accountant. *Credit: John Glatt*

ABOVE: Their 1989 wedding was a grand affair at the First Church of God in New Albany, presided over by David's uncle Leland. To the left of them are Kim's parents, Frank and Janice Renn, and to the right are Don and Susie Camm. *Credit: The Camm Family*

LEFT: David and Kim seemed to have everything going for them when they became man and wife. *Credit: The Camm Family*

ABOVE LEFT: Soon after the wedding, David became a member of the Indiana State Police and was on the fast-track to promotion. *Credit: The Camm Family*

ABOVE RIGHT: The Indiana State Police Post 45 in Sellersburg, Indiana, where Trooper Camm was based. *Credit: John Glatt*

ABOVE LEFT: A young David Camm, relaxing at home. *Credit: The Camm Family*

ABOVE RIGHT: Handsome and debonaire, David Camm got the ladies' attention. *Credit: The Camm Family*

ABOVE LEFT: Brad and Jill loved to dress up in outlandish clothes and play games together. *Credit: The Camm Family*

ABOVE RIGHT: Brad always looked out for his younger sister, Jill, and was an unusually thoughtful little boy. *Credit: The Camm Family*

LEFT: Brad and Jill with some of their cousins at the inauguration of the playhouse, just days before they were murdered. *Credit: Debbie TerVree and Phyllis Rhodes*

ABOVE LEFT: A diagram of the crime scene in the Camm garage. *Credit: The Indiana Superior Court*

ABOVE RIGHT: PT's Strip Club in downtown Louisville where David Camm knew most of the strippers from his frequent visits. *Credit: John Glatt.*

ABOVE LEFT: Veteran Floyd County Prosecutor Stan Faith spared no expense to prosecute David Camm for the alleged murders of Kim, Brad and Jill. *Credit: John Glatt.*

ABOVE RIGHT: The Georgetown Community Church Gym where David Camm played basketball the night his family were murdered. *Credit: John Glatt.*

ABOVE LEFT: Defender Mike McDaniel put up a valiant nine-week battle on behalf of his client, David Camm. *Credit: Matt Stone,* Snitch

ABOVE RIGHT: The New Albany Superior Courthouse played host to Indiana's trial of the century. *Credit: John Glatt*

ABOVE LEFT: The garage on Lockhart Road, New Albany, where Kim, Brad and Jill were slaughtered in cold blood. *Credit: John Glatt*

ABOVE RIGHT: David Camm is escorted from Floyd County Jail during his trial by Lt. Danny Emily (*left*) and Sgt. John Alee (*right*). *Credit: Michael Hayman /* © *The Courier-Journal*

LEFT: David Camm's house was a police crime scene for many weeks after the murder of his family. *Credit: John Glatt*

LEFT: David Camm's aunts Debbie TerVree and Phyllis Rhodes were among his staunchest defenders after he was arrested for murdering his family. *Credit: John Glatt.*

LEFT: The Ford Bronco, where Kim and her children died, was still on display at the ISP Post 45 in March 2004. *Credit: John Glatt.*

ABOVE LEFT: David Camm's brother Donnie with his daughters—Kara, 11, and Lauren, 7 (*left to right*)—who were in the same classes as Brad and Jill. *Credit: John Glatt.*

ABOVE RIGHT: Frank Renn talks to the press outside the Floyd County–New Albany Courthouse in early 2002, after his son-in-law David was found guilty of murdering his daughter Kim. With him are his daughter Debbie (*left*) and wife, Janice (*right*). *Credit: Bill Luster/© The Courier-Journal*

Later she would describe his tone of voice over the phone. "He was very rational," she said. "Very factual."

Later that day, ISP Detectives Darrell Gibson and Charlie Scarber arrived at Aegon to search Kim's office. After they finished, Sharon Long called Kim's parents, arranging to personally deliver her belongings, including her favorite pictures of Brad and Jill, which she always kept on her desk.

Soon after he put down the phone, Camm and his sister, Julie, drove to Frank and Janice Renn's house for an emotional meeting. Earlier that morning Camm had asked if anyone had broken the terrible news to Kim's parents, and Julie had told him how Sam and Leland Lockhart had gone over the night before.

"He wanted to go see Frank and Janice," said Julie. "I went with him."

When they knocked on the front door it was opened by Kim's Uncle Mark, who immediately started hugging Camm, as he took him inside the house. There he found his heartbroken father-in-law, Frank, sitting on a chair by a desk, and his mother-in-law, Janice, on a couch.

Camm sat down on a recliner by the kitchen, his eyes red from crying. He kept telling them how he could still hear his son calling, "Daddy, Daddy!"

"We just cried a lot," said Julie. "Very hard. Dave broke down more than I had seen him so far. I felt that it was as close to being near Kim as he could be."

David explained the visitation hours and funeral arrangements they'd made, and after an hour, he and Julie left.

"We went to the cemetery to find burial plots," said Julie. "And then we went by the doctor's office . . . as Dave wanted to talk to him."

At midday they returned to Lockhart Road to check up on the investigation, and try to get some fresh clothes. There were troopers everywhere and state conservation officers had brought in a specially trained dog, now scouring the woods behind the house for a murder weapon. There was also a team of ISP divers searching a nearby pond.

Television crews and reporters were everywhere, trying to get interviews and family photographs. To avoid them, Dave and Julie went over to their grandfather's house, where Sam Lockhart was already waiting.

"The media had called the kids' school, wanting pictures," said Julie. "They were starting to bug people and look up names in phone books and everything to get pictures."

ISP Press Officer Marvin Jenkins recommended they give the media photographs of Kim and the kids, so they wouldn't be pestered. Camm, who was not allowed in his house as it was an active crime scene, told a trooper where to find the pictures.

At about 1:00 p.m., Detective Sean Clemons spotted David Camm, his Uncle Sam and Julie sitting on lawn chairs in Amos Lockhart's garden. He came over to see how his friend was doing and to ask if he needed anything.

While they were talking, Camm surprised the detective by asking if investigators knew what had caused the broken windshield in the Bronco. The small hole, just over the dashboard, had been so hard for Clemons to see in the badly lit garage the previous night, that it had taken him more than two hours to even spot it, although Nelson Lockhart claimed to have spotted it immediately. So he carefully noted that Camm was not only aware of it, but apparently concerned about what had caused it.

Then Camm gave the lead detective the name of a neighbor and a colleague at United Dynamics, urging him to question two Mexican friends of his. Sam Lockhart gave Clemons the relevant phone numbers, and he promised to contact them as soon as possible.

A couple of hours earlier Detective Clemons had interviewed Camm's Aunt Debbie and her husband, Bob Ter-Vree. During the interview Debbie mentioned hearing "banging noises" at about 9:30 Thursday night. Later she claimed that when he asked if they were gunshots, she said no.

"I said, 'Sean, they were not gunshots,'" she remembered. "I know what gunshots are. My husband's an ex-cop and I worked for the police department and shot guns."

Then she banged on her desk with her fists several times to show him what they sounded like.

Two days later in his signed probable cause affidavit, Detective Clemons would write that Debbie had heard "three distinct sounds at the time of the murders that could be interpreted as gunshots."

After leaving their grandfather's house at 1:43 p.m., Camm and Julie returned to their parents', and he finally fell asleep for a couple of hours on the sofa. While he was sleeping Trooper Shelley Romero telephoned to check up on him.

Julie answered the phone and explained her brother shouldn't be disturbed, telling her about the funeral arrangements.

"I didn't know his sister," said Romero. "I said, 'Do not wake him, but if he wants to talk to somebody when he gets up, have him call me,' and I left my number."

Over the next several days, Shelley had many conversations with David, feeling torn between their long friendship and her responsibilities as a state trooper.

"Half of me was being a really supportive friend and really caring how he was doing," she explained. "The other half of me is still the policeman, keeping my eyes open, listening."

During their conversations Camm would continually fish for information on the investigation, and the course it was taking. But Romero had been quietly warned by a superior officer not to discuss the investigation with him, so she would pretend to know nothing.

On Friday evening David, Julie and their parents

watched the six o'clock news, to see how the murders were being reported. They were horrified to see the old footage of David's beating incident being shown repeatedly.

Julie was so furious she called her Uncle Sam to discuss what action the family should take.

"And because we're pretty aggressive people," Julie explained, "we were on the phone to the news channels, and the next day we had a press conference. In hindsight maybe we weren't right."

Later that evening Pastor Leland Lockhart became the first member of the family to give a press interview, speaking to reporters outside the crime scene.

"The family's hurting terribly," he told *The Courier-Journal*. "Kimberly was like a daughter to me, and those kids, they were like grandkids."

As his uncle was being interviewed, David Camm's New Albany High School friend Lisa Sowders turned up at his parents' door to offer moral support, after hearing about the murders on television. As a good neighbor, Lisa had cooked a pot roast in case they needed dinner.

"I just knew that's what you do [in an emergency]," she said. "You cook food and you take it to somebody."

When she arrived, Camm was out but his parents were there, as well as Julie and her 3-month-old baby grandson, Parker.

While she was commiserating with the family about the murders, Lisa, who runs a crime-scene cleanup business with her husband, Rick, picked up the little baby.

"When David came in I was holding his nephew," said Sowders, "and he said, 'Is that yours?' But then he realized it was his nephew and I knew he was out of it."

As she was leaving, Camm walked her out to her car and gave her a big hug. Then she says he surprised her by asking her to clean up the black Bronco, in which his family had been slaughtered, twenty-four hours earlier.

"I told him that should be the least of his concerns now," she said. " 'Don't worry about it. We'll get around to that later.'

Though Camm would later deny Lisa's allegations, she says, "And he asked me a total of three times that night about cleaning his vehicle. He was anxious to get it done."

Three thousand miles away in Portland, Oregon, crime-scene reconstructionist Rod Englert briefed his partner Robert Stites about the Camm murders. Earlier that day, Floyd County Prosecutor Stan Faith had called him to discuss the murders, hiring him to investigate the blood evidence and reconstruct the crime.

Englert was speaking at a conference that weekend so he asked Stites to fly out to New Albany instead and start work.

"My task was just collect the information for him at the crime scene," said Stites, who brought a large suitcase full of lighting and other specialized equipment.

The former police officer, who has worked homicide cases for U.S. Army and Naval Intelligence, first heard about the case at 1:30 p.m. Pacific Time. Ten hours later he was on the red-eye flight from Seattle–Tacoma airport to Louisville to begin.

22

"My Wife Is Looking Down from Heaven"

At 7:00 a.m. Saturday morning David Camm telephoned Trooper Shelley Romero, on the verge of suicide. Ironically, it was also the wedding day of Stephanie McCarty, the woman he had left Kim for six years earlier.

"Please just tell me my kids are in heaven, Shelley," he sobbed uncontrollably.

Fearing that he was serious, she begged him not to hurt himself and made him promise not to do anything rash until the murderer was caught, so he would know what had really happened.

"I'm not much of a God-fearing person, but I knew he was," explained Romero. "And I said, 'Dave, do you believe in God?' And he said, 'Yes, I do.' I said, 'Well, there's your answer—you know your kids are in heaven.'"

Romero tried to keep him talking on the phone to calm him down. And he told her he'd done "some pretty interesting shopping," buying three plots in the cemetery. His one-time girlfriend then asked him what clothes he planned to bury his dead wife and children in. David said he had thought about dressing Brad and Jill in the same Kentucky baseball jerseys, as they had recently been to a game and enjoyed it.

"But he wanted something nicer for Kim," said Romero.

She then asked what he planned to wear for the funerals and Camm said he was penniless, as the investigators refused to let him back in his kitchen to get his wallet and paycheck, as it was still a sealed crime scene.

Shelley said that was "no big deal" and she would give him the money. Then she offered to come straight over and take him clothes shopping that morning.

" 'I'll take you to get a suit,' " she said. " 'That is the least of your worries now.' I just kept telling him, 'Whatever you need just, you know, tell me and I'll take care of it for you.' "

As soon as she put the phone down Trooper Romero called her ISP superior officer Lieutenant Jim Biddle, to report back about her conversation with Camm. She noted that he never mentioned his wife's or children's deaths.

"It made me curious," she would later explain.

And just a few hours later, when detectives asked Camm who he suspected had killed his family, he told them they should take a close look at Trooper Shelley Romero.

After their conversation, David Camm telephoned the Sellersburg post, asking to speak to Detective Sean Clemons.

"He wanted his wallet and his payroll checks out of the residence, so he could have some money to purchase some clothing," recalled the lead detective. "It was decided that we would obtain these articles."

After hanging up, Clemons and another detective collected the wallet and UDI paycheck from 7534 Lockhart Road, personally delivering them to David Camm at his parents' house. Camm answered the door and hugged his old friend before asking how the investigation was progressing.

"I told him that we were working on things," said Detective Clemons. "And we were doing everything we could to solve the crime and that we had everybody working diligently."

Then the detective asked if Camm would be willing to submit to a suspect kit to clear his name, as blood and DNA samples were being taken from the scene. Suddenly David got very upset, asking why *he* needed to be tested.

Clemons tried to calm him down, saying it should be done to eliminate him as a suspect. But it didn't have to be done immediately.

"I asked him to give it some thought," said Clemons.

After Clemons had left, David telephoned his Uncle Sam to see what he thought. He told his nephew he should definitely be tested, even arranging an appointment that afternoon at Floyd Memorial Hospital with detectives.

Most of the morning Camm lay prostrate on a couch in his parents' living room, heavily medicated. He hadn't showered or shaved since the murders, and was wearing the same badly fitting clothes he had been given at the post early Friday morning, including his borrowed Indiana State Police jacket.

So his sister, Julie, took matters into her own hands and went to a nearby Kmart, buying him clothes, a razor and shaving cream. When she returned he took a shower, so he would be clean when the hospital nurses took the suspect kit.

On Saturday afternoon, the Lockhart family held a press conference in the parking lot of the Georgetown Community Church. With an American flag flying half-mast next to a large cross as a background, David Camm's uncle, Pastor Leland Lockhart, flanked by a dozen members of his family, addressed the media from notes he had written.

"This tragedy has left a very deep hole in our parish family," he said sadly. "Our pain is enormous."

Other members of the family told reporters about their grief at losing "the perfect family" in such an unspeakable manner.

"Why do this?" Sam Lockhart asked a reporter from *The Courier-Journal*. "It was senseless. We have a family here that had their hearts ripped out by a heinous crime. Our lives have been changed."

Asked why David Camm had not attended the conference, Sam told reporters his nephew was "experiencing a loss that cannot be put into words."

At 2:55 p.m. crime scene reconstructionist Robert Stites was officially logged in to 7534 Lockhart Road to begin his investigation. He'd only had a couple of hours' sleep after his all-night flight, and the Portland State professor—who teaches the only blood spatter university course in America—was greeted at the crime scene by Floyd County Prosecutor Stan Faith.

Inside the garage Stites saw the black Ford Bronco, which had been towed to Sellersburg on Friday night for testing, but was now back exactly where it had been at the time of the murders.

"When I walked in there," Stites later testified, "I immediately looked at a large pool of blood that was on the concrete floor, in the middle of the garage."

Then the blood expert got to work, documenting everything that he saw in the double garage.

"The first thing I did was just graph the whole garage out," he explained. "What was the size of the doors? Where was the blood located?"

He then sketched the blood patterns that he observed on the ground and inside the Bronco, as well as measuring the vehicle, to ensure he had an accurate picture of the crime scene, in case something was moved later. It would also be used back at Rod Englert's Portland laboratory for his later experiments, along with all the other evidence being collected.

Then Stites turned his attention to the long trail of colorless liquid running out of the garage.

"I observed some interesting things," he said. "There was a trail of bleach on the deck that looked like somebody dropped a bunch of bleach as they were walking. You could see where they poured it off. It was on the rail and then it went back in the house."

He followed the trail into a small utility room, where he found an open container of bleach, a mop and a bucket. In the garage he noticed a white residue on the floor, which he mistakenly concluded was dried bleach. There were also stains on the concrete garage floor, as if, he surmised, some bleach had also fallen there.

Then he looked above the stairway linking the garage to the house, and saw some red stains on the overhead garage door. He believed they were "blood drops," which could have been high-velocity blood spatter from Kim.

As he toured the crime scene, carefully taking notes and sketching blood patterns, several state troopers followed in his wake.

Using his white-surgical-gloved hands to make points, he explained the difference between forward and back blood spatter, high-velocity impact spatter and blood contact transference.

The professor told the troopers that a .38-caliber bullet, like the ones that had killed Kim, Brad and Jill, travels at 682 mph. When the bullet penetrates the skull the pressure inside the head increases, resulting in fragments of the skull, blood and brain matter bursting out through the hole.

Invisible to the human eye, the impact of a 682 mph bullet penetrating a human head produces fine droplets of blood, resembling a mist, known as high-velocity blood spatter.

"We're primarily interested in the high-velocity impact spatter, the mist, that comes out of there," said Stites. "It's a wonderful tool and the interesting thing about this is that it only travels four feet at the most."

Stites likened high-velocity blood spatter to a snapshot in time. And when found deposited on a person, it provides incontrovertible proof they have been within four feet of where the bullet entered the body.

There is also back spatter. This occurs where a bullet continues its course, compressing brain tissue and blood in the head and pushing more material out in front, causing intense pressure on the skull wall. Therefore the exit wound tends to be bigger than the entry wound, and the back spatter distribution is far wider.

Thirdly there is transference, where blood is inadvertently picked up by another person coming into contact with it.

At 4:42 p.m. Stites left the crime scene with his diagrams and drawings and telephoned Sean Clemons, saying he had news. After a cursory examination of the bathroom shower curtain, Stites erroneously believed he had detected signs of high-velocity blood spatter. He said he planned to go back and do extensive tests with luminol, a highly sensitive blood reactant.

They arranged to meet back at the crime scene that night, so Stites could take Clemons on a guided tour of his findings so far.

Earlier, Sean Clemons had requested the services of Floyd Memorial E.R. Nurse Cathy Doan, trained in forensics, to take the necessary samples from David Camm. Nurse Doan had known the ex-trooper for about ten years, from when he would bring in prisoners to be tested.

The Indiana State Police Suspect Evidence Collection Kit involves taking samples of pubic hair, head hair, blood and saliva. It can take anywhere between thirty minutes to two hours, depending on the suspect.

Detective Clemons met Camm just before 6:00 p.m. in a small private lounge used by emergency room technicians, well away from the public areas. A few minutes later Detective Darrell Gibson arrived as an official witness.

While they were waiting for Nurse Doan to prepare her equipment, Camm suddenly looked Detective Clemons straight in the eye, declaring, "If that expert puts me in jail, I'm gonna come back and kill you two!"

Later Camm maintained it was merely a joke between friends to break the tension in "an extremely humiliating situation." But the two detectives were not amused.

"Anytime somebody threatens my life, I take it seriously," Clemons would later testify. "I didn't know how to respond."

Then Nurse Doan came into the room and shook Camm's hand, offering her condolences. She explained she would be performing the examination and then left to get the necessary paperwork, arranging for them to use a more private emergency room at the back of the hospital.

"I went to triage and instructed them no visitors were to be allowed back until I gave them a phone call," she said. "I instructed staff to pull all curtains and shut all doors."

She then returned to the lounge and took Camm and the detectives down a rear hallway to Room 15, where the testing could be done away from prying eyes.

After he signed the consent form, the nurse asked Camm to undress from the waist down, handing him a gown and sheet to cover himself for the sake of decency.

But then to her embarrassment, Camm declared he "just felt like letting it all hang out," and didn't need anything to cover himself with.

"[He] proceeded to get up on the OB-GYN table," said Nurse Doan, "just dropped his underwear and his pants and sat down on the table. Well, it made me a little uncomfortable."

After he refused to put on a gown, she handed him a sheet, which he put across his lap.

A few minutes later, as she was explaining the procedure for collecting samples, Camm gave a boyish smile as he nodded agreement. But suddenly he became agitated and upset when the nurse mentioned extracting a semen sample.

"I'm not going to jack off into a cup!" he declared angrily.

"He made that comment a couple of times," said the

forensics nurse, "until I stopped him and [said] that wasn't going to be necessary. We weren't actually going to obtain a semen sample in that manner. I tried to lighten the situation a little bit and he seemed to calm down."

During the intimate evidence collection, the detectives watched as Nurse Doan ran a comb through Camm's pubic hair to obtain samples. But suddenly, he broke the uneasy silence, declaring, "So this is what they do to you when you kill your wife and kids? My wife is looking down from heaven and shaking her head."

Astonished at his strange outburst, Nurse Doan stopped combing, taking him to task.

"[I told] Mr. Camm that the reason why I was collecting the evidence kit was to actually provide known standards for the people who were directing the investigation."

Detective Clemons was also surprised by Camm's words, which only made everyone there even more uncomfortable.

Then Camm himself plucked a few hairs from his short brown crew cut, allowing the rest of the samples to be taken in silence. The nurse gave each sample to Clemons, who placed it in a small envelope, before carefully writing up a property record and receipt.

After the tense forty-minute examination, Clemons took the samples back to the Sellersburg post, where they were secured in a temporary evidence locker, until needed for testing.

Sean Clemons, who had virtually grown up with David Camm, took the threat on his life extremely seriously, believing his family could be in danger.

"I moved my wife and children," he later testified, "to her parents' home in another county."

After leaving the hospital, Sam Lockhart drove David and Julie to the Seabrook Dieckmann Naville Funeral

Home on East Market Street in New Albany, to check on the arrangements.

"[We] picked out the caskets," remembered Sam. "Then we went over to the gravesite and picked out graves, where they could be buried. I made the financial arrangements to purchase the lots."

Then they discussed what Kim, Brad and Jill should be dressed in for the Tuesday funerals. They decided to go to Dave's house and pick out some clothes.

It was almost dark when they arrived at Lockhart Road, parking in their grandfather's yard. Then Sam Lockhart and his nephew walked across the road toward the garage, where Detective Darrell Gibson and several troopers had gathered in a circle, discussing the investigation.

Camm told Gibson they needed access to his house, to get clothes for the funeral and some family pictures. But when Gibson denied them entry, saying the house and garage was still an active crime scene, a loud argument ensued.

The highest ranking state trooper at the crime scene was Lieutenant Jim Biddle, who had served with David Camm and knew him well. When he heard the raised voices he walked over to see what was going on.

Sam Lockhart told him they needed clothing and photographs for the funeral, and had been refused entry to the house. He demanded to know exactly who had final authority over the crime scene. Biddle told him that as the lieutenant in the Bureau of Criminal Investigations, he was the ranking officer and ultimately responsible for the overall investigation.

"Mr. Lockhart didn't understand why he would not be allowed into the house," Lieutenant Biddle remembered. "I explained to him that it was still part of the crime scene, and as such we were not letting people into it."

Biddle explained that evidence technicians were still processing the entire crime scene, and a backhoe had even been brought in to search for the murder weapon.

"I told them both that I would do my best to get what information or items they needed out of the house for the funeral," said the lieutenant, "but I'd have to run that by the prosecutor," although he didn't hold out much hope.

Refusing to take no for an answer, David Camm demanded to know exactly what the evidence technicians were doing in his house. But Biddle told him he couldn't go into details. Camm wanted to know why the house was part of the crime scene, when the murders had taken place in the garage.

"[I told him] he should relate back to his police experience, when he was an officer for us," said Biddle. "That we couldn't allow people into the scene on account of contamination issues."

When Biddle tried to end the conversation, saying he would call them as soon as he heard something, David Camm took a step back, puffing out his chest in anger.

"Jim," he said, his voice rising, "I just want to get in the house to get those things."

Then suddenly Camm stepped forward, physically bodychecking Biddle in a fit of aggression.

"I braced myself for the impact," said the lieutenant. "When we were chest-to-chest, I looked down to Dave and I said, 'Dave, I can't understand exactly what you're going through, but we're doing all that we can do. This isn't helping anything. Please step back.'"

Finally to defuse the situation, Sam Lockhart stepped forward, touching his nephew's arm to restrain him. Camm reluctantly stepped back, calling the Indiana State Police a "bunch of dumb asses," for the way they were conducting the investigation.

Then he stormed off, kicking a cardboard box being used for the ISP trash as hard as he could, sending soda cans and empty food wrappers spilling into the yard.

"Keep the fucking trash out of my yard!" he screamed, as he strutted back to his grandfather's house, followed by his uncle.

During all the commotion, Sean Clemons was inside the garage talking to crime-scene technicians. Hearing the arguing, he looked out to see what was going on, just in time to observe Camm kick the trash.

"He seemed to be very upset," said Clemons.

The ex-trooper's violent outburst soon became the talk of the crime scene, and hot gossip back at the Sellersburg post. Word had also started to filter through from the medical examiner's office that little Jill Camm may have been sexually molested in the hours prior to her death.

Soon, all sympathy for their one-time colleague had evaporated, turning into suspicion that maybe he had done the unthinkable and murdered his entire family.

From now on, his state trooper friends would avoid him like the plague. It didn't take long for David Camm to read their aloofness and realize he was now the prime suspect in his wife's and children's murders.

Later that night Professor Stites took lead investigator Sean Clemons on a tour of the garage, so he could see what had been found so far.

"I then followed him through the crime scene," recalled Clemons. "He pointed out several things to me as we moved through."

The crime reconstructionist began by drawing Clemons' attention to an area of the concrete garage floor which was discolored, as though it contained dried blood. Then he led him to the back of the garage and up the stairs to the rear deck, pointing out several small areas that also looked like blood.

Then they went into the Camm house, where Stites took Clemons into the laundry room.

"I observed a mop bucket in a utility basin," Clemons would testify. "I subsequently smelled the mop bucket. It had a strong odor of bleach."

They then went back out into the garage, where Stites

pointed out what could possibly be high-velocity blood mist on the door.

That night, as they walked out of the crime scene, both Clemons and Stites agreed they were on the right track to finding the killer. And they knew the clincher could come as early as tomorrow morning, when Professor Stites would travel to the Sellersburg post to examine Camm's basketball clothes for signs of high-velocity blood spatter.

That night David Camm appeared to be sliding into an abyss. As he lay on the couch in his mom's living room for the third night running, he refused all offers of food and had hardly eaten since Thursday night.

His sister, Julie, became so worried about him that she telephoned their Uncle Sam for advice.

"Julie, you've got to get him to eat something," he told her. "He needs to eat something."

She cooked him up some soup, but he just stared, refusing to eat it.

"I tried making a milkshake with orange juice and bananas, thinking he's got to have some nutrition," she remembered. "But he just didn't want anything. Our advice to him is just keep breathing. He feels like he doesn't even want to do that."

23

Under Suspicion

After snatching a couple of hours' sleep, David Camm telephoned Lieutenant Jim Biddle at 9:50 a.m. Sunday morning, apologizing for his violent behavior at the crime scene. But Biddle suspected he was also fishing for information about exactly where the investigation was heading.

"I know you guys are doing everything you can," said Camm. "This wasn't personal against you. I just needed to vent a little bit and you just happened to be there."

Biddle told him not to worry, saying that he regretted they had drifted apart in recent years and weren't as close as they once had been.

"I just can't imagine the pressure that you're under," he told Camm. "That's why there's no problem with me. It's a non-event."

Then Camm asked why so many state troopers he considered close friends were cold-shouldering him. The lieutenant said that probably, like himself, they didn't know what to say after the murders. They were keeping quiet so they didn't make matters worse.

"You're so well-liked," Biddle told him. "I mean, you're just one of the guys . . . good guys. So don't give it another thought."

Biddle thanked him for the "patience" he'd shown in allowing troopers and evidence technicians free rein in his house.

"We're exhausting every lead," said Biddle. "Every bit of information."

Suddenly Camm became highly emotional, once again begging to be allowed into his house to get clothes and personal possessions.

"This is killing me," he told the lieutenant. "Jim, all I ask is just try and see things from my perspective. I'm not saying give in and violate the rules."

He then asked Biddle to think back, to seeing Kim's, Brad's and Jill's bodies lying in the garage.

"[That's] also my last scene which I have to live with, over and over again," he told Biddle. "Not to mention the fact that I wasn't there to stop it."

Biddle urged him not to blame himself, saying that was a dangerous "mode" to fall into.

"My family," sobbed Camm. "My family, we were perfect. My kids were the greatest . . . they were angels."

The lieutenant recalled seeing Brad once at the post and thinking, "That's a little Dave."

"My wife," sobbed Camm, "she loved me unconditionally. Truly unconditionally."

Camm expressed "frustration" at not being on the "inside" of the investigation, and being left in the dark about developments.

"I need some information," he suddenly declared. "Do we have any suspects? Do we have any solid leads? You know I was a policeman for a long time and I know we should hopefully [be] developing some at this point. If we don't have any solid suspects at this point, the longer it goes the worse it's going to be."

Refusing to be drawn, Biddle compared Camm's situation to his and his registered nurse wife, when he had medical problems.

"Sometimes too much knowledge is a bad thing," he said. "We are pursuing every angle and we've had all our detectives out. We're going to continue going full guns until we find the person that did this. And I appreciate your patience."

Then Camm asked the officer ultimately responsible for finding the killer of his wife and children to give him "a big hug" and have "faith" in him.

"You guys are still like my extended family," said Camm. "You know, sometimes I need a little pat on the back. I mean, you hate to tell somebody that. But I have so many of those guys I just love like brothers. They just stay away from me. It hurts me. It hurts."

He then asked if investigators believed he might have murdered Kim, Brad and Jill.

"Do they think that I did this for real?" he wept. "You know that question runs through my mind. These people have known me for just so long too . . . that's just ludicrous. And I don't know [how] to handle this."

The lieutenant, who knew his detectives had Camm firmly in their sights, was evasive. Calling it a delicate situation, he said he could not discuss the investigation.

"We're struggling with that too," he told him. "I'm really glad that you've got such a good family there to support you. But it's just difficult for us to be able to do so, as much as we want to."

Camm then agreed to do whatever was needed to clear his name, once again offering to take a polygraph test. After the lieutenant told him he wished he had a "crystal ball I could look into" to solve the three murders, Camm fell apart like a desperate child.

"Please, I'm begging you. I'm begging you," he sobbed. "If this was a wager, the three most important people in my life have been set up on the table, and I just can't win them back.

"It's like a rollercoaster, Jimmy. You know I cried and then I get to the point where I can't cry anymore. It just hurts like a pit. I blame God. And you know I don't want to blame God."

In one final frantic attempt to get back into his house to get the clothes to bury his family in, he told the detective why it was so important.

"[It will be] the last images in my mind of Kim laying there as she was."

Again Lieutenant Biddle promised to call Prosecutor Stan Faith at home, and get him an answer within a couple of hours.

Then Camm calmed down and asked whether detectives had found something incriminating in the house, without telling him.

"Is there more of a [crime] scene?" he asked. "Is there something inside the house that we don't know about? I mean, none of that stuff's been told me. If there is, then I can understand why we can't go in."

Biddle said the detectives were having an investigation status meeting later, and he'd try to get him some answers. But Camm was hardly listening, now pleading with Biddle to accompany him on a tour of his home.

"Jimmy, you come right along with me, because I'll walk you through our bedroom, and the kids' rooms. And I'll show their pictures. I'll tell you their story."

After promising he'd get the clothes "one way or another," Biddle asked where he could get hold of him later that morning.

"I'm going to church," said Camm. "Then probably back at my mom and dad's. You know I'm trying to be too much of a policeman when I'm not out there. I overanalyze and I just can't describe it to you. I love all you guys. And please let them know that I'm counting on them pretty heavy."

Then Lieutenant Biddle put down the phone and turned off the audiotape recorder that had captured every word of their conversation.

He then put the tape in a small manila envelope and logged it in to the evidence room.

In another part of Post 45, crime reconstructionist Robert Stites was carefully laying out the basketball clothes David Camm had worn the night of the murders. Using three

600-watt halogen light bulbs mounted on tripods that he had brought from Portland, he was searching for any signs of high-velocity blood mist.

First of all he examined Camm's dark blue shorts under a ten-power magnifying lens, but could find no blood spatter. He then put Camm's white tube socks under the magnifying glass, finding traces of blood on the toe of one of them. But unfortunately the evidence technicians had failed to mark whether it was the right or left one.

Stites then turned his attention to the size eleven Converse tennis shoes Camm had been wearing. He observed bloodstains on the right shoe, on the laces and along the side, although it was contact blood and not high-impact mist.

"[After] finding the stains," Stites explained, "I circled them with a black permanent marker."

At 10:30 a.m. David Camm's gray Indiana State Trooper tee-shirt was removed from the evidence bag and placed on a table under the hot halogen lights. Using his ten-power magnifying glass the professor studied the shirt, observing eight tiny red specks, forming an unmistakable pattern. Later DNA testing would reveal it was Jill Camm's blood.

"I saw that right away," said the professor. "That was very obvious."

Stites immediately called Prosecutor Stan Faith's cell phone with the stunning news.

"I'll never forget that morning," said Faith. "I was sitting in church, when I received a phone call that they thought they had found high-velocity impact spatter on his tee-shirt. I left church immediately and drove straight over to the post to start making arrangements."

As Stan Faith was driving to Sellersburg, convinced he now knew who the murderer was, David Camm and his family were arriving at Georgetown Community Church for a special service. The previous day Pastor Lockhart had told the media that it would be an opportunity "to cry on each other's shoulders."

Under a long-standing arrangement, Julie Hogue's new grandson Parker was due to be dedicated in church that morning. Under the tragic circumstances she called her Uncle Leland, asking if they should cancel. The Pastor told her to bring the 3-month-old baby to the church anyway, saying that if it felt right he'd do the dedication, otherwise they'd reschedule. So Julie and her daughter, Emily, prepared to take Parker to the Georgetown church.

"Originally Dave wasn't going to go," said his sister. "But while I was getting ready he changed his mind."

Julie had been "real afraid" to have Parker around her brother, but when she walked in, David was gently holding Parker in the rocking chair.

"Somehow that made a difference to him," said Julie. "He said, 'Now I see why God sent Parker.' And he decided he wanted to go for the baby dedication."

Georgetown Community Church was packed for the 11:00 Sunday service. The press and cameras had been barred from entering, but the Lockhart family had promised they would give interviews outside after the service.

Dressed in a navy sweater and jeans, David Camm sat surrounded by family. He was crying uncontrollably, asking how God could have allowed such a terrible thing to happen to Kim and his children.

"It was excruciating," said Julie. "I saw Dave show more open anguish, pain, hurt—maybe a little anger with God—than I'd seen up to that point."

Somehow Camm composed himself enough to hold up baby Parker for his dedication. And later in his sermon Pastor Lockhart told the congregation that the devil had visited them, taking away three of their flock.

"Evil showed its face this past week," said the preacher, "in the most ugly way you could imagine."

Throughout the service, Camm wept uncontrollably, continually wiping his eyes with a handkerchief.

At the end of the service more than forty of the congregation joined David at the altar, laying their hands on his shoulders and gently rocking with him in a comforting motion.

"I came in searching within my heart," he told them from the pulpit. "Just looking for some sort of peace."

As his family led him out of the church into the bright sunlight, the press rushed up to him for an interview.

Clutching a handkerchief to his mouth, his sister Julie's arm protectively around his shoulder, Camm looked a broken man as he addressed the television cameras.

"I want my family back," he sobbed. "I want my babies back, and my wife. But that doesn't look like it's going to happen. There is no rational explanation for this."

He spoke of memories of his family forever burned into his brain. And he remembered the first time he'd set eyes on his wife, Kim, and how she'd taken his breath away. Then he mentioned the "tackle war" games he'd played with Jill and his son, Brad, who could outswim a fish.

He told of one final "precious" memory the night before the murders, when Brad had climbed into bed with him and Kim, curling up to go to sleep.

"I don't know if it was a personal attack on me," he continued, "or meant to be a personal attack on my wife. But if they have any decency, any compassion in their body at all, they'll turn themselves in."

Then an interviewer asked what he would say if the killer happened to be watching him on television now.

Then Camm lost it.

"Turn yourself in," he sobbed, dabbing his lips with his handkerchief. "You can't live with the guilt. What you did was such an irrational, ridiculous, ludicrous, demonstrative, Satanic thing—you cannot live with that guilt."

David Camm's dramatic interview outside the church led off Sunday's early news bulletins. And his friend and mentor Randy Hubbard was reading his Sunday newspaper when his wife, Martha, who also knew Camm well, saw the interview on their television.

"I was about halfway paying attention," remembered the Floyd County Sheriff. "Then my wife, Martha, turned around, looked at me and she said, 'That's Susan Smith,'" referring to the South Carolina mother who drowned her two boys in 1994, before going on national television to appeal to their killer.

"I said, 'What are you talking about?' and I looked over to see David on TV, being interviewed outside the church. And she said, 'That's Susan Smith all over again. He's not sincere. Look, look, look—it's that look.' And then I focused in, looked at those phony tears and thought she might be right on this one."

Back at his parents' home after his press conference, David Camm sought further reassurance from his old friend Sammy Sarkasian. At 1:30 p.m. he called the evidence technician at the post, and was put through immediately. The sergeant had already been briefed on the preliminary high-velocity mist findings on Camm's tee-shirt, and was now recording the call.

"Sam, nobody will talk to me," said an anxious Camm, getting right to the point. "I just want to know what's going on."

Sarkasian, who was overseeing the technical parts of the investigation, had been close to Camm and was now in a very difficult position. He knew David would probably be arrested within hours, so he was noncommittal, only saying everyone was working really hard to "get all ducks in a row." Then Camm asked whether the ducks were "headed in one direction" or "in a mess."

"It's a difficult case," replied Sarkasian, "from an emotional standpoint on everybody. [It's] personal. I know your family. We've got that expert from Oregon. We're just trying to put it together here. And we want to go back over things and make sure everything's correct."

Then Camm complained that all his old friends in the department "just walk right past me," saying he was "very hurt." As Lieutenant Biddle had done, Sarkasian explained how uncomfortable everybody felt making small talk at a time like this, saying it was "awkward" for them.

Then he changed the subject, asking Camm if he had had any time to "reflect" on things over the last two days, and come up with any motives or theories as to who would have killed his wife and children.

Maybe someone had been "stalking" Kim, Camm conjectured, although she'd never mentioned anything.

"Our lives were perfect," he suddenly told Sarkasian. "We were at a point where things were perfect."

Then the sergeant said there was "a lot of anger" in how violently they had been murdered, prompting Camm to wonder if someone was out to get him.

"Kim's never done anything to anybody," he said. "But to also take out my two kids. I think they were waiting for me. You try to rationalize it but you can't help but think as a policeman."

Camm said his police training made him believe someone had seen Kim at the swimming pool, either forcing his way into the Bronco, or following her home.

"But the shit obviously happened in the garage," he said.

Then he asked why one of the detectives couldn't just sit down with him and say, "Dave, look. Here's what is going on. Here's what we're doing."

It wasn't that simple, replied Sarkasian, explaining that "the brass" want to know everything.

"It's nothing against you," he told him. "They're just doing their job, forging ahead. And you'd rather be out there forging ahead and doing their job."

Camm agreed, asking if they had any good evidence so far.

"Got some great evidence," said Sarkasian cryptically, with some dramatic irony. "And they're getting the qualified people to explain [it]. As soon as they come to a conclusion, I'm sure you're gonna know. We don't want to be wrong."

Camm told him that his family was "praying for you guys," explaining how he'd just returned from a pretty "emotional meeting" at church.

"I didn't want to go," he said. "But God told me I needed to be at church today and I went. About three hours of crying in church."

Then Camm confided he believed God had spoken to him in church.

"We prayed for some peace this morning for me," said Camm. "And I know that he spoke to me."

Camm started to ramble. He returned to "the clothing issues," and Sarkasian assured him detectives would make sure he got some for the funeral on Tuesday.

"Well, I about ripped Biddle's throat out last night," he told Sarkasian. "I know I shouldn't have lost my temper but I just couldn't help it."

Once again Camm fished for information, saying he felt he was under suspicion as the killer.

"What are you asking about?" replied Sarkasian, becoming increasingly uncomfortable.

"I'm asking my friend Sam Sarkasian to tell me, 'I know, Dave, that you didn't do this.' "

"Well, Dave," said the trooper, "I've got to be objective about everything, everybody. I'm not excluding or including anybody—okay?—until we come to a conclusion. That's Sam Sarkasian the policeman speaking. You know I have a hard time dividing that guy sometimes. I mean, I've had six hours' sleep in the last four days. I'm a little soup silly myself."

Although he considered Camm a friend, he said he could not let his emotions interfere with the investigation.

Camm then questioned why Shelley Romero had not visited him at his parents' house as they'd arranged. He wondered if "somebody [had] nixed that," as it might look bad for her to be seen with him, emphasizing she was just a friend.

Just before putting the phone down, and without being asked, Camm explained why he had called the post after finding his family dead, instead of making the usual 911 call.

"I wanted my people there," he declared. "If I'd wanted a screwed-up investigation done, I'd have called the sheriff's department instead of the state."

24

Probable Cause

Late Sunday afternoon Lieutenant Jim Biddle telephoned David Camm, inviting him to come to his house and get whatever clothing he needed for the funerals. As Kim's parents also wanted to be there to help select clothes, they met Dave, Julie and Sam Lockhart for the highly emotional task.

"They wouldn't let us in the house," said Julie Hogue. "And so [the troopers] would go in and look through drawers and closets. Then they'd bring the clothes out and lay them on the hoods of the cars for us to pick. Frank and Janice made the decision, and they needed a few things. I guess probably it was more difficult for Janice, than even myself."

Because of the state of the bodies after autopsy, they needed long-sleeved clothes, as there was a one-hour open casket for the family.

"The funeral director allowed us to see them," said Julie. "There was so much work to make them presentable."

Unfortunately the troopers couldn't find anything suitable to adequately cover the children, so Julie went off to a nearby Target to buy pantyhose for Jill and a decent shirt for Brad.

After they finished, David Camm and his Uncle Sam wanted to stay at the house a little longer, so Julie agreed to meet them later at the funeral home.

Then Lieutenant Biddle came over, saying they needed to speak to Camm once again at the post in Sellersburg.

Sam waited while Biddle took his nephew to one side, and after a few minutes he returned.

Remembered Lockhart: "[Dave] told me, 'Sam, I need to go with these fellows.' And I said OK. And that's the last time that I saw him before I learned of his arrest."

That Sunday afternoon Sean Clemons had been busy, writing up a probable cause affidavit, accusing David Camm of the murders of Kim, Brad and Jill. Then, after it was signed by a judge, a warrant was issued for his arrest. But Camm would not be aware of this for the next several hours.

Indiana State Police Detective Sean Clemons swore out the following probable cause affidavit against his childhood friend, who had once encouraged him to become a policeman and had helped train him.

1. I am a Detective with the Indiana State Police.

2. On the 28th day of September, 2000, I was called to David R. Camm's residence at 7534 Lockhart Road, Georgetown, Floyd County, Indiana, where I had found three people who had been shot: Kimberly Camm, Bradley Camm, age 7, Jill Camm, age 5.

3. The following evidence has been processed from the crime scene at the above mentioned address:
   a. The crime scene was manipulated by use of a high Ph cleaning substance.
   b. The tee shirt worn by David R. Camm on the above mentioned date had high velocity blood mist which occurs in the presence of gunshot at the time of the shooting.
   c. The cleaning substance was thrown over the back deck of the above-mentioned house also leaving a trail from the garage area, along with a transfer of blood on the house.

d. A witness said that between 9:15 p.m. and 9:30 p.m. she heard three distinct sounds that can be interpreted as gunshots.

e. Jill Camm, aged 5, had a recent tear in the vaginal area consistent with sexual intercourse.

f. There is a wet mop in a bucket in the utility room of the house at the above-mentioned address with the strong odor of bleach.

g. Witnesses playing basketball with David R. Camm said that he left the game on or around 9:00 p.m. and David R. Camm told them he was headed to his house, the above-mentioned crime scene.

h. There was a flow of blood from the garage that is inconsistent with the viscosity of blood and was aided in its flow by the presence of water and cleaning substance.

i. Kimberly and Jill Camm were killed by gunshot wounds to the head from a certain .380 caliber firearm.

j. Bradley Camm was shot in the chest which exited in Bradley's back eventually killer [sic] Bradley Camm.

4. The above mentioned information was gleaned from statements or reports made to me by Tracy Corey Handy, M.D., all pathologists, Robert Stites crime scene re-constructionist.

5. I make these statements not as complete recital of all facts, but to establish probable cause.

6. All of which gives me probable cause to believe that David R. Camm has committed Murder, in Floyd County, State of Indiana.

Signed: Sean Clemons
ISP 5751

25

Interrogation

At 5:50 p.m., Sunday, October 1, 2000, Indiana State Police Detectives Mickey Neal and Darrell Gibson began their second interview with David Camm, who had no idea of his imminent arrest. In the two days since their first interview, the detectives' images of him had changed from grieving friend to murder suspect.

This time the interrogation room video recorder was working, and after pushing the RECORD button, Mickey Neal began by saying that, as the case was so high-profile, the prosecutor's office had ordered everything to be by the book, and all witnesses must be advised of their rights.

"This is an advice-of-rights-interrogation," explained Neal. "You have the right to remain silent. Anything that you say can and will be used against you in court."

Camm said he had no problems. He told them he knew the rights statement by heart, having read it to suspects numerous times during his career as a state trooper. Then Neal asked him to repeat what had happened Thursday night, after the basketball game.

Once again Camm ran over his story of finding Kim, Brad and Jill shot dead in the garage, saying his "police mode" had kicked in. But this time, he told detectives, he wasn't certain whether he had administered CPR to Brad before or after calling the state police from his kitchen landline.

The detectives were suspicious, pumping him with questions about the exact sequence of events to try to catch him out.

"When I first got there I found the kids," said Camm. "I went in and I make the phone call. I came back out. I pulled Brad out. I did the CPR. I knew I was fucked. And that's when I ran over to get Nelson."

Detective Neal asked what was in the garage when he came home, and whether he noticed anything out of the ordinary. Suddenly Camm took the detectives into his confidence, focusing on how his state police training had guided his actions when he found Kim's body.

"It took me a while to figure out that she just had panties on," he explained. "And I haven't told everybody in the family what I suspect may have happened. And I looked a couple of times and it looked like tan pants or shorts that were lying there. I don't know for sure what they were or whether they were ripped or torn.

"Then I finally realized that all she had on was panties, so assumed the worst there. But I didn't stop and analyze any of that stuff. It's like, OK, she's been dead. She's probably been raped. I didn't give her a kiss or anything. I didn't touch anything. I didn't bother anything.

"It's hard to believe, guys, that I would be thinking that. But I'm telling you, I went into this mode of shocked but rational. And I think it just falls back on my training and the things that I've seen in the past."

Camm continued his stream of consciousness, telling the detectives how he wished he'd done more for his little daughter Jill, apparently unaware that she may have been sexually molested.

"It really breaks my heart," he said in a quivering voice. "I think I was scared to raise Jill's head up. I didn't do good. I didn't really do a whole lot for her or with her. I didn't even look at her little face. Now maybe, you know, God had me not do that for a reason. I don't know. But I could just see her hair. All her pretty hair."

He told detectives how he had seen Brad's face, as it was slumped over the divider in the back of the Bronco.

"I mean, buddies, I just grabbed him, and out of there I came."

Detective Neal then asked about the children's sleeping arrangements. Camm said they usually slept in their own separate rooms, but occasionally one of them might get into bed with him and Kim, as Brad had the night before his murder.

"Pretty crowded?" Neal asked wryly.

Camm agreed, saying that sometimes he or Kim had to go and sleep on the couch.

At 6:34 p.m. Detective Neal switched off the videotape and finally leveled with him. He told him bluntly that they were not satisfied with his account of Thursday night and had probable cause to believe he murdered Kim and his children.

Camm lashed out at them in total disbelief, furious and hurt that he was now under suspicion by his one-time friends. Slamming his fists down hard on the table, he was yelling at the detectives when Neal turned the video recorder back on at 6:38 p.m.

"You guys are morons! Morons!" screamed Camm, stomping his feet in anger. "I cannot believe this! I cannot believe this!"

"What do you mean?" snapped Neal angrily. "Can't believe what?"

"You are going to try to blame me for killing my children and my wife."

Neal told him that he was trying to explain some of the "physical evidence" they now had and that they had "some problems."

"I'm going to do this one time," said Camm. "I'm going to sit here and I'm going to look both of you dead in the eye, man-to-man. And I'm going to tell you, and you can believe this in your heart and soul, or you can not. I leave this choice to you. I did not do this, Darrell! Mickey! I did not do this!"

Neal assured him everybody at Post 45 wanted to believe he was innocent too, but the evidence against him was compelling.

"We took your clothing and it's been analyzed," Neal told him. "There's high-velocity blood spatter on your shirt, David, and other articles of your clothing."

Camm explained he had picked up Brad, which accounted for the blood over him. But then Neal, who had been carefully briefed on the different types of blood spatter, said it was not "transfer" but a high-velocity mist.

"Guys!" said Camm emotionally. "You better find somebody else to do those tests, because, Mickey, they're wrong!"

Over the next few minutes the detectives confronted Camm with some of the evidence that Stites had found. But they also tried to trap him, claiming that he had been wearing a gray sweatshirt and they had proof of it, although they actually had none. A sweatshirt with the name "Backbone" handwritten on its collar had been discovered near Kim's body in the garage.

When Camm denied knowing about it, Neal lied, telling him that they'd interviewed everyone at the basketball game, all of whom said he had been wearing it.

"OK," said Neal, "I'm just going by what these people told us over there."

"It's not right!" screamed an exasperated Camm. "It's not right, guys! You're wrong! You're wrong! Something's not right here! Now fix it!"

Neal told him he now had an opportunity to explain what really happened. And he knew Camm had been in the laundry room "as some things were transferred from you. Think hard."

There was a long silence and then Darrell Gibson took over, telling him to "just relax," and asking why he had gone to the laundry room. After almost a minute passed without any response, Gibson asked if he remembered going into the room.

"No I don't," Camm hissed.

"We *know* you went in the laundry room," Detective Neal said forcefully.

"We *don't* know I went in the laundry room," replied Camm.

"Well," Detective Neal continued, "I'm going by what I've been told by technicians. And they've got a mop. [You] tried to clean some of the blood up."

Camm said that was "ridiculous," and when Gibson then asked him about "some bleach," Camm lost it.

"No! No! No!" he shouted, pounding his fists on the table. "I didn't clean up shit, guys. I was in the house long enough to make the phone call. I ran outside. I went and got Nelson and he ran over with me. I didn't try and clean up shit! Somebody may have, but it wasn't me! That person is your suspect! I am not that person! And I am not your suspect!"

Now going for a full confession, Detective Neal bluffed, saying that investigators now knew where Camm had hidden the murder weapon, and it was being retrieved at that moment.

"Can you share that?" asked Camm, sounding surprised.

Neal said they were searching a pipe inside a drain on his deck, which housed two septic tanks, and Camm said he knew where they meant.

"We suspect that the gun is down in there," said Neal.

"Mickey, I swear to you, brother, I did not do this," said Camm. "I don't know what you're talking about."

Then Gibson took over the questioning, adding a bluff of his own about a neighbor seeing Camm throw something incriminating over the back porch.

"I want you to think hard, OK?" said Gibson. "I mean, we're just trying to explain [things], you know."

As David Camm proclaimed his innocence, refusing to be drawn, Detective Neal told him the big problem was the eight drops of high-velocity blood spatter found on his tee-shirt.

"I'm only dealing with facts here," said the detective. "Not rumors or innuendos. I'm dealing with facts."

Camm told them the "blood people are wrong" and they needed to find other experts.

Then, taking a new tack, Darrell Gibson asked if, when he had arrived home and found his children dead, he had thought Kim responsible.

"You're way off base," said Camm. "You're both way off base."

Neal suggested he might have come home and gotten into an argument with Kim, and things had gone terribly wrong.

"Was she leaving?" Neal asked. "Taking off for some reason?"

As Camm kept denying anything bad had happened, Detective Neal played his trump card.

"Well," he began, a new sense of gravity entering his voice. "I'll tell you we know a thing about Jill,"

"What about Jill?" Camm asked.

"We know the fact that she had been sexually molested," said Neal.

"I don't know anything about that," replied Camm. "So how could you know something about that?"

"Well," replied Neal, "because that was determined at the time of the autopsy."

"Well, then, Mickey, whoever did it, if she's been molested, whoever the son-of-a-bitch was that killed them, did it to her."

Then Camm told them that if Jill had been sexually molested it must have happened "that night."

"You guys are wrong here," he said in a straining, high-pitched voice. "You're wrong! Mickey! I did not do this! I did not do this! Gosh, Darrell . . . Doggone it . . . I didn't do it. This is my family!"

Neal then asked who, if it wasn't him, had killed Kim and the children? Camm told them it was their job to find out.

Camm told the detectives how his life with Kim and the kids had been perfect, painting a scene straight out of the classic TV show *Leave It to Beaver*.

"My life had never been so good," he sobbed. "At home, at work, with the kids—everything. It could not have been any more perfect, I'm telling you.

"We didn't fight. We didn't argue. We paid our bills. Everything was perfect. My wife loved me through thick and thin, literally. And I the same for her. And my children . . . I worship those children. I worship the ground they walk on. And she took care of my babies. I did not do this. I'm not a rape master, liar—I'm just like one of you guys."

Camm told the detectives that while they were talking, there was a "perverted, sick individual" out there free, and they were not looking hard enough.

"We've got the wrong boy sitting here," he said. "Anybody that would kill my kids, molest my child and do who knows whatever to my wife, is a messed-up individual. And you guys need to switch gears here, Mick. I'm not your man."

Detective Neal told him a highly paid expert had found the damning evidence against him.

"There's blood on your shirt," accused Neal, "and I had it DNA analyzed, This is a presumptive test [and it] is high-velocity blood spatter. It's scientific documentation."

Neal explained that the only way it could have gotten on his tee-shirt is from "blow-back or blow-out" from a gunshot wound.

"They're minute particles that travel at extremely high speeds, and they come in contact with a surface and they stick to it. I don't know how much expertise you've got in spatter."

"And that is supposed to be on my tee-shirt that I played ball in?" asked Camm.

When Gibson said it was there, Camm told him to get another expert, as any blood on it had to have come from the Bronco or from carrying his son, Brad.

Neal then told him that they were going to analyze DNA samples they had taken from Jill.

"Did somebody rape my little girl?" asked Camm, his voice shaking with emotion.

"She'd been sexually molested," replied Neal. "Is there a possibility at some point . . ."

"There's some perverted motherfucker out there that's done this to my family, all right? You need to find out who they are."

Then Neal asked if he had sexually molested his 5-year-old daughter.

"No," said Camm.

"Have you ever touched her in a sexual way?" Neal demanded.

"No."

"In her vagina?"

"No," said Camm resolutely. "I have given her a bath and dried her off."

"Yeah, sure," said the detective. "I'm not talking about that."

"OK," said Camm. "When those samples [are analyzed by the medical examiner's office] and they determine it's not me, you both owe me one huge humungous apology. You guys are disturbed. You just can't see it."

Neal then asked if Camm had had any recent girlfriends or sexual affairs with married women. Camm said the only one was Anita Asher at the Heritage Weekend, but they hadn't actually had sexual intercourse.

"I've got nothing to hide," said Camm, who had been on the other side of the interrogation table many times as a state trooper. "As bad as you want to get me to confess to something, it ain't going to happen, Mick, because I didn't do it."

Then, after more than an hour of cold, intense questioning, the detectives tried a friendlier tack.

"Let me tell you one thing, Dave," said Neal. "We don't want to be sitting here. This is hard on us just like it is hard on you. You think it's easy? Hell, we were shift partners. We worked together for a long time."

"Now imagine this," said Camm. "If the roles were reversed and you were sitting here, having to answer these questions. And it was your wife and kids and you were innocent."

Then Neal told him that they had witnesses who'd heard gunshots at 9:20 p.m., about the time the murders were thought to have happened.

"Now these are just the facts," said Neal, in true Joe Friday style. "I'm just telling you what we know. When you came home there's nine minutes in the air that are missing."

Calling them "wrong" and "confused," Camm said their "time element" was totally off.

"Well, we've gone over this time line pretty close here," explained Neal. "It doesn't take you nine minutes to find your family and then go in and call."

Detective Neal changed the subject, asking if he had any life insurance on his family. Camm explained they'd changed their policies after he had left the ISP, using his little brother, Dan, as a broker.

"I lost all my retirement," he told them. "We redid all that after I left the department to try and head back in a better direction. We paid our bills. Money was not an issue. I didn't do it, Darrell, I didn't do it."

Now Detective Gibson took over the interrogation, trying to relate to David Camm as a friend, saying there had be some explanation why he had done it.

"Dave, when we started this," he began, "no one would have believed you would have done this, OK? Because the Dave Camm I know wouldn't do this. And I love you—I still do. You probably don't think so. That's the truth."

Gibson asked if something had happened to make him lose control. Camm replied by pounding the table with his fists, shouting, "No, no, no!"

"Well, Dave," Gibson continued, "there's a lot of things that are just not adding up."

"The bottom line is I didn't do it," said Camm with increasing frustration. "Things were good. I didn't lose it. I didn't blow my top. Something is a mess here with this shirt. I don't know what it is. You guys will find out what it is. OK, you'll solve that mystery somehow."

The detectives asked about the large amount of Viagra found at his house.

"Do you take Viagra?" asked Gibson.

"I've taken it," replied Camm defensively. "I've had to take it. We had it for a little while [when] I was going through a problem."

David Camm maintained that his and Kim's sex lives had been "great," saying they'd last made love the Sunday evening before she was murdered.

Gibson asked what had caused his temporary impotence, and Camm said it had been stress-related.

"[Viagra] was just to get me over that fear of not being able to get an erection," he explained.

Then Neal spoke up, asking if he ever cruised the Internet, trawling for sex.

"I've been on the Internet before and looked at the pictures and that kind of stuff," he said. "I've chatted with people online."

"Did you go into a sexual chat room," questioned Gibson, "or something where you chat sexually with people?"

Camm said no. He had sent instant messages to a mother from Greenwood, Indiana, on America Online, trading pictures of their kids. And he had also instant messaged a 16-year-old cheerleader in Florida, while he was still a state trooper. He said he had warned her to be careful who she talked to on the Internet, and never meet them in person.

Mickey Neal wanted to know if he frequented strip clubs and Camm admitted that he did periodically.

Then Neal asked about a blonde Kentucky woman's driver's license that investigators had discovered hidden in his house.

"She's a stripper," Camm replied. "I tried to track her down."

Camm's story was that when he was a trooper he had arrested a man a couple of years earlier, and found the driver's license in his car. The man had claimed it was his ex-wife's, who worked as a stripper in Lexington, so Camm had confiscated it, concerned for her welfare and intending to try to track her down.

"I called a bunch of strip clubs down there," explained Camm. "And none of them had heard from her or anything. Tried to get a phone number and I couldn't get hold of her. It was very innocent."

He said he had never drawn a case file on it or even run it through the police computer.

"I should have thrown it away a long time ago," he said. "There's nothing to that, Mick."

Then, out of left field, he suddenly boasted of having a signed picture of Miss Kentucky, which she'd given him after he had stopped her car. He said he had even tried to get a dinner date with her later on, when she was returning from the Miss USA Pageant, but it didn't work out.

Neal asked him about all the traffic violation tickets they had found in his basement, which had never been turned in to the Indiana State Police Department.

"Well I made a lot of mistakes like that," he told his old colleagues. "I probably wasn't as good a policeman as everybody thought I was."

Towards the end of the two-hour interview, David Camm announced he wanted to go home. Darrell Gibson told him he was the "low man on the totem pole" and could not make that decision.

"If you guys take me down to jail," said Camm desperately, "you'll be putting an innocent person in jail for murder [and] whoever is really guilty is going to walk. It's wrong! Wrong!"

Then Camm asked sarcastically if they were to lock up an "innocent man, who has just had his wife and kids killed," would it be a "big feather in the state police's cap?"

"You're one of our own," said Gibson. "No, you're wrong about that, Dave."

Gibson cryptically asked whether he had ever "messed around" with Felix Grant's (not his real name) granddaughter. Camm said he didn't even know who Grant was, and asked where this was going.

"I can't remember," said Gibson. "I don't recall right now."

Gibson ended the interview, saying he had work to do.

"Are you going to lock me up?" asked Camm.

Gibson said he didn't know and Neal asked him to wait in the investigation room, as they had to check on something.

"I want you to be comfortable," said Neal. "You know this is kind of like a black hole back here."

A few minutes later Detective Neal summoned David Camm to another interview room, to have him demonstrate how he had tried to resuscitate Brad with CPR. Although he had learned CPR as part of his basic training in law enforcement, and won a Bronze Star for performing it several years earlier on a drowning man, Camm described how he had been uncertain of how to do it on his son.

"When I first did the breaths I forgot to tilt his head," he said. "I gave him a couple of breaths in his mouth and it came right out of his nose. Then I could see something. I don't know if it was bubbly or something out of his nose and then I realized, 'Shit, you big dummy, the air's coming right out of his nose.' "

He burst into tears, telling Neal that if whatever got onto his shirt from Brad's mouth or nose sent him to jail, that was all right.

"As God is my witness," he sobbed, "I'm being persecuted."

Then in a long, bizarre rambling monologue, Camm compared his suffering to what Jesus Christ must have endured two thousand years ago.

"Jesus came to save us," he told the detective. "You know that's why he was there. And all people had to do was listen. And they're the ones that persecuted. All they had to do was open themselves up and listen to his message."

Neal told him he wasn't trying to persecute him, but Camm continued anyway, casting himself as a martyr in the first of many religious diatribes he would make over the next two years.

"Mickey, persecute me," he wept. "And if it's because I gave my son CPR, then so be it. My wife and I never fought. We never argued. She loved me and I loved her and we loved our children. And our children were perfect little angels."

At 8:45 p.m. Sunday night David Camm was arrested on three counts, for the first-degree murder of his wife, Kim, and children, Bradley and Jill. As he was being led into a police car by Indiana State Trooper Charlie Scarber, Shelley Romero rushed out of the post to talk to him, saying she knew he was innocent.

He was then driven to New Albany to spend his first night behind bars in Floyd County Jail, which was run by his mentor and good friend, Sheriff Randy Hubbard.

    And as Sheriff Hubbard was formally booking him into
jail, Camm denied he had murdered his family.

    "There were a lot of mixed emotions," said Hubbard, who
put him on suicide watch that night on the advice of his jail
psychiatrist. "It's sad, it's upsetting. I hoped it wasn't him."

26

"I Will Bring Justice to Those Who Violate Those I Love"

At 9:00 a.m. the following morning, David Ray Camm was arraigned at Floyd Superior Court in front of Judge Richard Striegel, who had already been appointed to the case. Three innocent pleas were automatically entered on his behalf and he was represented by attorney George Gesenhues Jr., who Sam Lockhart had hired late Sunday night.

Camm, who was on tranquilizers and migraine medicine, sat impassively in the dock, as his attorney requested he be allowed to view his family's bodies at Graceland Baptist Church that night. Judge Striegel gave his permission, but denied Camm bail, explaining that he refused to set a bond as Prosecutor Stan Faith considered him "a flight risk."

Then Striegel set another hearing in twenty-four hours to reconsider setting a bond, and the sobbing prisoner was led back to Floyd County Jail to meet his attorney.

Outside the court Gesenhues told reporters that the prosecutor's case against Camm was weak. He said the probable cause affidavit did not even link Camm to the murders, and neither did the allegation of Jill's sexual abuse.

"It's such a prejudicial nature that I think it shouldn't be included," he said.

Prosecutor Stan Faith said he had still not decided whether to seek the death penalty against Camm.

"This is a very serious case," he explained.

David Camm's family were shocked by his arrest, as he'd been playing basketball with at least six of his relations when the murders were supposed to have been committed. The family had always protected David since he was a baby, but now, in his time of need, they would close ranks to fight for his innocence.

Intially Kim's parents believed him innocent too.

"I just couldn't believe that the person I knew, thought I knew, could do that," said Janice Renn.

But in the weeks after his arrest, that would all change, and the Camm and Lockhart families and the Renns would turn against each other, with the former believing in his innocence and the latter certain he had cold-bloodedly butchered his family.

"We knew exactly where he was," said his brother Donnie. "There's no way."

Sam Lockhart visited his nephew in jail soon after his arrest, and began organizing his defense and appeal to be freed on bail.

Lockhart believes there was a rush to judgment by the Indiana State Police, based on the assumption that the spouse is usually guilty in domestic murders. Then, according to Lockhart, they came up with a probable cause affidavit to conveniently fit their theories.

Ultimately he would be proven right, as almost every part of Sean Clemons' PCA would turn out not to be true.

"They automatically look at the spouse," said Sam. " 'Cause that's the highest percentage that they knew killed them. So they jumped to conclusions based on percentages."

Lockhart says the ISP assumed Camm's guilt from the outset, unleashing a witch hunt. And the terrible pressures placed on his nephew made him act badly under intense interrogation.

"Well, how does someone act after finding their family dead?" he asked. "Dave was not like this before."

Lockhart claims that after crime-scene reconstructionist Robert Stites confirmed blood spatter on Camm's tee-shirt, the detectives stopped pursuing any further leads.

"Once that statement was made," he said, "the state police said, 'By golly, we've got him. If that's high-velocity blood spatter, then he had to have been there when the kids and Kim were shot.' So they went ahead and made the arrest, right after he'd picked the clothes up for his kids' and his wife's funeral.

"Then all other avenues of investigation of the murders ceased. The investigation then focused in on finding evidence to prove that they had arrested the right man."

That Monday morning Brad and Jill's classmates were back at their desks at Graceland Christian School, for the first time since the murders. Principal Kevin Wilson and a group of volunteer counselors and pastors talked to more than four hundred children that day, trying to console them and make them feel safe and secure.

"We are confronting the loss and telling them that it's OK to be sad," Wilson told Amany Ali of the New Albany *Tribune*. "We know that Jesus loves us and that's never going to change. They're told that [Kim, Brad and Jill] are at home with Jesus."

Graceland Baptist Church's senior pastor, Dan Hall, whose daughter Lydia had been in kindergarten with Jill, helped organize the grief counseling sessions. And as a father it was an ordeal trying to explain "such a violent and senseless act" to his daughter. The children were also confused because just two days earlier they had been attending prayer vigils for David Camm, who was now accused of their murder.

A few minutes before 10:00 p.m. that night, David Camm was led into the sanctuary of Graceland Baptist Church, where Kim's body lay by the side of Brad and Jill, in two matching pearl white open caskets. Earlier that day the rest of the family had viewed the bodies, someone placing a miniature toy car by Brad and a favored doll next to Jill.

When Pastor Hall came forward to greet the weeping prisoner, Camm looked him in the eye, saying: "I didn't do it."

Then, dressed in an orange prison suit, handcuffed and in leg irons, he stood sobbing by his murdered family. The entire time he was there he was guarded by Sheriff Hubbard and three of his officers, who never left his side in the empty church.

After spending fifteen minutes with the bodies of Kim, Brad and Jill, he was led out of the church and back to Floyd County Jail.

"What his true reaction was," said Sheriff Hubbard, "I wasn't really sure. I mean, he posed himself to be like any of us would under the circumstances, a grieving male spouse and father."

At 9:00 the next morning, David Camm was back in Floyd County Superior Court, applying for bail. After Defense Attorney George Gesenhues and Chief Deputy Prosecutor Susan Orth made their various arguments to Judge Striegel, a weeping Sam Lockhart took the stand, pleading for his nephew to be granted bail.

"I would be the first person to say that if David Camm did this, then he would need to be in jail," said Lockhart, who said David was like his own son. "He loved his children so much. The thought of him hurting [them] is so foreign to me."

Judge Striegel remained unmoved and denied Camm bail, saying he'd have to remain in Floyd County Jail without bond. He set the next pretrial hearing for November 14, with an omnibus hearing for December 12, when he expected to set a trial date.

As Camm was taken back to his cell, more than a thousand people gathered at Graceland Baptist Church to bid final farewells to Kim, Brad and Jill. It was an unusually warm October day as the mourners took their seats in the church. The press and television crews remained outside, respecting the families' wishes.

After the congregation sang "What a Friend We Have in

Jesus," Pastor Hall eulogized Kim as the "consummate mother," who was always cheering on Brad and Jill in their various sporting activities.

He remembered Brad as a well-mannered "short adult," who enjoyed life and was carefree. His sister, Jill, said the pastor, could light up a room with her "smiles and giggles," and was always outspoken.

Then Pastor Leland Lockhart gave a short speech at the funeral, but although the Camm, Lockhart and Renn families were cordial in church, there was already an uneasy tension between the two factions as to David's innocence.

"To me it was surreal," said Camm's sister, Julie Hogue. "I just remember sitting there and thinking why I was crying. Whether I was crying for Dave or Kim, Brad and Jill."

Julie felt it was different for her family as they were "torn" between grieving for Kim and the children and supporting her brother, who she believed to be innocent.

"The whole thing was, we had to switch," she said. "And then there became that connotation that because we supported Dave, we didn't care about Kim, Brad and Jill. But our focus had to be on Dave. It had to because we couldn't save them, but we could help Dave."

After the service 350 mourners walked behind the pair of black hearses and two limousines to a busy intersection at Charlestown Road, which police had closed off to traffic for fifteen minutes, as a mark of respect. Then the funeral procession turned south to Kraft-Graceland Memorial Park for the burials.

At the gravesides Jeff Barbour, who was head of Graceland's pastoral ministries, as well as the Indiana State Police chaplain, read a moving passage from the Book of Revelation. At the end of the reading, several white pigeons were released over Kim and her children's graves.

Then the mourners began filing out of the graveyard, leaving the two floral-covered caskets gleaming in the bright sunlight.

On Wednesday, Janice and Frank Renn's attorney, Nicholas Stein, called a press conference on behalf of Kim's family. Stein told reporters that the Renn family had not yet made up their minds if they considered their son-in-law responsible for the murders.

"They have questions," said Stein. "They hope it's not true. And they're going to reserve comment until the investigation is over. [Then] it will be time to start answering the questions."

Stein said the Renns had not spoken to Camm since his arrest, and harbored "no grudges or ill feelings" towards the Camm or Lockhart families.

Later Donnie Camm would complain the Renns had not pulled their weight and helped with their daughter and grandchildren's funerals.

"Actually, Sam, my sister, Julie, and Dave went and took care of making all the arrangements," he said. "The Renns did none of it and they also didn't spend any money."

27

In the Hole

Over the next few months the Indiana State Police doggedly pursued the David Camm investigation. For almost a week after his arrest, 7534 Lockhart Road remained an active crime scene, guarded twenty-four hours a day by state troopers. Day after day investigators combed through the house inch-by-inch, looking for the elusive .380 murder weapon. They seized Camm's day planner/address book and interviewed and reinterviewed everyone in it.

But they paid special attention to Camm's bedroom, taking samples of the sheets and bedspread for DNA analysis. And they also seized six unspecified sexual devices from one of his drawers, as well as a large supply of Viagra.

Searching for a motive, prosecutors subpoenaed insurance policies, bank statements and telephone records, as well as a family journal about Amos Lockhart's medication, bodily functions and the daily duty roster to look after him.

But despite all their efforts detectives never did find the .380 murder weapon.

On October 5—one week after the killings—Prosecutor Stan Faith made one final tour of the crime scene, and, satisfied the prosecution had everything it needed, released it back to the Lockhart family.

From the night of David Camm's arrest, Sam Lockhart

took over his nephew's affairs and led the fight to clear his name. He and Donnie Camm would devote most of their time and energies over the next four years to trying to vindicate him.

"I will do anything I possibly can to try and correct a wrong," said Sam. "It was not a campaign to save Dave Camm, because if I had thought he had killed Brad, Jill and Kim, they probably wouldn't have had to arrest him. He was my nephew, but I would have fought just as hard to have Dave Camm convicted if I'd known that he had killed them."

Sam assumed Camm's power of attorney, paying his mortgage and all the other bills for the house, which was eventually rented out to some cousins. And United Dynamics would suffer as Sam devoted himself to the case, pouring more and more money into David's defense. He also read every one of the thousands of pages of discovery, following up leads and doing whatever was necessary to find new evidence to free David.

One Thursday night in early November, Lockhart arrived at David Camm's house with a loaded .380 gun. He wanted to disprove the prosecution's claim that his sister, Debbie TerVree, had heard three gunshots the night of the killings.

In order to re-create the scene as accurately as possible he wanted it to be a Thursday, so everyone was in place as they had been the night of the murders.

"I went inside the garage," Sam would testify. "And I opened the garage door on the side the Bronco was parked and I had the other garage door down. And, yes, I have a .380 caliber weapon, the weapon they say was used in these particular killings."

Inside the garage he fired the gun three times to simulate the murders, before walking back to see if Debbie and Bob had heard anything.

"They did not hear it," he said. "I went over to my dad's house across the yard to ask Nelson if he heard it, and he didn't know I was going to do it. He had not heard it."

Then without telling them what he was going to do next, Lockhart fired three more shots outside the garage, which the TerVrees heard clearly.

Then he called Detective Sean Clemons, who collected the .380 Sig Sauer P230 handgun and the spent cartridges. The weapon was later analyzed and found not to have been the one used in the killings.

In mid-November, Floyd County Superior Court Judge Richard Striegel appointed public defender Pat Biggs to represent David Camm. He also allowed a motion from the Renn family to freeze Kim's assets, preventing their son-in-law from taking advantage of her $680,000 life insurance policy.

But the Renns' attorney Nicholas Stein told reporters that, despite their decision, Frank and Janice Renn had still not "taken a position," on David's guilt, preferring to wait for all the evidence to come in.

During the early weeks of the investigation, detectives focused on David Camm's womanizing and infidelities throughout his marriage. Ultimately ISP detectives would interview almost twenty women who had been sexually propositioned by Camm. Some had been willing sex partners, turned on by his being an Indiana State Trooper.

"He was a very sexually active individual," explained Prosecutor Stan Faith, looking for a possible motive as to why he might have murdered Kim and his two children. "You always try and get into the other person's mind if you can, but it's hard to get into his."

During the course of his investigations, Stan Faith consulted with a criminal profiler in California, to try to unlock the *real* David Camm.

"He said he had every earmark of a sociopath," said the

prosecutor. "And that basically, inside their head the universe revolves around them. Everything in this house was for David: NASCAR, hunting and so forth. Very little for Kim. So it was obvious in that household he had been the center of attention. Everything basically was for his benefit. Very self-centered.

"Now there's a morality there. The morality is himself; and what is good for him is moral and what is not good for him is immoral. I think that's how his universe works."

Faith believes it is impossible for Camm to understand social mores like normal people. And he had a "perfect storm" of motives, resulting in him killing his wife and children, says Faith.

"People wipe out their families on a regular basis for very many motives," said Faith, "all of which he had. There's the molestation, there's the money, there's the women, the sex angle, and wanting to appear really great in front of his uncle [Sam] that he admired."

The veteran prosecutor believes that David Camm molested his daughter, citing Janice Renn seeing a redness in the child's vaginal area, and pathologist Dr. Tracey Corey's findings of trauma to Jill's genitalia and petechial hemorrhaging to her chest and arms.

So why didn't Faith charge Camm with molestation?

"I made a strategic decision not to charge him with that," explained Faith. "I believed we had probable cause, but I didn't want the jury to say no on that, because it was circumstantial, and then [find him not guilty] on everything else."

The prosecutor said his early career as a salesman had taught him that when a customer starts saying no for one thing, they tend not to buy anything.

Faith believes that somehow Kim discovered Jill had been molested by her father in the last few hours of her life, and then come home to confront him.

"That was explained by the scuffle," explained Faith, "and by the extreme cold-hearted attack."

But Faith had some real problems to contend with. First, the medical experts concluded that, if Jill was molested, this most likely occurred a few hours before her death. But, by all accounts, Camm had not seen her since early that morning. And with eleven witnesses swearing that David Camm had been with them, playing basketball that Thursday night, Faith would have difficulty proving how David Camm could possibly have committed the crimes.

Initially he believed that Camm had returned home a little after 9:00 p.m. and killed Kim, Brad and Jill. But that theory would alter radically several times, as fresh new evidence emerged in the months leading up to the trial.

At the end of November, Sheriff Randy Hubbard became so concerned about David Camm's safety, he put him in solitary confinement for 130 days. Worried other inmates might attack the former Indiana State Trooper, the sheriff transferred Camm into a tiny cell for his own protection.

"My concern was that we had an ex-cop in the facility," said Hubbard. "He could potentially be injured or killed by any of these other inmates. So we had a security issue."

Having David Camm as such a high-profile inmate at the Floyd County Jail presented many problems for the sheriff. At one point he was accused in print of favoring his friend, after a jail employee anonymously told a reporter Camm was "King of the Jail," even having his own hairdresser to cut his hair before court appearances.

But the sheriff strongly denied any preferential treatment, blaming it on a dirty tricks campaign to stop him from being reelected. According to Hubbard the truth was that he tried to avoid any contact with his prisoner, because of their previous friendship.

"It was an emotional thing for me," he explained. "I checked on him but didn't spend a lot of time with him."

On several occasions Sheriff Hubbard, who thought Camm guilty, asked him if he had committed the murders, but his prisoner never got angry.

"All he kept saying was, 'Somebody did this just to get at me and hurt me,'" said Hubbard. "'Just to hurt me.'"

28

The Sacrificial Lamb

On November 16, 2000, David Camm sat in solitary confinement at Floyd County Jail and wrote a letter to the commander of the Indiana State Police, Superintendent Melvin Carraway. He then gave the letter to his Aunt Phyllis Rhodes, a trained reporter with Green Banner Publications, a group of free newspapers around Indiana, who typed it up and sent it to ISP headquarters in Indianapolis.

"I'm not writing this letter to beg you for your help [or] sympathy," the letter began. "I know you to be a Christian man, as I am."

Writing in the third person, Camm likened his plight to a martyr in some kind of bizarre fairy story.

He portrayed a man in his mid-thirties with a "beautiful, loving wife and son and daughter," who had recently found a new job for the sake of his family.

"Most importantly, the man has gained a new relationship with Jesus Christ," he wrote. "Every aspect of the man's life is glowing with a newness and a happiness that is as perfect as it can get here on this earth."

But one night, after playing basketball at a church hall, he came home to find his family slain in his garage.

"It's getting close to 9:30," he wrote Superintendent Carraway, "when the man pulls into the driveway and starts to pull into the garage and sees what he first believes is his five-year [old] daughter lying on the concrete floor.

"The door of the car is open and there is a lot of blood. The man thinks at first his little girl has fallen out of the car and hit her head, but no, as the man runs to the car he can see that it is his wife and she is lifeless. The man grabs his wife by the shoulder and as he looks at her totally blue face and streams of blood running from her head, he screams Kim, Kim, Kim, no, Kim. The man knows she's gone."

Then he writes how the man, "who is beside himself," calls the Indiana State Police, but soon realizes he has become the prime suspect as the killer and is arrested.

"Superintendent," he wrote, "how does an innocent man accused of killing his family survive after being falsely imprisoned?"

Writing that the man's grief "runs so deep with loss," he turned to God as his "only source of support.

"How can such a travesty take place? As the man looks at the situation from a far off, with all the lies they are trying to cram in-into a tidy box and place upon the man, it seems ridiculous, but the forces outside are working even harder now to make the man look bad so they can be justified in their own minds.

"Superintendent, as you know, the man is me and this is exactly how it happened, my family taken, my family taken from me then State Police Detectives throw me in jail and refuse to really search for the truth. Now, read this again and pretend you are I, see if you can begin to feel a small portion of my pain. I want truth. . . ."

Superintendent Carraway did not respond to David Camm's letter.

29

A Family Feud

Crime-scene reconstructionist Rod Englert left Portland, Oregon, on December 13 to fly to southern Indiana, but only got as far as Chicago because a heavy snowstorm had paralyzed air traffic in the Midwest. He finally arrived in New Albany on January 2, 2001, where he spent four days scientifically reconstructing the murders of Kim, Brad and Jill.

He interviewed the medical examiners who had performed the autopsies and ISP investigators, spending most of his time at the Sellersburg Post 45, examining Kim's Ford Bronco, now secured inside a large garage. He also viewed videotapes and saw photographs of the crime scene, taken straight after the murders.

He also visited the ISP Laboratory at Evansville, Indiana, closely examining the tee-shirt and other articles of clothing worn by David Camm the night of the murders. He met with lead investigator Sean Clemons and evidence technician Sam Sarkasian, as well as catching up with his old acquaintance Prosecutor Stan Faith, who introduced him to other key members of his team.

He spent hours working inside the Bronco, drawing detailed diagrams of every bloodstain, for later scientific analysis back in his Portland laboratory. To Englert every bloodstain at the crime scene told its own story about how a murder had been committed.

But the most damning evidence he discovered was on David Camm's gray Indiana State Police tee-shirt, with its eight microscopic drops of his daughter's blood.

"[It] has a pattern consistent with high-velocity mist," said Englert. "It's consistent with blow-back spatter of a person between Jill Camm against the right passenger seat."

Englert also discovered more evidence against Camm in the form of smudged droplets of Kim's blood on one of his basketball sneakers. He believes her own hand could have spattered her blood onto David's shoe as she dropped to the floor after the fatal shot to the head.

On January 5, Englert flew back to Portland to carry out additional tests and prepare his report for the prosecution. Before he left he told Stan Faith he was satisfied David Camm had slaughtered his family, and had the scientific evidence to prove it.

In the first week of January 2001, Sam Lockhart hired a prominent New Albany criminal attorney named Mike McDaniel to lead David Camm's defense. The 58-year-old, white-haired lawyer with a walrus mustache had once reportedly fought Muhammad Ali, in his early days as Cassius Clay in Louisville, in a local "Tomorrow's Champions" tournament. In a distinguished thirty-four-year career McDaniel had defended more than five hundred cases, several of them against Stan Faith.

The folksy attorney, who looks like a youthful Wilford Brimley, was overweight with a history of heart problems. Recently, on doctors' orders, he had been on a diet and given up smoking his favorite Doral cigarettes, but the stress of defending David Camm would soon see him fall off the wagon.

As their original attorney, George Gesenhues Jr., had had no experience with capital cases, the Lockhart family had gone shopping for a replacement.

First the family met with a prominent attorney in Louisville, but he was too expensive.

"He started talking about a hundred-thousand-dollar retainer," remembered Julie, who used connections her ex-husband had in law enforcement, "He said it would be at least a half a million dollars."

They looked to securing the services of a public defender, but when none could be found, Floyd County agreed to pick up a percentage of McDaniel's fees, with Sam Lockhart paying the rest.

"Mike was supposed to be the best there was in southern Indiana," said Julie. "So we thought we were going to get somebody good at a better rate. In hindsight, I think everybody would say we should have spent the money."

On January 10, McDaniel made his first appearance at Floyd Superior Court, at a bail hearing, to decide if David could go home before his murder trial, now scheduled for March 12.

McDaniel, who had only just received the results of blood tests, told Judge Striegel there wasn't enough evidence to keep his client behind bars before his trial. He also demanded an evidentiary hearing, claiming several key parts of the state's case were suspect.

The veteran defender said he had reviewed the reports, and found the DNA samples taken from Camm's tee-shirt were so similar, they could have come from either Brad or Jill.

Floyd County Chief Deputy Prosecutor Susan Orth, who would work the case alongside Stan Faith, strongly disagreed.

"The blood on that shirt belongs to Jill," she told Judge Striegel. "And that alone establishes probable cause."

McDaniel also denied that 5-year-old Jill had ever been sexually molested, claiming her genital injury was the result of a playground accident a few days before her murder.

Urging the judge to deny the defense's motion for an evidentiary hearing, Orth claimed that it amounted to nothing more than a fishing expedition for state evidence.

The hearing ended dramatically when the judge delayed making a decision on the evidentiary hearing, or whether to grant bail. Suddenly David Camm lowered his head down on the defense table, exhaled and burst into tears. Then, as bailiffs led him out of the courtroom, he began shaking his head and weeping, on his way back to the adjoining Floyd County Jail, where he remained in solitary confinement.

The following day, Judge Striegel released a statement ordering full depositions to be taken, before ruling on an evidentiary hearing. And he also subpoenaed Indiana lab technician Lynn Scamahorn, who had conducted the DNA testing, to appear at a special hearing to explain her findings.

Outside the court, Mike McDaniel told reporters that David Camm had now been held in solitary confinement for more than one hundred days.

"That's enough to make you crazy," he explained. "He is starved of human communication."

But the defense lawyer said he worried about releasing the former police officer into the general population, as he would be a "flight risk." So Camm stayed in solitary, reviewing the escalating volumes of discovery from his case and helping prepare his defense.

Finally, at the end of January, after nearly five months in solitary confinement, Camm was released back into the general population and placed in a cell with four other prisoners.

"I demanded it," he would later explain. "I was told it was at my own risk."

On February 7, David Camm's paternal grandmother Fern Camm died at the age of one hundred. The following week an angry letter to the editor from David's mother, Susie, appeared in the New Albany *Tribune* Mailbag.

She wrote that her mother-in-law's life had been "full of losses," with almost everybody she loved dying before her.

"However," wrote Susie, "she fought courageously to live on, putting her faith in God. The final losses in her life were the cruelest and hastened her death."

In the letter she said Grandma Camm's great loss of three close members of her family was magnified by "an unfair, inept judicial system" and "political power and ego."

The family had deliberately not told the old woman about her grandson David's arrest for the murders, but somehow she had found out.

"With that knowledge she gave up her fight for life. She stopped eating, drinking and talking," wrote her daughter-in-law. "Grandma Camm knew her grandson as a Christian husband and father and knew he was incapable of such an evil act."

The letter then went on to defend David Camm as an innocent man persecuted by "dishonest, self-serving" policemen.

"Our family has been lied to," claimed her letter, "and efforts have been made to intimidate us by those who do not want the truth to be known."

On February 27, Judge Richard Striegel postponed David Camm's trial until June 18, to allow attorneys more time to study the many volumes of evidence. There was already a growing bitterness between the two sides, as Mike McDaniel had accused his old rival Stan Faith of withholding pretrial discovery from the defense.

"They're dragging their feet," Sam Lockhart angrily told *The Courier-Journal*, as a recent gag order from the judge now forbade all the attorneys connected with the case from talking to the press. "They have not turned over evidence."

Chief Deputy Prosecutor Susan Orth denied the allegations. In a court motion she claimed her office had already turned over more than three hundred police reports, transcribed interviews and other investigation documents.

At the end of the hearing, McDaniel asked Judge Striegel to set a bond for his client, still claiming there was not enough evidence to hold him in jail.

"Murder is not a bailable offense," the chief deputy prosecutor told Judge Striegel, who agreed.

The decision to deny Camm bond was met with loud sighs of frustration from no fewer than twenty-five members of his family who were in the public gallery. Then the tearful prisoner was escorted out of the courtroom, shaking his head in disbelief.

In mid-February, Detective Sean Clemons spent several days at Floyd Memorial Hospital, as a procession of women connected with Camm visited the emergency room to give blood or saliva for DNA testing, because the mysterious gray sweatshirt, bearing the word "Backbone," had been found near the bodies at the murder scene, and been found to contain blood and several hairs which could not be accounted for. So over a two-week period evidence samples were taken from: Anita Asher, Jamie Spurgeon, Beth Minnicus, Lisa Korfhage, Tamara Lynch and Trooper Shelley Romero. But after the DNA testing, all the women were cleared of having anything to do with the murders. And the mystery of whose DNA and hair was on the Backbone shirt remained unsolved.

March 14, 2001, would have been Kim Camm's thirty-seventh birthday, and her husband, now accused of her murder, wrote her an emotional birthday card from his jail cell. With a cluster of forget-me-not flowers on the front, the card bore the inscription: "May your birthday be filled with the kinds of special moments that will become the treasured memories of tomorrow."

And inside the card, in neat childish letters he wrote to his "beloved Kim":

Words can never describe my pain here without you.
How can I begin to thank you for all that you have done
for me over the last few years especially our little ones.
You have always been the one to sacrifice for love, never

complaining about my hobbies and always giving, never asking for anything of yourself.

Why God chose to allow you and the kids to be taken from me in such a manner, I will never understand. Not until I join you in heaven where we will be together again. If you are present with God and are aware of what they have done to me, I pray you see through God's eternal eyes of understanding, and are aware of his plan. I can't believe God is not working some greater plan out of this terrible situation to try and bring some good for his glory to balance out so much bad and evil.

Your family is constantly on my mind and I hope that the love that was shared will not be lost.

I stay strong not for me, but for you, Brad and Jill. For the three of you have suffered the greatest injustice of us all. I will continue to walk with you in my heart each and every day.

You will always be my wife no matter the circumstances. I wish I would have told you more often how much I appreciated you, and you're [sic] importance in my life. Though I have in the past, I will never miss another birthday, anniversary, or Valentines Day.

> *I love you always,*
> *Your Husband,*
> *David*

The birthday card would never be sent to Kim's family, but is now at his parents' house, in a large album devoted to pictures of their tragic son, his wife and children.

Over the next few months the case against David Camm would be increasingly played out in the media. It was now attracting national attention, and a production team from CBS-TV's *48 Hours* had arrived in New Albany to do the groundwork for a one-hour investigative special on the David Camm case. And the prosecution and the defense had signed an agreement with producer Shoshana Wolfsonto to be interviewed on camera, on condition she did not disclose what either side had told her to the other. A second stipulation was that *48 Hours* not air the show until after the trial.

In early April, Prosecutor Stan Faith filed a brief, claiming that Camm had killed Kim and the children to leave him free to pursue extramarital affairs. Prepared by his deputy Susan Orth, the sensational brief was in direct response to a motion by Mike McDaniel, who wanted to suppress any mention of his client's infidelities at trial.

McDaniel argued that his client's past conduct had no bearing on the murder charges, and was just an attempt to prejudice the jury. This crucial issue fell under Indiana's evidence rule 404(b), meaning the prosecution cannot simply introduce evidence of a defendant's previous bad character or adulterous behavior to pursue a murder conviction against a spouse. It must show evidence of motive and cannot just be used to influence a jury.

Judge Striegel's subsequent ruling to allow the sometimes damning testimony from almost a dozen women at trial would have monumental results.

On April 9, Sam Lockhart filed his own detailed time line of the night of the murders, attempting to prove it was impossible for David to have carried them out. Citing the prosecution's theory that Camm had left the basketball game at 9:22 p.m., driven home and then reported the murders seven minutes later, Lockhart believed he just would not have had enough time.

"The defense can establish and prove beyond any doubt," wrote Lockhart, "that David would have had only 90 to 120 seconds to get into an argument with his wife, struggle with her, beat her, kill his wife and children and then dispose of the gun so well that it has not been recovered."

The next day Sam Lockhart gave an exclusive interview to the New Albany *Tribune*, explaining his time line and discussing the toll the killings had taken on his family.

"The family was devastated when it first happened," he told reporter Jennifer Bland. "And at first, we all thought that maybe David had done it. And if that were true, then yes, I believe that David should be behind bars for the crime."

He claimed that he and other members of the family had conducted their own investigation of Kim, Brad and Jill's murders, "as thoroughly as any of the prosecutors on this case."

"My family has been in law enforcement for over eighty years now," declared an emotional Lockhart. "This has shattered my image of the justice system in this country. The way they are handling the case is just ridiculous."

The following day the Renn family finally broke their silence about the murders, giving an exclusive interview to a Louisville television station. For the first time they publicly stated they believed David was guilty and had murdered Kim, Brad and Jill. Frank Renn said he had decided his son-in-law was guilty, after seeing the scientific results from Rod Englert.

"There's no doubt in my mind David did it," said Frank Renn. "It's kind of hard to accept, I mean, of all people, David would do this."

The Renn family was persuaded after Prosecutor Stan Faith met with them in his office, explaining how Rod Englert believed Jill's high-velocity blood mist was on David's shirt.

"That convinces me one hundred percent," said Renn, "that David, and nobody but David, did this."

Kim's younger sister, Debbie Karem, who reportedly has multiple sclerosis and can never have children, said she too believed her brother-in-law was *the* worst kind of murderer.

"He's the father of those kids," she said. "I can't imagine looking into those eyes and killing your children. I can't imagine anybody doing that."

Then Frank Renn said he had just one question he wanted to ask his son-in-law, if he happened to be watching from jail.

"You killed your wife and you killed your children," he said, staring straight at the camera. "If you and Kim were having problems, and you felt like you had to kill her, then why didn't you turn that gun around and shoot yourself before you shot those two little kids?"

From now on the Camms and Lockharts would avoid the Renns. David's first wife, Tammy, and his 18-year-old daughter, Whitney, had sided with Kim's family. Initially after his arrest, Tammy had corresponded with her ex-husband and even visited him several times in jail. But then she and Whitney turned against him, deciding he had murdered Kim and the children.

"Whitney's mother has taken the side of the Renns and thinks that Dave did it," said David's sister, Julie. "She's been influenced by her mom."

Whitney then broke off all contact with her father's family, refusing to take their calls.

"We've not been able to get to her," said Julie. "It's easier for Whitney just to block it off and act like her dad doesn't exist."

The Lockhart and Camm families even boycotted Karem's Meats, owned by Kim's brother-in-law Greg Karem, where they had shopped for years.

When David's family decided to erect a stone bench as a memorial to Kim and the children in the churchyard where they were buried, Don Camm called the Renns for their input.

According to Don they refused to take his call, so the Camms and Lockharts went ahead anyway. The bench was placed by a path near the graves. On one side, facing the path was engraved, "Donated by the Camm–Lockhart family," and on the other, facing into the cemetery were the names Kim, Brad and Jill.

"It was something that David wanted," said his mother,

Susie. "He drew it up and he did everything. And I wanted a big one."

The Renn family was furious, considering it "offensive," viewing it as more of a tribute to Kim's in-laws than the murder victims.

"I raised a stink about that," Frank Renn told a reporter.

Finally Sam Lockhart agreed to turn the memorial bench around, so Kim and the children's names could be more prominent.

After that both families' attorneys, Nicholas Stein and Mike McDaniel, agreed that they should not have any further communication with each other.

30

In His Own Words

Soon after his arrest, Phyllis Rhodes had drafted a set of questions to her nephew, so he could explain what had happened in his own words. A freelance reporter for Green Banner Publications, Rhodes said it "hurt to ask those questions," but she primarily did it so the family could know what had happened. She also saw it as a possible book after the trial.

She was going to submit it to her editor with a view to publication, if the defense team agreed and the paper considered it newsworthy.

"I [wanted] to answer questions to everyone's satisfaction," explained Rhodes. "We already knew for sure that David didn't do it."

So over the next few months, Phyllis sent off her questions to him in jail. And David sent back his answers in longhand, two or three pages at a time, some of it almost illegible because of his dyslexia. Then his aunt would type up his responses and send them back for his approval. Her probing questions took a no-holds-barred approach to his case, asking difficult and often personal questions.

Ultimately prosecutors would obtain a copy of Camm's answers and use them against him.

Dear David:
Here are some questions we can form an interview from. Some of them will be hard because we want this to be a real interview. The hard questions will also give you a

chance to answer some of the rumors; charges and spec-
ulation put out by the prosecution, or have simply formed
in some people's minds. If I miss asking you something
that you think should be asked, add that to your answers.

Q. Give your time line of that night. (I can pretty much
get this from the letter to the superintendent, but if you
have remembered any other detail, cars you passed, people you spoke to at the gym, phone calls by you or others
to help establish the time, add that).

A. I got home around 5:30 or so from work. Kim knew I
was playing ball that night and I knew she would be dealing
with Brad's swim practice and Jill's dance with the assistance of her mo- of Kim's mother. The Schwan's man arrived around 6:40 or so, I bought a few tings from him,
then headed for the gym at about 7:00 p.m. Several others
were already there and Jeff Lockhart was just pulling up.
He unlocked the doors and turned off the alarm. I remember we played until after 9:00 p.m. when several of the guys,
there were 8 of us left, wanted to play one more game.
I agreed. It was about 9:10 as I recall. The game ended
quickly. I collected a few dollars from the guys to give to
Kim for assistance on the electric bill, as Jeff set the alarm.
Several of us were talking about playing golf the next day
as we walked out. I thought it was about 9:20–9:25 when I
left. Phillip was in front of me, Jeff was behind me. I made
no phone calls while at the church or from any phone in my
truck while on my way home. I arrived home around 9:27
or 9:28 and called the post at 9:29 p.m.

Q. When you got to your driveway, exactly what did
you see?

A. The house was dark, Kim's garage door was open, and
mine was shut. I opened it with my automatic opener. As

I started to enter the garage, that's when I saw the stream of blood running toward-toward the garage door. The blood led toward the Bronco where the passenger door was open. I saw what I thought at first was Jill's body and I thought in my mind she had slipped and fallen from the car and hit her head. I thought it was Jill because I couldn't see Kim's legs lying under the-the Bronco and because Kim was in her panties. I thought it was Jill still in her dance outfit. I got out of the truck as quickly as I could and ran into the garage when I realized it was Kim. I knelt down beside her. There was blood all around the right side of her body as well as the stream following toward the garage door. Her eyes were half open and face blue. I knew she was gone. Then I thought where are the kids! I climbed into the passenger front seat and saw Brad at the far right side of the back seat. I then turned my head left and saw Jill with her head lying in her lap, face down, as I recall. I remember blood. I grabbed Brad, pulled him to me, picked him up, and carried him out of the car. I laid him on the floor and tried to give him CPR. His little eyes were half open. I had difficulty remembering how to do the CPR properly. Once I did get in a few breaths and compressions (45 seconds or so after I got him out) I knew I needed help.

Q. Were you able to think as an officer at some point and view the scene for possible clues?

A. I never really looked for clues. My mind was unable to process anything at that point. I just remember not being asked to hold still, continuously walking and moving, talking to myself. I felt sick to my stomach like I was going to throw up, but yet I was so numb I found it difficult to cry. Everyone wanted to hug me and I just wanted to scream. I paced constantly thinking it was a dream.

Q. Did any of the officers say anything to you that night that indicated you were at that time the prime suspect? Did anyone say anything about "getting you off" or "nailing you for the crime"? Did you sense any animosity or "agenda attitudes" from any law enforcement officers?

A. Sean Clemons stated "Dave you know we have to clear you before we can do anything else." It was obvious to me that their agenda was to focus solely on me from the beginning. They arrested me without any evidence, just the word of an individual that was hired by the prosecutor's office. Everything else in Sean Clemons' Probable Cause affidavit he lied about. At least as far as I am concerned, once this is over, I believe he should be fired and many others demoted or reprimanded for their inept actions, and total disregard for the rights of my wife and children. Now the prosecutor's office is throwing money at the screwups to try to save face because their egos are more important than justice. And it seems to be condoned by the judge.

Q. Were you and Kim having marriage problems? Had Kim indicated she wanted to leave or divorce you? Had you had marriage problems before? What and when? How did you rectify them? Had you been faithful to Kim all your married life? Had she been faithful to you?

A. Kim and I had NEVER EVER been happier. My love, my love, my love for her was greater than the day I married her. We had matured and grown through some tough times and she loved me unconditionally. I know that with all, I know that with all my heart. It was not out of the question, it was not out of the question for us to have another little one. My job was going great and we had whatever we wanted. I miss her more than words can describe and those who think we were having problems and all the other garbage that's been put out there by the State Police and prosecutors, are lies. Those who believe the lies are simply foolish and didn't know Kim and me very well. I had been unfaithful to Kim. I've made no secret of that. Don't let the police make you think that they have through some in-intensive investigation found things from my past that were hidden deep dark secrets. Almost all of the information that they have concerning any incidents they have, I told them in the beginning in my best attempt to try and locate any and all persons I believe could be remotely considered suspects in the killings of my family. These incidents occurred while I was with the State Police and only one was an affair, that occurred six years ago and Kim and I had long since moved beyond it. Unfaithfulness is not uncommon among police officers and I could not shake the reputation I carried after that incident. The rumors around the Post were like being in a soap opera. The employees there were always gossiping about someone. I believe it's one of the reasons why I was prejudged and that the latest allegation publicized that I killed my family to pursue affairs is the stupidest thing I've ever heard! The prosecutor's office must have no idea how desperate that makes them appear. Even many of the inmates here that saw the story on the news just shook their heads and remarked what a ridiculous assumption it was for them to pursue such garbage as a motive for a man to kill his wife and children. It's not true, it's National Enquirer garbage.

Q. There have been many theories of motive for you to murder your family. Did you have any improper sexual contact with your daughter or your son?

A. Sean Clemons' accusations of sexual intercourse having taken place with Jill and his asserting I was guilty of such a thing shows the intelligence level of this "lead" investigator. It was not true. He made such allegations yet on the stand during the bond hearing (5 months later) he stated he was in a position of the autopsy reports but had not had time to read it. Don't you think if a 5 year old has allegedly been forced to have sexual intercourse, he (Clemons) would be anxious to read Jill's autopsy report? If he had taken a few seconds to look at it, he would have seen that the hymen was intact as it was supposed to be and he should have immediately apologized to me and my family. He doesn't have the guts for something as noble as that.

Q. Do you have any suspicions as to who might have reason to kill your family? Has your life ever been threatened?

A. I originally thought it was someone waiting to kill me, someone that I had dealt with while with the police. I gave the police any and all information I could that I thought might be helpful, but they didn't follow up on many of the leads.

Q. Talk about what has happened to you since your arrest. How long were you in solitary? How have you been treated by inmates and guards there?

A. I was in shock from the time I found my family until at least a week or two later. I spent 118 days in solitary confinement until I demanded to be removed regardless of the threats made against my life. Since being placed in a cellblock, I have made many friends and most did not prejudge. It doesn't take long before they can see through the propaganda on the news and realize I am innocent. I spend most of my time studying and reading my bible. I know that Kim and the kids are in Heaven and in the presence of our Lord and He walks with me as I travel down this path. I have grown in the sense of not seeing things so one dimensionally. Many of the people in here did not choose the lifestyles that led them to jail, but their life circumstances forced them because it was the only thing they knew . . .

The best way to describe the justice system is to simply say that it is unjust!

Q. Talk about your day-to-day existence. How have you coped?

A. My day-to-day existence consists of dealing with each individual moment as it comes. As it comes. Focusing on God's promise to never leave me nor forsake me. I study in the, in the Word. I kiss Kim's and the kids' pictures at least a dozen times a day and tell all that I love them and miss them. If I focus too much on how much pain I have inside, I would break down and not be able to make it. I stay strong for them.

Late one night in his Floyd County Jail cell, David Camm had a vision. He told his mother how he had been a little boy riding his bicycle when he found himself in a place where he had never been before.

"He told me he had glanced to the right and seen Paul the Apostle," said Susie Camm. "He was sitting at a table writing and they looked at each other. Then he spoke to David through his blue eyes, without saying a word."

According to Camm, Paul told him that God understood that he was suffering unjustly and would lead him to salvation.

31

A Circus

In early May 2001, Mike McDaniel appealed to the Indiana Supreme Court to grant bail for David Camm, after Judge Striegel refused bond for the third time. His latest grounds for freeing Camm were that he had now been in jail six months without a trial.

"It wasn't a big surprise," said McDaniel after hearing of the judge's refusal. "I do believe I have a valid point in asking for a discharge."

At the hearing the Renn family complained to a television reporter that the whole case was turning into a "circus," prompting Donnie Camm to lash out.

"We don't think this is a circus at all," he said angrily. "We just want the truth to come out. Obviously we take this very seriously."

David Camm's family were leaving nothing to chance at the upcoming trial, now scheduled to start in just five weeks. They had launched a campaign to influence possible voters by drawing up a six-page pamphlet explaining why David was innocent. A number of volunteers, including a uniformed New Albany police officer, Dan McMahel, were distributing it to the public.

Prosecutor Stan Faith was furious when he found out, labeling it "propaganda." He immediately filed an administrative complaint against the officer with the New Albany Police Department, who immediately launched an internal investigation.

Judge Richard Striegel was so worried about the effects

of the propaganda campaign that he called a hearing in mid-May to discuss moving the trial out of Floyd County because of all the publicity. The Reverend Leland Lockhart was called to the stand to explain the pamphlet.

"We felt a need to tell our side of the story, because the truth wasn't shown through the media," explained David Camm's uncle, under oath. "We offered it to the church family and it was made available to anyone who wanted it."

Chief Deputy Prosecutor Susan Orth asked the pastor if the family had wanted a uniformed officer handing it out to local businesses.

"Not that I'm aware of," said the pastor. "I have no strong feelings on whether he should've done it or not."

At the end of the hearing, Judge Striegel ordered a jury be picked from upstate Johnson County, finding the Floyd County jury pool to have been tainted.

Two weeks later, no less than thirty-four members of David Camm's family put their names to a letter to the editor, printed in the New Albany *Tribune* on the Mailbag Page. It strongly condemned the newspaper's coverage of the court hearing about the pamphlet, as well as including all its points about why the family thought David innocent.

Under the headline, "Camm Family Upset with Media Coverage," the letter ripped into the media, also taking potshots at the prosecution and the Indiana State Police.

"David Camm's wife and two children were murdered in September," it began. "David was arrested and charged with the killings three days after he came home and found his family shot to death."

The family were upset the readers might think its pamphlet had been intended to influence public opinion, saying it was made available to any church member interested in learning how David's case was progressing.

"Copies were made available on a table at the back of the church for those who wished to have one," it pointed out.

The letter also accused the media of "incomplete and often inaccurate" reporting of the case, and the prosecutors of wrongly referring to the pamphlet as "propaganda."

"If the document in question is propaganda, it said, "it is propaganda straight from the prosecution's own discovery documents that have been filed and are available to the public."

It then accused the media and prosecution of being "cruel and unethical," by driving a wedge between the two sides of the family. And the letter pledged to continue the fight to clear David's name, claiming he had been victimized by "the egos and ambitions" of certain politicians and law enforcement officers.

"David would prefer to join his family in heaven," it continued. "But he and the rest of his family cannot rest knowing that the person or persons who killed our loved ones are still out there."

The letter concluded, "No one else is looking for the truth."

It was signed by no fewer than thirty-four members of David Camm's family.

Noting that there were no other suspects and no investigation to find any, the letter criticized the police and the media for ignoring the "Backbone" sweatshirt found at the scene, even though it had unknown DNA on it.

"And by the way," the letter dramatically emphasized, "none of David Camm's DNA was found on the shirt, because it is not his."

"According to the letter, not only had investigators resisted trying to match the unknown DNA with any on file, but the shirt had not been tested for gunshot residue. The letter closed by saying the family would have put its trust in God that the truth would be found.

On the same day the letter was published, Judge Striegel delayed the triple murder trial until August 20, to allow defense experts more time to carry out DNA testing on clothing found at the murder scene.

Deputy Prosecutor Rob Colone said the State of Indiana was ready to go to trial, but welcomed the delay.

"[This] gives us more opportunity to prepare our case more thoroughly," he said. "I would say that we're ready."

Then a month later in July, defense attorney Mike Mc-Daniel filed a motion to delay the trial even further, claiming he had not been given adequate time to prepare.

Sam Lockhart told the press that the prosecution was to blame.

"We still haven't had access to all the discovery we should have had," he explained. "The prosecutors have not been forthcoming with evidence."

After considering McDaniel's motion for a continuance, the judge postponed the trial yet again until October 15.

But if some questioned whether David Camm's family were showing signs of paranoia, when a portion of his Aunt Phyllis Rhodes' questions and answers was taken from Amos Lockhart's house by one of his nurses and then given to prosecutors, their fears seemed well-founded.

"It was stolen," complained Debbie TerVree. "There were a couple of days for a few hours that she was there with dad in the home. She took them."

Even then it took weeks for the prosecution team to realize that Phyllis was Camm's aunt. At that point Judge Striegel ruled that she must hand over the complete interview with her nephew, which would then be used in evidence. Rhodes cited freedom of the press and refused, but the judge disagreed.

"The defendant has made a statement in writing to a family member," said Deputy Prosecutor Susan Orth at a superior court hearing to discuss it. "We feel we are entitled to a copy."

The David Camm Q&A was eventually given to the prosecution and later read by the jury.

On August 9, New Albany Police Officer Dan McMahel appeared before a police commission, accused of improper conduct for distributing a pro–David Camm pamphlet while in uniform. With his job on the line, the twenty-seven-year veteran told the investigating officers he had grown up with the Camm and Lockhart families and believed David to be innocent.

"I really didn't think I was doing anything wrong," he explained.

The Police Merit Commission disagreed, suspending him for four months without pay for violating the department's standard operating procedure with four acts of conduct unbecoming a police officer.

A dozen members of David Camm's family showed their support by attending the public hearing.

"Obviously we're disappointed for Danny," said Donnie Camm. "A police officer has integrity enough to stand up for the truth, and this happens. The only mistake he made was doing what he did while in uniform."

In late September, a couple of days before the first anniversary of the murders, David Camm was led into Floyd County Superior Court, wearing a polo shirt and slacks. This latest court hearing was for his attorney Mike McDaniel to file a belated alibi plea. In the wake of the recent September 11 terrorist attacks, security was tight, with all spectators being searched for weapons in the hallway.

On one side of Judge Striegel's courtroom sat the Camm and Lockhart families, to lend their support to the defendant. And on the other side, behind the prosecution table, sat Frank and Janice Renn and half a dozen of their family members.

The ten-minute hearing was a technicality, to allow Mc-
Daniel to officially file Camm's alibi into the court, claiming
he could never have committed the murders, as he was playing basketball at the time, and eleven other players would
swear to that.

The defense was confidently telling reporters that the
prosecution had gotten it all wrong. Its blood experts had
proven conclusively that Kim and the children must have
been killed at least two hours earlier than the prosecution's
estimate of 9:30 p.m. Kim's blood had coagulated and broken down into a watery serum when she was found, a process that takes several hours.

A few days later another hearing was called to discuss
the incendiary 404(b) issue, and whether to allow sixteen
women romantically linked with Camm to testify at trial.
At the last minute it was postponed, prompting the October 1 edition of the New Albany *Tribune* to run an editorial, labeling all the delays "ridiculous" and unfair to the
defendant.

"David Camm has been in Floyd County Jail for nearly
a year," noted the editorial.

Referring to delays in hearing dates and wrangling over
the character evidence the prosecution had gathered, the
editorial claimed it could be another year before Camm's
case finally went to trial.

"This is bordering on ridiculous," said the editorial,
questioning how someone could sit in jail for more than a
year without a trial. The editorial acknowledged that this
was no ordinary trial. "A man's life is at stake here and
both sides want to make sure they have all of their evidence in order."

But does it take a year to gather that evidence? We
think not.

The editorial noted that, given the way the case had

proceeded, it was no wonder that "people take a nega-
tive view of our legal system." Noting that further delays
would not only be unfair to Camm and his family, but to
Kim's family as well as to the taxpayers of Floyd County,
the editorial urged, WE DON'T NEED TO SEE ANY
MORE DELAYS."

Judge Richard Striegel apparently never read the editorial, as the next day he postponed the trial until January 7,
2002. This time his reason was air travel and all the diffi-
culties the experts were having getting flights, after the
World Trade Center and Pentagon attacks.

"Unfortunately, the tragic events caused interference
with experts coming in for depositions and to look at evidence," explained Shane Gibson from the Floyd County
Prosecutor's Office. "You don't want to rush into it."

The following day, October 16, the prosecution and defense teams drove sixty miles north to Franklin, Indiana, to
start picking a jury who would try the triple murder case in
New Albany. They interviewed 230 prospective Johnson
County jurors, whittling them down to one hundred. The
plan was for the final cut of twelve jurors and three alternates to be selected in Franklin on January 7, with opening
statements expected in New Albany a week later.

Floyd County Deputy Prosecutor Rob Colone voiced
many people's frustration, admitting there had been too
many delays.

"I hope it starts on the seventh," he told reporters. "The
community is ready for this to move forward."

So far the Camm case had cost the taxpayers of Floyd
County more than $200,000 for expert witnesses, DNA
testing and flying in out-of-state witnesses. But that would
more than double once it went to trial.

With a new trial date set, for the fifth time Mike Mc-
Daniel asked Judge Striegel to release David Camm on
bond, so he could spend the holidays with his family. Citing

new evidence that would prove his client's innocence, McDaniel claimed that the defense crime-scene experts had found much of the prosecution case scientifically lacking.

"This is a brand-new perspective," McDaniel optimistically told Meghan Hoyer of *The Courier-Journal.* "Once we started taking expert depositions, it became apparent that there was nothing there."

Prosecutor Stan Faith described the defense motion as "a beautiful piece of propaganda that's not worth one spit."

Accusing the defense of attempting to try the case in the media, Faith said he would use the "proper forum," presenting his case in front of a jury.

He also lodged an official complaint with Judge Striegel, that key depositions from the defense experts had been leaked to the press before the prosecution had even seen them.

But after an emotional bond hearing on November 5, attended by more than sixty family members from all sides, Judge Striegel once again refused to set bond, without giving a reason.

A month later, David Camm received another blow when Judge Striegel finally handed down his decision on the controversial 404(b) issue, agreeing to allow evidence of his extramarital affairs to be introduced by the prosecution.

After hearing the decision, which would change defense strategy for the trial, Mike McDaniel announced he planned to call several Indiana State Troopers to the stand, and question them about morality and extramarital sex in the department.

"It's probably going to be an embarrassment for everybody," said the defender. "What we're trying to do at this point is educate the judge that we have a situation."

That December, David Camm spent his second Christmas behind bars, just two weeks away from his high-profile murder trial.

"My life is on the line," he told *48 Hours* reporter Richard Schlesinger in a tearful jailhouse interview. "I'm not just fighting for me. I want justice for my wife and my children."

Several weeks before his trial, Floyd County Corrections Officer Diane Heavrin accused inmate David Camm of sexually propositioning her. The officer, who was soon to be married, was on duty in the East Pod of the jail when Camm called her over, asking for a medication request form. Reportedly his family were now spending $3,000 a month on all his various prescribed drugs for migraines, anxiety and allergies.

"He congratulated me on my upcoming wedding and asked if he was invited," Heavrin later testified. "[He said] he would be out in time for it."

Then, according to her testimony, Camm smiled, saying she still had time for one last sexual fling with him.

"I was shocked," said the corrections officer. "He just turned around and went back to his pod."

On Monday, January 7, 2002, jury selection began in a Franklin courtroom for the David Camm trial. It was hoped the Johnson County community knew little about the case, which hadn't been covered extensively in *The Indianapolis Star*.

The remaining ninety-seven men and women were all asked to fill out a seventeen-page questionnaire, jointly drawn up by the defense and prosecution. It asked their opinions on adultery, and whether it was acceptable; if they were divorced; and even if they knew anyone who had ever called a psychic hotline.

David Camm sat on the defense bench, carefully watching the jury being questioned by Mike McDaniel and Stan Faith and his team of prosecutors. During a court recess, the defendant gave an impromptu press conference.

"We're right and they're wrong," he declared.

When a reporter asked him if justice was coming, Camm replied, "Absolutely. For my family, that's most important for my wife and children. We don't want that to be lost."

Back in New Albany, Judge Striegel's courtroom was undergoing a high-tech makeover, with workmen installing thousands of dollars' worth of sophisticated audio and video equipment to make the complicated scientific evidence more palatable to the jury.

Outside, in almost every grocery store, bar or restaurant in Louisville and southern Indiana, David Camm loudly proclaimed his innocence on the front page of *Snitch*, a free newspaper specializing in covering local crime. His Aunt Phyllis Rhodes had given the paper a copy of her controversial Q&A with David to reporter Mat Herron, who printed choice selections.

Born in Louisville, the 22-year-old investigative reporter had studied journalism at the University of Kentucky. The Camm trial had previously been covered for *Snitch* by a freelancer, but when she left, Herron was called into his editor's office and given the assignment.

"We were going to take an O. J. Simpson approach," he said. "My boss likes to do wall-to-wall coverage and it was a pretty challenging task."

Two weeks before the trial he met with David Camm's father, Don, and Aunt Phyllis, and was handed the previously unpublished Q&A as an exclusive.

"[Phyllis] kept saying over and over again," remembered Herron, " 'if David did this, we wouldn't want him in our family or around our kids.' And it became almost like a mantra for the entire family."

But their constant barrage of pro–David Camm propaganda seemed to be having the opposite of the intended effect. Public opinion had turned against the ex-trooper and his family, with many people thinking them arrogant and overbearing.

"At the trial we were bad," said Julie Hogue. "Now we were the enemy. There was a newsman who commented to one of my aunts, 'These people are crazy.' Maybe · we looked that way. Maybe we did—we're vocal."

On Wednesday morning the jury was finally selected, comprised of seven women, five men and three alternates. They consisted of two nurses, a librarian, a restaurant manager, a special education teacher, a printer, a commercial banker, a realtor, a landscaper, a sales manager, a pharmacist and a highway engineer.

Starting that Monday, for the duration of the trial, they would live at the Holiday Inn, in Clarksville from Sunday to Thursday night, and be allowed home for weekends. They would not be sequestered and would be able to go out for dinner, although there was an 11:00 p.m. curfew.

The trial was expected to last six weeks, and perhaps longer. The pressures on each of the jurors would be tremendous, and some would ultimately crack under the strain.

"I think we're satisfied," David Camm told reporters after the final selection. "It's time to get the truth out."

32

A Jury of His Peers

David Camm's long-anticipated murder trial finally started at 9:00 a.m., Monday, January 14, at Floyd County Superior Court. The night before, the jurors had been bused into New Albany and had spent their first night at the Holiday Inn, a few miles away.

The Camm trial was the hottest ticket in town. The first people started arriving as early as 5:00 a.m. that freezing cold morning, several hours before the deputies came to open up the drab concrete building. The same people would line up every weekday morning for the next nine weeks, hoping to secure one of the eighty available seats in the courtroom to watch southern Indiana's own trial of the century. They were admitted on a first-come, first-serve basis and most days some unlucky ones would not get in.

After David Camm ate breakfast and took his medication, Sheriff Randy Hubbard and several deputies arrived to escort him from his jail cell through an underground passage to a holding pen next door, directly under the court building. They then took an elevator up to Judge Striegel's second-floor courtroom. Camm had changed from his bright orange prison suit into a suit and tie, which was hanging off him, as he had lost so much weight.

The corridor outside the courtroom was a hive of activity, as several camera crews and print reporters had stationed themselves for interviews, jockeying for the best position. And to add to the excitement the celebrated *48 Hours* reporter Richard Schlesinger was there with his producer and crew to film the first day of the trial. He would return to New York the next day, leaving behind a skeleton crew to cover the rest of the proceedings.

"September twenty-eighth is starting all over again," sighed Frank Renn, looking pale and drawn as he entered the courtroom.

The atmosphere inside was electric, as everyone took their seats. The Renn family were seated on the right-hand side of the courtroom, second row right, behind Stan Faith's prosecution table. With them sat David Camm's first wife, Tammy, who had taken time off work at Floyd Memorial Hospital, and would attend the entire nine weeks of the trial, taking copious notes.

Just a few yards across the aisle to the left were the Camm and Lockhart families, on the defense side. David's father, Don, wore a burgundy jacket with a United Dynamics logo, a pen and notebook at the ready. His wife Susie remained at home, as she was too sick to attend.

A little after 9:00 a.m. there was a hushed silence as Judge Richard Striegel entered the courtroom, taking his seat overlooking the proceedings. The judge favored an air of informality in his domain, only requiring the court to rise when the jury entered the courtroom, and not when he did. And he never buttoned up his black robes of office, as if emphasizing his individuality.

"Bring in Mr. Camm," he told the two deputy sheriffs standing guard at the back of the court.

A metal door slowly opened and the public gallery had its first glimpse of the defendant. Pale and thin, Camm was wearing the new suit his family had bought for the occasion, and there was a blankness in his eyes, as if he were under the influence of one of his many prescribed drugs.

He gazed over at the spectators and then walked down the aisle, between the two sides of his family, looking alternately from one to the other, like a little boy searching for approval.

Once the defendant had taken his place next to Mike McDaniel, Judge Striegel turned to the clerk of the court, asking, "Are we ready?"

The court rose to its feet as the twelve jurors and three alternates entered the courtroom, taking their places in their box, next to the press table.

The first order of business was a separation of witnesses order. None of the potential 174 witnesses would be allowed to stay in the courtroom until they had testified. That meant most of David's family would have to wait in the corridor. And some, like his brother Donnie, would have to wait outside the entire trial, as they never testified.

Frank Renn remained in court. He was not on the witness list, but his wife, Janice, was. She spent the entire trial in the prosecution office, watching the proceedings on closed circuit TV, as the defense persuaded the judge her presence in the courtroom would be prejudicial to the defendant.

Stan Faith, who was up for reelection that year, looked smug. The canny prosecutor had said little about his case before the trial started. But his Chief Deputy Prosecutor Susan Orth was about to deliver a bombshell.

The 43-year-old career prosecutor looked all business as she slowly walked up to the podium to deliver the prosecution's opening statements. Next to her was an overhead slide projector. She would be using photographs and computer graphics to illustrate key points.

"Welcome to New Albany," she began, addressing the out-of-town jurors. "During the evening of September twenty-eight, 2000, in a garage located in a home in a secluded, private neighborhood, the defendant shot and killed his wife, Kim, and their two children, Brad and Jill. The defendant, an experienced marksman and gun expert, fired three shots, three bullets, that resulted in the death of three people."

The jury sat riveted in their box as Orth dramatically

led them through the prosecution's version of the events that had led to the murders.

"On the surface they seemed to have a picture-perfect marriage," she told them. "But you will hear that just under the surface were the lies, the deceitfulness, and the darkness."

After describing the night of the murders, she told how Camm had become "violent" in the days following, before his arrest.

She also told the jury how the Kentucky medical examiner believed 5-year-old daughter Jill Camm had been sexually molested, suggesting that her father was responsible.

Then, to the astonishment of the defense, Orth revealed the prosecution had what she described as incontrovertible evidence that Camm had made a telephone call from his home at 7:19 p.m. the night of the murders, ruining his alibi that he had been at church, playing basketball at the time.

"You'll see the evidence will show the defendant wasn't playing basketball from 7:00 until 9:00 continuously as he says," she told the jury. "The evidence will show he was home and he left proof of it, a phone record. And Kim and the kids arrived home after seven-thirty."

After a short recess Mike McDaniel strolled up to the podium to deliver the defense's opening statements, which would take almost three hours. In his syrupy Southern drawl, the warhorse of a defender waxed folksy for the jury, first apologizing for not being as technically savvy as the prosecution.

"I started out using a manual typewriter," he explained, his hands wedged into his trouser pockets, under a large protruding stomach. "Carbon paper, onion skins and dial-up telephone."

Then, getting down to business, he warned the jury he would be showing them some "disturbing" photographs, as it was important to set the scene.

"David was born into a diverse family," he began. "Widely, laterally expanded family. Had many aunts and uncles. Has two brothers and a sister. His family were country people. They were conservative in their outlook on business, religion and law enforcement."

He described David Camm's succumbing to temptation during his early days with the Indiana State Police, comparing Post 45 to a "sophomore boys' locker room." He told jurors how the "bonding" and "brotherhood" of officers included entering into "sexual competitions," and "bragging about their conquests."

McDaniel then walked them through the night of the murders, saying it would have been impossible for David to have left the basketball court for fifty minutes, the time he would have needed for the killings, without being seen by anyone. As to the allegations of sexual abuse of Jill, he claimed her vaginal injuries could have been caused by the Bronco's seat belt.

When McDaniel showed pictures of the bodies of Kim, Brad and Jill, taken at the crime scene, David Camm wept uncontrollably.

And at the conclusion of his opening statement, McDaniel promised to call two blood spatter experts, who would testify that the notorious eight drops of Jill's blood found on Camm's tee-shirt were not high-velocity blood spatter. In fact, they were blood transfer, picked up while he was taking Brad out of the Bronco.

"The State of Indiana is going to make David out to be a monster, suggesting he molested his daughter," McDaniel told the jury. "They're telling you he was a womanizer. Doing anything they can to smear this guy. And I'm gonna tell you, if David was a monster sitting here, he would not be the monster that murdered his wife and children."

During a lunch recess, before the first prosecution witnesses were called, McDaniel told reporters he was pleased with the jury.

"The jury had to absorb a heck of a lot with two openings," he said. "There was no fidgeting, looking at the ceiling, no yawning . . . I think they tracked extremely well."

After lunch Deputy Prosecutor Robert Colone led off the state's case, playing David Camm's dramatic emergency call to the Sellersburg post, reporting his family dead. Later that afternoon ISP Detective Sean Clemons took the stand, describing how he'd been the first on the murder scene and become lead investigator. The youthful red-haired trooper told Prosecutor Faith he'd known David Camm for more than twenty years, and had been encouraged to join the force by him.

He vividly described the murder scene, seeing Kim and Brad's bodies on the garage floor, and Jill's still seat belted into the rear Bronco passenger seat.

There was an air conditioning problem at the courthouse which would plague the first two weeks of the trial, as it was either too hot or too cold during the long courtroom sessions. At about 3:45 p.m. Mike McDaniel asked Judge Striegel to recess, saying the packed courtroom was stifling, and making him feel ill.

The judge agreed and adjourned for the day, admonishing jurors not to discuss the case with each other. He also warned them to disregard any newspaper or television coverage of the case, if they left the hotel before the 11:00 p.m. curfew.

Detective Sean Clemons retook the stand at the beginning of the second day of the trial. Carefully avoiding his onetime friend's withering gaze, Clemons looked straight at Deputy Prosecutor Colone, as he answered questions simply and to the point. Several times, when disagreeing with Clemons' testimony, Camm would shake his head at the defense desk, in full view of the jury.

The lead detective took jurors on a vivid tour of the crime scene, noting how the garage floor was discolored and there were stains on the back deck. He noted how he had found a mop and bucket inside a utility room that smelled of bleach, saying he believed the crime scene had been manipulated, as it was just "too neat."

When the prosecutor asked why the detective had not asked Camm about the discoloration and stains on his deck, Clemons said he hadn't bothered as David would only "lie" about it.

"I move for a mistrial," declared Mike McDaniel, jumping to his feet. "That's outrageous."

The jury were then dismissed and McDaniel told Judge Striegel the stains were months old, and Clemons had "grossly misled" the jury about the defendant's right to remain silent at the time.

Judge Striegel denied the mistrial, ordering the jury back into their box to continue.

Then, prompted by the deputy prosecutor, Clemons described how Camm had threatened him the night of the murders.

"[He] pounded my chest," said the detective, "and told me he wanted this 'fucking done right.' "

Clemons told of Camm's outburst the next day at Floyd Memorial Hospital, when he said he would kill Clemons and Detective Gibson, while giving samples for DNA analysis. Asked by Colone if he had taken Camm seriously, Clemons replied he had immediately moved his family out of town.

After a short recess, Mike McDaniel began his cross-examination, slowly and methodically picking apart Clemons' testimony to try to discredit him. He asked Clemons about the three banging noises Debbie TerVree had heard at about 9:30 p.m. on the night of the murders. Clemons conceded he no longer believed they were gunshots, as he had stated on his signed probable cause affidavit. He had changed his mind, he said, after new evidence that Camm had made a phone call from his kitchen at 7:19 p.m.

"At the time I signed it," he declared, "it was a fair and accurate representation of the information we had at the time. Due to subsequent investigation, we since learned of the 7:19 p.m. phone call, which gave Mr. Camm the opportunity on two occasions to return to his residence."

McDaniel tried to belittle the detective, goading him to answer the questions, instead of "doing little lectures." Stan Faith objected, accusing the defense of "badgering" the witness.

Then McDaniel turned to Camm's alleged cleanup of the crime scene, asking if he knew that the thirty-foot plume of colorless liquid seeping out of the garage was Kim's blood breaking down into serum, and not bleach as he had claimed in the probable cause affidavit. Clemons denied seeing the results of any tests that proved it was not bleach.

At the end of his cross-examination, McDaniel suddenly asked if Clemons had considered the defendant a close friend before the murders. When Clemons agreed he had, the defender suddenly asked out of the blue if "your friend David" had ever given him a citation for causing a car wreck. When Clemons said no, the attorney apologized, saying it was "an unfair question" and he'd made a mistake. Then, rephrasing the question, he asked if Trooper Camm had ever put him down for causing a wreck. This time Clemons said he had, but denied ever asking Camm to file a stolen car report for him, after his car was taken from a Clarksville nightclub. The odd line of questioning ended there and was never explained.

Clemons remained on the stand most of the second day, and would be recalled constantly during the course of the trial.

On the third day, jurors got to hear the audio- and videotapes of David Camm's interrogations by Detectives Darrell Gibson and Mickey Neal. The jury were all ears as Camm

tearfully described finding his wife and children slaughtered in his garage.

They heard his impassioned pleas to his former friends,
as he realized he was about to be arrested for the murders.
Throughout the tape, Kim's sister, Debbie Karem, sat
transfixed, rubbing a silver cross for comfort.

At one point, while the tape was playing on a boom
box, two reporters saw a blonde juror named Stephanie
Jones start crying and then mouth what they thought was
an obscenity at the defendant.

At the next break they reported the juror to Judge
Striegel, who immediately called an in-camera hearing, to
have them explain further on the record and under oath.

"I was just doing my thing," explained New Albany *Tribune* City Editor Amany Ali. "The juror, I don't know her
name, she's blonde, real tiny. She was crying, sniffling,
staring at Mr. Camm a lot, like someone who would be
staring a hole through someone. She mouthed what appeared to be an obscenity, 'You son of a bitch.'"

Then WMPI Radio reporter Doug Williams confirmed
it, telling the judge that he too had seen juror Jones staring
at Camm in tears, and calling him a "son of a bitch" under
her breath.

Judge Striegel summoned Jones to the stand. She explained that the reporters got it wrong. She had merely
been apologizing to a male juror, for becoming so upset
during the tape.

After Jones was sent back to the jury room, Prosecutor
Stan Faith told the judge he had seen a television reporter
sneaking a look at one of the juror's notes.

"I don't know what Mr. McDaniel feels about this,"
Faith told the judge. "And I'm sure not going to defend
[him], he's quite adequate himself. But he's got a bunch of
vultures behind him in the form of reporters."

Judge Striegel told both attorneys to keep an eye on the
reporters and let him know if they saw anything else.

But the incident with the juror would cause much friction with the other reporters covering the trial, who were angry at their two colleagues.

"Striegel almost kicked us out," said *Snitch* scribe Mat Herron. "Because you just don't fuck with the jurors."

Paradoxically, even if Prosecutor Faith considered journalists "vultures," he and McDaniel were always available for interviews in the corridor outside the courtroom. Like sports commentators, they would opine on every twist and turn of the trial during breaks in the action.

"There was a real urgency in the way that we reported this story," said Herron, "because every single time they went out they gave an interview. They just wanted to control the perception of the crime."

On the fourth day of the trial, after jurors were played a second videotaped account of David Camm's version of events the night of the murders, Stan Faith told reporters he wished to point out "contradictions" in Camm's story.

"He seems to have a switch like a very young child," Faith said outside the courtroom.

For his sound bite of the day, Mike McDaniel focused on the fact that Detective Mickey Neal had admitted lying to Camm several times during the interviews, to get a confession.

"[Dave] didn't try and make up a story to go along with the facts," McDaniel told Channel 32 TV's Abby Miller. "To me that's an indication of truthfulness."

Later on in the trial one particular radio station even sent Mike McDaniel a thank-you note for publicly "slugging it out" every day, as it was good for ratings.

David Camm's family also made themselves available for interviews towards the end of the trial, deliberately courting the press for favorable coverage. Sam Lockhart, Donnie Camm and Julie Hogue were all highly articulate, and knew just how to get their points across in David's defense. But as potential witnesses they could not speak on the record until the case went to the jury.

"It was uncanny," said Herron. "It was almost like they thought the entire family was on trial. The minute you turned on a microphone or camera—*Boom*, instant interview."

But Frank Renn was not so eloquent, always reaching for the right words to express himself.

"Frank could not articulate his emotions," explained Herron. "He was so pissed off, so angry and so grief-stricken. He was this huge, tall guy and very polite and very nice. But you'd talk to the guy and he just could not elaborate."

As the trial finished its first week, the attorneys, reporters, family members and jury soon fell into a comfortable routine. Much of the long, often laborious trial would be taken up by hours of chain-of-custody questions, to formally introduce evidence. Some of the expert witnesses would spend as long as three days going over the finer points of highly technical blood analysis.

The first of the experts, crime-scene reconstructionist Professor Robert Stites, took the stand on the first Friday of the trial. Rod Englert's pupil and partner had flown in from Portland, Oregon, to testify.

He started by giving the jury a brief class in blood spatter analysis, using a Magic Marker and a whiteboard. Extravagantly using his hands, he demonstrated what happened when a bullet traveling at 682 mph hits someone's head.

Stites told the jury he had discovered eight tiny dots of Jill's high-velocity blood mist on the tee-shirt David Camm had worn that night. According to Stites, the only way that the spots, invisible to the human eye, could have gotten there was if the defendant had been within four feet of her when she was shot.

McDaniel's low-key cross-examination focused on the professor's academic credibility and qualifications as an expert in blood analysis. Stites said he had a bachelor's degree in economics, but did not have an M.A. or Ph.D., both of which he was presently working on.

But although he took extensive notes at the crime scene, Stites could not remember the names of most of the detectives and technicians he'd spoken to, or just what he'd told them at the time.

"He was never intended to be *the* expert," Faith later told reporters in the corridor.

The trial resumed on Tuesday, January 22, as the court had been closed for Martin Luther King Day. All the jurors had been allowed to go home to Johnson County and spend the three-day weekend with their families. But under the judge's orders they had reported back to the Holiday Inn late Monday night.

The first witness on the stand that morning was Sergeant Sammy Sarkasian, the ISP crime-scene investigator and evidence technician, who had been in charge of ensuring all the evidence was collected properly and safely logged. Wearing a smart blue suit, starched white shirt and tie, the severely crew-cut Sarkasian appeared straight out of central casting.

He explained to jurors the prescribed way to set up a crime scene and how he had interfaced with Sean Clemons at David Camm's house. Like the lead detective, the sergeant had also become suspicious about how neat and clean the murder scene had been after the murders.

"I didn't see a lot of footprints or tracking in the blood," he told Deputy Prosecutor Robert Colone in his by-the-book monotone. "I'd been given information prior to me walking up to the scene, and I anticipated to see some disruption."

Sarkasian told jurors how he'd spent nine hours at the medical examiner's office in Louisville, observing all the autopsies. At one point during Jill's, he had walked out to take a phone call when Dr. Tracey Corey suddenly called him back.

"She met me at the doorway and she said, 'It appears this child's been molested,'" testified Sarkasian. "She had the child undressed and she showed me the genitalia area of Jill Camm. It was red, inflamed, swollen, traumatized. And her preliminary examination [was] that the child had been molested."

In his cross-examination Mike McDaniel asked Sarkasian why ISP investigators had not called a medical examiner to the crime scene to figure out the victims' time of death. The sergeant replied that it was medically impossible to ascertain an exact time of death, as detectives do on television.

"I've been told the only way you can tell exact time of death," he told McDaniel, "is if you're an eyewitness."

McDaniel grilled Sarkasian about the chain of custody he supervised, but failed to find any holes in his methodical collection of evidence.

That afternoon a procession of the basketball players who would provide David Camm's ironclad alibi took the stand to testify. Martin Dickey, a former employee of David Camm at UDI, and his brother Jeff, both agreed that David had sat out a game at about 7:30 p.m. But they couldn't say exactly what time he had rested, or be any more specific.

After the court adjourned for the day, Prosecutor Stan Faith told reporters there was one big problem with all the players' assertions that Camm never left the church gym—the 7:19 p.m. telephone call allegedly made from his house.

"Telephones don't dial themselves," said the prosecutor. "I think the jury sensed that he could have left any time he wanted to, and come back any time he wanted to."

The next day the prosecution called each of the remaining basketball players to the stand. The players testifying included two of David Camm's cousins and several other distant relatives or family acquaintances. None of the players could say with certainty how long any of the games had lasted, or which ones the defendant had sat out. Some remembered playing just two-on-two and four-on-four games, while others rested on the sidelines. But others said they played five-on-five the entire night.

As they testified one after another, the jurors took careful notes, but looked visibly confused at the discrepancies.

"It's porous," Stan Faith later told reporters at one of his impromptu press conferences outside the courtroom. "You can drive a semi through it. They don't have times. They don't know when it happened. It's very easy for people to lose track of people for a very long time."

Mike McDaniel then presented his take on what had happened in the courtroom to reporters. "It's just incontrovertible proof that David was playing basketball" when the murders occurred, he said. It was as if there were two separate David Camm trials; one in the courtroom in front of the jury and the other outside for the court of public opinion.

On Thursday, January 24, day eight of the trial, the jury took a field trip to the Georgetown Community Church, so they could get a firsthand view of the gymnasium. The fifteen jurors spent half an hour closely examining it, checking exit doors and walking around the perimeter to get a better idea of its layout.

Looking up to the ceiling, they saw two large quilts hanging above the bathroom entrance. Halfway down one of them was a picture of 7-year-old Bradley Camm, his name neatly embroidered underneath in blue. And just above it was another picture of his cherubic-looking sister, Jill.

Floyd County Sheriff Randy Hubbard and his team of deputies worked full-time during the trial, handling the complicated logistics of twenty-four-hour surveillance of the jury, as well as using a rotating team of five officers to secure Judge Striegel's courtroom.

Hubbard, who had recently announced he was standing for a second term as county sheriff, observed most of the trial from his security vantage point inside the courtroom.

Under Judge Striegel's orders the jury was bused back to neighboring Clarksville every lunchtime, for one of their three meals a day, purchased by Floyd County taxpayers. The judge was very flexible about luncheon court recess, which could run two hours or longer.

When Stan Faith was asked by a reporter if these long lunches were prolonging the already expensive trial, the prosecutor thought the question preposterous.

"What are we, on a deadline?" he replied. "This trial will take a year if it has to."

33

A Ladies' Man

There was an air of expectation in the courtroom that Friday, when David Camm's mother-in-law, Janice Renn, was called to the stand to testify against him. Kim's mother and Brad and Jill's grandmother wore a somber white sweater and gold necklace as she walked over to the witness stand to be sworn in. Her husband, Frank, and daughter, Debbie, sat by the prosecution bench, lending emotional support to what would be highly emotional testimony.

She told the jury how Kim had been devastated in 1994, when David had left her for another woman while she was pregnant with Jill, saying he no longer wanted to be married. But after her granddaughter was born, Kim reconciled with David.

Gently led by Chief Deputy Prosecutor Susan Orth, Janice said her daughter had become anxious again in August 2000, two months before her murder. When she asked Kim what was wrong, she said she was getting headaches and was just rundown.

Orth asked her about Jill's painful vaginal irritation. Kim had first brought it to her attention in May 2000, and Janice had looked and thought it was a diaper rash. She'd first advised using Diaperene, and then taking Jill to a doctor if it didn't clear up.

She told the jury that the Sunday before the murders, she was babysitting her grandchildren while their parents went out to see *The Perfect Storm*. After Jill took a bath,

Janice was drying her with a towel when the little girl complained of pain between her legs.

"I put Vaseline on it," she said. "That's all they had at the time."

At the end of her testimony Stan Faith asked her to identify blown-up photographs of Kim and her grandchildren, so they could be introduced into evidence. Janice then broke down sobbing, explaining how the picture of Kim, taken when she was a high school senior, had been a special Christmas present from her daughter.

At that point Susan Orth finished her questioning and the judge turned to the defense for its cross-examination.

"Your Honor," said Mike McDaniel. "We have no questions."

On the morning of Monday, January 28, the start of the third week of the trial, the jury was shown pictures of the crime scene on a large screen, in the front of the courtroom. Lead investigator Sean Clemons had been recalled to the stand to guide the jurors through the heartbreaking photos.

At the prosecution table Stan Faith, his wide bulk tightly packed into a bright red shirt and black suit, a silver cross hanging from his neck alongside a four-leaf-clover pin, placed the slides in an overhead projector, one-by-one. Eventually the jurors asked Judge Striegel if they could take a trip to 7534 Lockhart Road, so they could see the crime scene for themselves.

That afternoon the twelve jurors and three alternates were driven to Georgetown in two vans to see David Camm's house and garage, where the murders took place. Watching closely from his father's house across the road was Sam Lockhart.

Also standing in the yard observing the jurors that sunny late January afternoon, was Mike McDaniel. And it didn't go unnoticed that he was wearing a red tie with a scales-of-justice motif, saying "NOT GUILTY," in large white letters.

On Tuesday, Stan Faith was back in court, ready to give the media what it had been waiting for since the beginning of the trial. The first of a procession of young women—some of whom had had affairs with David Camm—were due to take the stand that morning and spill titillating details about the defendant's racy sex life.

It had taken the chief prosecutor innumerable hours of gentle persuasion to get many of the women to testify publicly. Some were married and had been unfaithful with David Camm, while others were state troopers or worked in law enforcement.

First there was the question of whether Judge Striegel would allow the defense to question witnesses about sexual mores at ISP Sellersburg Post 45. Deputy Prosecutor Robert Colone argued against it, claiming troopers' "extramarital relationships and sexual improprieties" were irrelevant, confusing and misleading to the jury.

But Mike McDaniel said that as Rule 404(b) was being used by the prosecution, it was only fair that it should not be used solely against his client.

"One of the marks of intelligence is that you learn from your mistakes," said McDaniel at an in-camera hearing, without the jury present. "Part of his defense to the claim of murdering his wife and children, so he could pursue extramarital affairs, is to show the conduct he engaged in while he was a state trooper was not serious. The evidence in this case will be that if one trooper was seeing a lady, another trooper would try and see that lady too. This was merely a competition."

The deputy prosecutor said what ISP troopers did in their free time had nothing to do with the case. Finally, in one of the few rulings for the defense he would make in the Camm trial, Judge Striegel said he would allow limited questioning on the sexual behavior of troopers, as long as no names were mentioned.

For the next several days the courtroom became a revolving door of women, testifying on anything from having sex in the back of police cars to harmless flirtations. A box of Kleenex had thoughtfully been placed on the stand to help some of the more emotional women get through their testimonies.

First on the stand was Stephanie McCarty, who had been married two days after the murders. She told the jury about her passionate affair with Camm when he left his wife, which ended after he pulled out a gun, threatening to shoot himself.

Outside the courtroom after her testimony, Prosecutor Faith told reporters he was calling the women to show motive.

"If you'll notice," he told one reporter, "he killed his family two days before Stephanie was married. Yes they [the women] were a motive. He wanted to be free to engage in his own interests. There have been people killed for a lot less than that."

Mike McDaniel disagreed, accusing his opponent of character assassination.

"They're smearing him because they don't have anything else," said the defender, who had described his client's romantic liaisons as only "slap and tickle" to a reporter. "We had one serious affair. Not every event was a score."

Most of the women who testified said that Camm had told them he was single or separated when he propositioned them, never wearing a wedding ring. Former State Police Dispatcher Beth Minnicus testified that he had told her his marriage was troubled in 1997. She said that one night after having a fight with Kim he'd bad-mouthed her, calling her "a bitch."

Minnicus said that on two occasions Camm had tried to come on to her, trying to kiss her and touch her breasts. Another time she had pushed him away, while he had tried to hold her down.

A young dental assistant named Michelle Voyles testified how she had had sex with Trooper Camm at a rest stop on I-64, just outside Georgetown. He had been on duty at the time and in the subsequent weeks she would often go riding with him late at night in his ISP cruiser. She described the day she claimed he shaved off her pubic hair, declaring: "Now, if I can do this without thinking I'm fucking a six-year-old . . ."

Tammy Rogers told the jury how she'd met Camm at a gun store, and he'd later given her shooting lessons. He'd told her he was separated, but there had been no sexual contact.

Emily Shepherd told of how in March 2000, the then state trooper had come to her rescue, after her car had broken down on I-62. She admitted sitting in the back of his cruiser after he'd told her he was not married, and letting him kiss and fondle her. The next day he'd left a message on her home phone, asking for a date. But she'd never called back, thinking him "too desperate."

Real estate agent Lisa Korfhage admitted having sexual relations with David Camm for about a month in 1997, after he visited her home to investigate some threatening phone calls. After she got married they stayed platonic friends, but Camm continually tried to resume the affair, she said.

The final woman to take the stand was Trooper Shelley Romero, who admitted to having sex with David Camm in 1992 and again in June 1993. She said they soon became platonic and "real good friends" over the years. But she testified that on several occasions in the weeks before the murders he had tried to rekindle the affair, asking if she wanted to have sex again.

Trooper Romero also testified about their "five or six" conversations straight after the murders. She said they had made her suspicious and she'd reported them to her superior officer at the post, Lieutenant Jim Biddle.

It would be the first time that David Camm's family had learned the full extent of his infidelities. And it hit hard with their strict religious beliefs. It was at this point, many believe, that the jury began to turn against David Camm.

"People started hating him," said his brother Donnie. "And they wanted to convict him because they didn't like him as a person. He was a bad character."

Sam Lockhart does not make any excuses for his nephew's infidelities and his betrayal of his wife and children.

"He was an adulterer," said Lockhart. "And he was not a very good husband, and I'm not very proud of him for what he did. But that does not make him a murderer."

On Wednesday, January 30—day twelve of the trial—the prosecution called Kim Camm's best friend, Marcy McLeod, to the stand. She would be a crucial witness for the prosecution, illustrating Kim's state of mind at the time of the murders, and providing a possible motive for the killings.

But before she even took the stand, Mike McDaniel had called a meeting with the judge, away from the jury, to protest a highly incriminating part of McLeod's testimony. He did not want the jury to hear Marcy's account of her final conversation with Kim, three weeks before her murder, when Kim had reportedly told Marcy, "History is repeating itself."

"It is clearly hearsay," argued McDaniel, stressing that his client was not having an affair. "Her testimony about what Ms. Camm said to her is inappropriate for the jury to hear."

Chief Deputy Prosecutor Susan Orth disagreed, telling the judge that in the context of the conversation it fell within the state-of-mind exception of the hearsay rule.

"Kim made statements to Marcy that she needed to get away," Orth told the judge, "she wanted to bring the kids to Florida, and that history was repeating itself, when asked directly, 'How are you and the defendant getting along?'

"This goes directly to Kim's state of mind near the time of the murders."

Judge Striegel agreed, ruling that Marcy could testify about the conversation, and show Kim's growing anxiety shortly before her murder.

During his cross-examination, Mike McDaniel attempted to get Marcy to admit that Kim was probably just tired and worn-out when she made the "history" comment. But Marcy stood firm on what she thought her best friend had been trying to say.

"I asked, 'How are you and David?' " she firmly told the jurors. "And she said, 'History's repeating itself.' "

Then McDaniel asked if Marcy had "selected to interpret" Kim's statement as a history of bad things?

"Yes," she replied. "Because of her state of mind."

Friday, February 1, would have been Brad Camm's ninth birthday, and the night before, the Renns had left court to attend a special Mass to commemorate him at the Holy Family Church.

Frank Renn described it as "teary-eyed," noting that another birthday was on the way, as Jill would have turned 7 on February 28.

As the prosecution's case reached a climax, perhaps no one, with the exception of David Camm, was under more pressure than Stan Faith.

The Floyd County Prosecutor was up for reelection in May, and his future could well depend on winning this case. After sixteen years on the job, Faith had almost become a

New Albany institution, and one of the town's best-known and well-respected citizens. But his politics were controversial. Active in the Democratic Party, Faith proudly displayed a picture of himself shaking hands with President Bill Clinton on his office wall. There was also resentment against him, and much support for his Republican rival Keith Henderson.

"He's certainly getting a lot of publicity about it," said the chairman of the Floyd County Democratic Party, Warren Nash. "If people don't know his name before, they do now."

The intense television and newspaper coverage the case was receiving daily was making everyone connected to it famous locally. Donnie Camm was now recognized wherever he went, and he hated it.

"It was horrible," said Donnie. "We were on the news every night, and it's not like our name was Smith or Wilson. We couldn't even go into a restaurant and put our names on a wait list, because everyone would stare and look."

And there were several nasty incidents at Graceland Christian School, where his daughters, Kara and Lauren, still attended. They stopped after the principal made it clear to teachers and pupils that he would not tolerate any discussion about the murders, even though Brad and Jill had gone there.

"It was nipped in the bud," explained Donnie. "It was an issue for the kids, but the school administrators took action early."

For the next several weeks there were few fireworks at the trial. Stan Faith methodically tried to nail down the prosecution case, supplying a shopping list of motives to explain why the defendant might have cold-bloodedly murdered his wife and children. He called Camm's younger brother Dan, questioning him about dubious life insurance policies the Camm's had taken out three months before the killings, in which he stood to receive a substantial amount if his family died. But the testimony also reflected that

David Camm had purchased far more insurance on his own life than had been purchased for Kim.

"They committed out-and-out fraud," snapped the prosecutor, referring to the policies not being signed in Florida, as required by law.

It was also noted that Dan Camm was the secondary beneficiary of the insurance policies and could receive the money. But Dan Camm explained this was intended to provide for the children if David and Kim were both to die, leaving Dan as their guardian. And Dan told the court that in the event that he were now to get the money, he would give some of it to the Renn family and his niece Whitney.

That Friday, as the judge sent the jurors home for the weekend, he ruled that they would be allowed to watch the Super Bowl on Sunday night at the Holiday Inn. But a deputy sheriff was under strict instructions to mute the television if there was any coverage of the trial whatsoever.

On Tuesday, February 5, forensic pathologist Dr. Donna Hunsaker took the stand to testify about performing Kim Camm's autopsy, less than twenty hours after her murder.

She told jurors there was strong evidence of a scuffle, and Kim had put up a fight before she was shot.

The pathologist used a plastic model skull and brain to illustrate the path of the bullet that wiped out her life. Kim did not die instantly and could have lived for up to five minutes, although Dr. Hunsaker said there was no way of knowing for certain just how long.

"I can say that she died quickly," she testified.

The following day Dr. Tracey Corey, Kentucky's chief medical examiner, testified about performing Brad and Jill's autopsies. During her testimony explicit autopsy photographs of the children were passed to jurors, some of whom were close to tears, finding it hard to look.

The attractive blonde medical examiner also highlighted a damaging inconsistency in David Camm's version of how he tried to revive Brad with CPR. For in one of his answers to Phyllis Rhodes' Q&A he had claimed he had his son's blood in his mouth.

"I didn't know whether to rinse it out or savor it," he had written. But Dr. Corey told the jury she found no blood in Brad's mouth during the autopsy.

Again and again in re-cross-examination, Mike McDaniel tried to blunt the damage to his client, trying to show other ways that mucus or something else could have gotten into Brad's mouth.

But Dr. Corey stood firm, declaring: "I found no evidence of blood within Bradley's mouth."

Moving on to Jill's autopsy, Dr. Corey told the jury how she had found trauma injuries to Jill's genitalia as she removed her panties. She also discovered numerous tiny petechial hemorrhages, caused by physical obstruction to the blood flow. This resulted in capillaries bursting with an overflow of blood, causing minute dots on the surface of the skin.

Once again in his cross-examination McDaniel tried to lessen the impact of Dr. Corey's powerful testimony, and Dr. Corey conceded that Jill's injuries could have been caused by a straddle fall.

"Children of Jill's age could suffer rashes or irritations from bubble baths?" he asked.

When the doctor agreed little girls could, the defender continued.

"There's another great big word you use to describe a medical condition that I think we call pinworms. One of them begins with an 'e' (Enterobios Vermicularis) and I won't even try and pronounce it."

"I know what pinworms are," said the medical examiner. "I didn't see any evidence of a pinworm infection."

From this point on, the trial would become a battle of the experts. Testimony would often go on for days, as the defense and prosecutors picked it apart to try to gain the most advantage. And the David Camm trial would prove to be highly lucrative for all the experts.

The prosecution was already running out of money, after spending more than $200,000 so far to bring Camm to justice. Now halfway through the trial, Stan Faith hadn't even called his much-touted blood spatter expert Rod Englert, and he needed more cash. So he asked Floyd County Council for an additional $75,000 to cover the escalating costs of the trial.

So far Englert had billed the state $80,000 for 250 hours' work on the Camm case, including a cool $8,000 for his testimony. His partner, Robert Stites, had also cost Floyd County taxpayers a further $30,000.

But the prosecutor assured county voters that the additional money required would come from his own personal diversion fund.

The prosecution also had high hopes for William Chaplin of the Chicago-based McCrone Laboratories, who spent two days lecturing on microscopic particles found on David Camm's tee-shirt. But along the way he seemed to lose the jury, as they became increasingly fidgety, attempting to digest the "mind-numbing" testimony.

Mike McDaniel, now being plagued by an old back injury, continually challenged Chaplin's finding of trace amounts of blood, bone and plasma on Camm's tee-shirt.

Lynn Scamahorn, the state's DNA analyst from the Evansville's state police laboratory, spent almost three days on the stand, revealing whose DNA she found and where at the crime scene. She confirmed that the already infamous eight drops of blood found on David Camm's tee-shirt belonged to his daughter Jill. But she also destroyed the prosecution's earlier claims that Camm had used a mop and bucket to clean up after the murders, testifying that no blood had been found on either of them.

She also did nothing to dispel the mystery of the gray

"Backbone" sweatshirt, saying the DNA she found on it was unknown.

The next witness was Wayne Niemayer, an expert on gunshot residue (GSR). He began by giving jurors a brief lesson in his chosen subject, using charts to illustrate particles of GSR on a sock belonging to David Camm, and inside the right pocket of his shorts. He also found traces of lead and copper on his tee-shirt.

Some of the experts' testimony was potentially explosive, including the revelations that there was unidentified DNA on the "Backbone" sweatshirt and other unidentified DNA found on Kim and Brad's pants. But these key facts were buried deep in hours of technical explanations. One reporter covering the trial observed a female juror briefly falling asleep during the testimony, and other members of the jury didn't seem far behind.

On Friday, February 15, when Stan Faith's final witness, Rod Englert, took the stand, the whole courtroom woke up. The former homicide detective, who'd left the police force after thirty-one years to start his own forensic consulting company, was a born showman. After days of long-winded, often tedious, scientific evidence, Englert had a knack for simplifying complex ideas and making them accessible.

First off Stan Faith asked his star witness to name some of the higher-profile cases he had worked on.

"I was involved in the O. J. Simpson case for three years during the prosecution phase," he replied, immediately getting every juror's attention. "The Bob Crane case, the person from *Hogan's Heroes*, and I also worked on Selena, the Tejano star that was murdered in Texas."

For once Faith said little, letting Englert do most of the talking. The Portland-based crime-scene reconstructionist testified he had consulted on almost three hundred cases and testified in twenty-four states, including Indiana, where he had appeared in the early 1990s in that very court, as Faith's expert witness in the Jonathan Whitesides case.

Then, using a series of tutorial charts and other props, Englert told the jury about blood spatter.

"Blood tells a story," he said, as he dropped some stage blood on a foam board, holding it up for the jury to see. "And in crimes of violence, bloodshed can be categorized."

Blood spatter, he explained, can be broken down into three different types—low, medium and high velocity.

Low velocity is plain blood transfer or smears, with no energy behind it. Medium is from blunt trauma, usually from a beating with an object like a club or hammer.

"The third category is high velocity, which comes from gunshot," he told the jury, pulling out a piece of foam board punctured by a 9mm bullet, with tiny red droplets surrounding the hole to illustrate his point.

Moving on to the Camm murder scene, Englert revealed his findings, after analyzing the Ford Bronco, the bullet hole through the windshield and blood spatter found above the back seat.

He was certain Kim was not shot on the floor, but was standing up near the open door of the Bronco, close to the running board.

Then, apologizing to the jury, he put a gruesome close-up picture of Kim's head, lying on the concrete garage floor, on the overhead projector. To one side of it were Brad's Nike tennis shoes.

One-by-one, Englert showed high-definition color photographs of Kim, Brad and Jill at the murder scene. Then David Camm began weeping, and Mike McDaniel put an arm around his shoulders to comfort him.

With each photograph Rod Englert dispassionately discussed its relevance. Slowly he moved to David Camm's tee-shirt, and what had become known as Area 30, where the eight tiny drops of Jill's blood were found.

"Four of them were tested and they came back as the blood of Jill Camm," he told the jury. "And there is a high-velocity mist pattern."

Then Faith asked the significance of the microscopic drops of blood on Camm's tee-shirt. Englert said it proved David Camm was standing between Jill and the right passenger seat when the gun was fired. The little girl was looking away, leaning into the back seat.

To reinforce Englert's scientific findings that David Camm had murdered his family, Faith pointed to a photo of the Indiana State Police tee-shirt the defendant was wearing that night and asked, "So that tee-shirt was there, in your expert opinion, at the very moment the blow-back occurred?"

"That would be my opinion," replied Englert. "Yes."

Soon afterwards Judge Striegel recessed for the weekend. As the jury left the courtroom, David Camm swung around in his seat and said to his father, loud enough for reporters to hear: "This is the most expensive whore in town right here!"

On Tuesday, February 19, the trial entered its sixth week. After a long weekend, Rod Englert retook the stand to be cross-examined by Mike McDaniel. Up to now McDaniel had adopted a soft-spoken approach, but this morning he came out fighting, like he did more than forty years ago in the ring with Cassius Clay.

"Mr. Englert," McDaniel began, tugging at the red suspenders worn over his lucky fifteen-year-old suit. "I'd like to talk a little bit first with you about your training, education, background. What brings you here today, OK?"

McDaniel had done his homework. His first question was whether the renowned crime-scene reconstructionist had ever taken a seminar in presenting expert testimony in court. When Englert said no, McDaniel asked if he had attended a 1992 course on the subject in New Orleans, hosted by the American Academy of Forensic Sciences.

"Yes, sir, that is correct," admitted the balding expert, rubbing his goatee.

The wily defender then went back even further, to 1960, when Englert was a law major at San Angelo University in Texas, before moving on to East Los Angeles Junior College, and taking a two-year associate degree in Police Science.

When the blood spatter expert confirmed that was correct, McDaniel asked if he had passed his classes in Introductory Chemistry and Intermediate Algebra.

"I don't know," he admitted. "My grades weren't that great, they were terrible in college."

Going down his CV, line by line, McDaniel questioned him about attending California State University in Fullerton in 1968, as he had told the jury he had.

"Yes, sir," said Englert. "I attended two semesters for the sergeants' exam."

Then McDaniel asked why the university had no record of him ever attending those classes.

"They changed over to a computer system and they lost it," Englert replied.

"Excuse me?" said the defender incredulously.

At this point Stan Faith stepped in to object, saying the defense wasn't allowing his witness to answer the question. This prompted McDaniel to tell the judge he didn't need a lecture from the prosecution on objections.

"You definitely need a lecture," said the prosecutor sarcastically, without missing a beat.

Englert admitted he had withdrawn from the class, as he had been a detective, working undercover narcotics at the time. He had gotten his $75 fee back and his professor had allowed him to audit the class, in return for telling his police colleagues about the Business Administration course.

"I can tell you every year of my life," said Englert, showing the jury his diary.

McDaniel then turned to Rod Englert's qualifications as an expert in the field of blood spatter, asking if he was certified in the subject.

"No, sir," said the prosecution's star witness. "We do not have any certification in our field."

Then McDaniel asked if he had ever testified under oath about having a "pseudo-certification" in blood interpretation. Englert admitted he had, although he couldn't remember which case it had been in.

"All right," said McDaniel. "Is that a certification that you gave yourself?"

"Probably more 'qualified,'" conceded the nationally recognized crime-scene expert. "I misused the word 'certification,' I should have said 'qualified and recognized.'"

Then in a classic *Perry Mason* moment, McDaniel slowly rose from his desk for dramatic effect and picked up a copy of *Black's Law Dictionary*. He then walked over to the witness stand, placing it right in front of Englert, already open right to the page defining "pseudo."

"Let me have you read here a definition," said the defender, savoring the moment. "First one up from the bottom."

Englert looked at Stan Faith, but the prosecutor was powerless to help his star witness in his public humiliation.

"Uh . . ." he began reading. "Pseudo is 'false, counterfeit, pretended, spurious.'"

But McDaniel still wasn't finished with trying to discredit the crime-scene reconstructionist. He then asked Englert about working as a homicide detective in the late 1980s in Multnomah County, Oregon, before joining the Housing Authority Police, a lateral move he called a promotion.

McDaniel then asked if that was the same time he had

endorsed a renowned psychic detective named Noreen Renier, writing that she "had a formidable record for honesty and professionalism."

Englert explained that he had been involved with Ted Bundy and the Green River Killer investigation, and he was merely demonstrating that she was not one of the many charlatans offering their assistance.

"Are you finished?" asked the defender sarcastically, as he brought out a copy of the endorsement he'd earlier downloaded from the Internet.

At that point Stan Faith stood up to object, calling it "totally irrelevant."

Then Judge Richard Striegel called a recess so the two attorneys could argue the matter, away from the jury's presence. Stan Faith told the judge that if he allowed this into evidence it would set a dangerous precedent.

"[Then we] will be able to bring anything off the Internet," he said.

When McDaniel said it was important for the jury to see it, by virtue of it existing, the angry prosecutor warned, "Remember this, Mr. McDaniel, when we get into some of your witnesses."

"Fine," said the defender.

"Well, you haven't seen all the Web pages we've seen," snapped Faith.

"I don't do porno," quipped McDaniel.

"I don't either, Mr. McDaniel, and I resent that," said Faith, bristling with anger and asking Judge Striegel what he was going to do.

The judge, who had written in his Internet biography of the importance of "Christian values," was dumbfounded by this unprofessional exchange between the two lawyers he had so often worked with in his twenty-three-year career on the Superior Court bench.

"I'm not going to let you guys go," said Striegel, raising his voice for the first time in the trial. "You cannot make off-the-wall statements that just insult the other side. Porno into this thing . . . that didn't happen."

After McDaniel apologized, a lengthy discussion ensued about whether Englert's endorsement for the psychic should be admitted. Faith then accused the defense of using "McCarthyite tactics from the 1950s," rendering his witness guilty by association.

Finally, with the judgment of Solomon, Striegel said the Website document would be inadmissible, but allowed the jury to hear Englert's actual endorsement.

At the next recess both Faith and McDaniel couldn't wait to give the press their own spin on Englert's credentials as an expert witness.

"He lacks credentials," said Defender McDaniel. "We've got a guy who's got no science background. He's results-oriented and obviously money-oriented."

Stan Faith maintained it was all "red herrings," accusing the defense of going back forty years, to distract the jury from the real matter—high-velocity blood spatter on David Camm's tee-shirt.

On Thursday, February 21, at 11:20 a.m., the State of Indiana rested its case against David Camm. It had taken twenty-six days and eighty-four witnesses to present. After sitting through almost four days of Rod Englert's violently explicit testimony, often illustrated by gruesome crime-scene photos, the Renn family told TV news reporter Abby Miller what it had been like.

"The pictures are hard," said Kim's sister, Debbie Karem. "You can't sit there and look and look at them. It's kind of like an emotional rollercoaster. You relive a lot and there's only so much you can hear."

Frank Renn said he had observed his son-in-law's reaction to the photos of his dead wife and children.

"I do keep an eye on him," said Renn. "And he doesn't have any expression."

His daughter agreed, saying she too had been watching David closely at the defense table.

"I look at David and I see nothing," she said. "He looks at them like they're an everyday occurrence."

And Renn said he was angered by Camm's whole demeanor at the trial.

"He comes in like he's King Kong or something," he said. "Like he's a lawyer. He's sitting there prancing around like he doesn't have any feelings about this at all."

34

The Day of Reckoning

Mike McDaniel planned to call between five and ten defense witnesses, sending the case to the jury within two weeks. He also assured reporters that David Camm couldn't wait to take the stand to defend himself.

And behind the scenes, Sam Lockhart and Donnie Camm had been working hard. Between them they had spent hours poring over phone records, trying to prove that David could not possibly have made that crucial 7:19 p.m. call on which the prosecution had based its theory of the murders.

"It didn't make sense," explained Lockhart. "I knew that Dave was not at his home making a phone call at seven-nineteen because I saw him playing basketball at the church. I knew that there had to have been a mistake."

So Sam and Donnie began comparing phone records from Amos Lockhart's house, to different numbers and calls from their cell phone back to his. Knowing that Amos had exactly the same Verizon phone service his grandson had across the road, if there was any discrepancy, it should be common to both. They also knew Indiana and Arizona are the only two states to have two separate time zones in the United States.

Then they struck gold. Donnie discovered that a glitch in the Verizon computer had mistakenly registered the call an hour later than 6:19, when it had actually been made. Sam Lockhart was ecstatic, knowing it could be pivotal to the whole trial and cause the prosecution's case to collapse.

"The prosecution was trying to pin it down that it was seven-nineteen," said Donnie, who had taken time off from his job at IBM to investigate the call. "They went out with a preconceived idea of what had happened, and they were going to try and mold it to fit their theory."

On Monday, February 25, Mike McDaniel called Verizon's billing supervisor David Eschweiler to the stand, as a surprise witness. He confirmed that the telephone company had indeed made a mistake, forgetting to adjust the computer covering several counties in southern Indiana to Daylight Savings Time.

"It was a mistake," explained Eschweiler. "It's going to add one hour to the start time of the call."

Later, outside in the corridor, Stan Faith said he was "extremely upset" with Verizon.

"We relied on their word," he told reporters. "And they all of a sudden go back on it."

But Mike McDaniel was jubilant.

"I'm so proud of Verizon to come in and say they made a mistake," he said.

The physical stress of the trial was taking its toll on McDaniel, who had a history of heart problems. Soon after the trial began he had gone off his diet and resumed smoking, to cope with all the pressures. Just before luncheon recess on Wednesday, McDaniel was taken ill.

"I've got a problem," he told the judge, who broke for lunch to give the defender time to recover.

David Camm's father, Don, who was in court every day of the proceedings, said he watched his son's defender become sicker and sicker as the trial progressed.

"There were days there when you would look up at him and you'd think he was going to keel over," he said. "And they would have to break at noontime because of his sickness. Once they had to take him right off to the hospital."

He worried that McDaniel's worsening health could have an adverse effect on his son's defense.

"Why did he take the case when he was in the condition?" asked Susie Camm.

That Wednesday, Sam Lockhart took the stand to testify about playing basketball with his nephew the night of the murders. He told the jury that he had sat out three games, of about twenty minutes each, before David sat one out. He said it was impossible that David could have left the gym to go home and kill his family and return without anyone noticing.

On his cross-examination Stan Faith tore in to Lockhart, stopping short of accusing him of lying to protect his nephew.

"Have you ever told [anyone] you would take it to your grave," asked the prosecutor, "if you knew that the defendant was guilty?"

"Absolutely never told anybody that," replied Lockhart.

When Faith questioned him about discrepancies between his account of when he said he'd played and what the other players had testified, Sam said they were "all mistaken" except for him.

Then the prosecutor asked if he had ever coached his relations and employees on their testimony, to protect David.

"No, sir," said Lockhart firmly.

The next witness was the defense's own highly paid expert blood spatter witness Terry Laber, who over the next four-and-a-half days would refute most of Rod Englert's findings. Laber ran a laboratory in St. Paul, Minnesota, and was being paid $80,000 by Sam Lockhart for his services.

Using pictures of the inside of the Ford Bronco, Laber pointed out spots of blood and tissue in the vehicle, echoing much of what Englert had testified to a week earlier.

But the defense expert maintained Englert had gotten it wrong, and all the blood evidence completely matched what Camm had told the police.

The defense expert also testified that the eight tiny dots of Jill's blood on David Camm's tee-shirt, as well as Kim's on his basketball sneakers, came from blood transference alone. He said they had come from the defendant simply walking through the crime scene, and were not high-velocity blood spatter at all.

Out of the infamous Area 30 of Camm's tee-shirt, said Laber, only four of the eight stains could be tested for DNA without being destroyed. Of those, two were from contact that could have been caused by "a bloody object," and the other two were smeared.

"I believe the blood spatter evidence," said Laber, "is consistent with what he said he did and what he observed at the crime scene."

On Tuesday, March 5, Stan Faith had his chance to cross-examine Terry Laber, and he would be just as vitriolic as McDaniel had been with Rod Englert.

"I want to congratulate you," began the prosecutor sarcastically. "I had sixteen pages of notes, and I don't take notes."

Taking a leaf out of McDaniel's book, Faith had studied some of Laber's old cases. For the next two days the prosecutor unleashed a non-stop barrage of questions, attempting to discredit the defense expert. First he tried to discount Laber's findings that the crime scene had not been cleaned up, as the prosecution maintained.

Faith showed Laber and the jury several photographs of blood and a clear serum flowing from Kim Camm's head, pointing out there were no footprints through any of the blood, as would be expected. But the defense expert repeated that the crime scene had not been cleaned.

Then the prosecutor asked Laber about the eight spots of Jill's blood found on Camm's tee-shirt, insisting they were high-velocity blood mist. Not true, said Laber, repeating that he believed they were the result of Camm brushing up against his daughter and resulting transference of her blood.

Finally, at the end of his testimony, in response to a juror's question, Laber conceded that two stains found on Area 30 could have come from high-velocity gunshot mist.

Later, at his daily media briefing outside the courtroom, Faith said he was certain jurors could tell that Laber was not to be trusted, as he was biased towards the defense, who was paying his bills.

"Does he know his business?" asked Faith. "I don't think he does."

On Thursday, March 7, the crowds came even earlier than usual, eager to see David Camm take the stand to defend himself. Some arrived outside the City–County Building as early as 4:00 a.m., and so many were expected that Judge Striegel arranged for a forty-five-seat overflow room across the hall from the court, so more people could watch the proceedings live on closed-circuit TV.

Since the trial had started back in January, the same curious members of the public were coming every day. Many of them admitted they were addicted and saw it as a real life whodunit. Now, on the thirty-sixth day of the trial, some considered themselves David Camm aficionados, freely discussing the finer points of the defense strategy with each other during recess breaks.

But all this "morbid curiosity" made the Renn family uncomfortable. They felt it trivialized the murders of Kim, Brad and Jill, turning the tragedy into entertainment.

"To see a lot of the hoopla diminishes from the severity of it," explained Kim's brother-in-law, Greg Karem. "Our family is reliving a lot of it. To have it exploited, it's a lot to take."

By 8:00 a.m. the atmosphere in the courthouse resembled a fairground. More than 120 would-be spectators had already gone through a metal detector downstairs, crowding the second-floor hallway outside the courtroom. As the Lockhart, Camm and Renn families pushed their way through the hubbub, flashes from a dozen cameras and the bright TV lights temporarily blinded them. Without saying a word they walked through the media gauntlet, shaking their heads in disbelief.

By the defense table Mike McDaniel looked confident. And like the proud manager of a championship sportsman, McDaniel hoped his client would put on a good show and impress the jury.

"It's like getting ready to play a World Series game and getting rained out," McDaniel told a reporter, describing his client's frustration with having to sit out six weeks of trial unable to say a word. "You know, you've got all the adrenaline and no place to go. So I think he's ready to testify."

Led into the court by two deputies, David Camm looked anything but heroic. All the bravado and confidence he displayed so often in court was gone.

After the jurors took their seats in their box, Mike McDaniel pressed his client's arm in reassurance, about to send him out into the ring.

"May it please the court?" said the craggy defender. "Call the accused."

Then all eyes were on the tall, painfully gaunt defendant, as he nervously walked over to the podium to be sworn in.

"For the record, will you tell us your name, please?" asked McDaniel.

"Yes, sir," stammered the defendant. "It's David Ray Camm—C-a-m-m."

At that point he burst into an uncontrollable fit of tears, lowering his head into his hand. One reporter could clearly see the vein in his forehead twitching, as if he were in the throes of a migraine. The one-time macho state trooper had been reduced to a sniveling schoolboy. His family looked on concerned, but there's absolutely nothing they could do to help him now.

Finally, after several minutes of sobbing he dried his red eyes with a handkerchief, ready to begin two days of often intense testimony.

"I was running a little late," Camm began, as his attorney gently led him through his drive home after playing basketball on September 28, 2000. "I figured Kim would've already got the kids ready for bed."

In a blank monotone he told the jury how he had arrived home and seen that the left door on their double garage was raised open, which was unusual. He had hit the automatic door opener for his side, waiting until it was high enough for him to drive his UDI van inside.

"I saw blood," he said dramatically, as a highly skeptical Frank Renn stared straight at his son-in-law. "And I thought it was Jill, I swear."

McDaniel calmly asked why he had thought that. Camm replied that Jill had been to dance class that night, so she would have been wearing a leotard.

"I just got out of the truck as fast as I could," he continued, "and when I ran into the garage I saw it was Kim."

"What'd you do?" asked his attorney.

"I kneeled down by her and I was yelling her name, just yelling at her, 'Kim!' Her face was just all blue and she was in a pool of blood. I made contact with her somehow, and I'm not sure whether I checked her for a pulse or not."

Then he described looking into his wife's eyes, which were barely open.

"There was no moisture on her eyes and I looked at the blood trail. And then it just hit me, 'Where are the kids?' "

Looking into the Bronco in the almost dark garage, he said he couldn't see anything, until he climbed up into the passenger seat and "peered" back.

"That's when I saw Brad," he said.

"What else did you see?"

"I turned and I saw Jill."

"Where are you now?" asked his lawyer.

"I was still in the front seat. Her head was laid down in her lap and her hair was kinda flowing down over the top of her. And I saw her little green shoe bag. It had blood on it."

"What'd you do?"

"Honest to God, I don't remember. I was afraid. I did not know what happened to any of them, and I was afraid to raise her head up. Because of what I might see on her face or what was done to her. I was scared and I didn't do anything else for her."

"Did you check Brad?"

"I grabbed Brad's hand and it was limber. It seemed warm and I just had to do something."

Across the courtroom the jurors were hanging on his every word. A couple had even put down their notebooks, so they could concentrate fully.

"The best way to describe it," he continued, shaking with emotion, "is that flight-or-freeze syndrome. And I've never been one to flight or freeze."

In Camm's earlier statements to Indiana State Police, he had described kicking into "police mode" straight after his terrible discovery. This was an important point not lost on Stan Faith, who would raise it later during his cross-examination.

Camm told the jury how he had reached over and picked up his son, lifting him over the driver's seat and carrying him outside, before laying him on the floor.

"I must have laid Brad on top of that sweatshirt," he continued, referring to the mysterious "Backbone" shirt with unknown DNA. "But I swear I do not remember that sweatshirt."

"When you laid him out," said his lawyer calmly, "how'd you start CPR?"

"I don't know . . . What did I do first? I think I started off by trying to give him a couple of breaths."

Then Camm explained he now knew he had done it wrong.

"I should've tilted his head back," he said, "and pinched off his nose and given him breaths into his mouth. And watched his chest to make sure it was rising to see if the air was going into his chest cavity."

He said that as he blew air into Brad's mouth he could hear it coming out immediately. Eventually he realized it was coming out of his nose.

"I gave him some compressions," he continued, wiping his reddened eyes with a handkerchief "And I did that wrong.

"On a boy that size you're supposed to use one hand, and I was using two hands, and I think I gave him about eight to ten compressions.

"And after, I was looking at his face, and that's when I thought to myself, 'You didn't pinch off his nose,' and I realized that's why, where the air was coming from or I'd assumed so, anyway.

"So the next time I went back to give him more breaths, I tilted his head back, I pinched off his nose, and I gave him the breaths, and I watched his chest and I could see some movement. I only went through about two cycles, two or three cycles.

"And again, like with Kim, the last time I gave him a compression I just looked at him in his face and his little eyes were just barely open and they were real dry, they had no moisture content in them. And I thought, 'That means that he's gone.'

"I was so used to just going and being the responder, I've never been the one that needed responded to before. I ran in to use the phone, because I knew I needed some help. I called the post."

"Why'd you call the state police post?" asked Mc-Daniel.

"There's a couple different reasons," he explained.

"Everybody at the post knows me. I wanted to hear a familiar voice, I wanted somebody that knew me. I wanted to talk to somebody that knew me. And when I said, 'It's Dave Camm and I need help,' that they knew I meant business."

He described running over to his grandfather's and calling his Uncle Nelson, who came over before the police arrived.

McDaniel asked him about his unusual behavior at Floyd Memorial Hospital, as he gave samples of his pubic hair and blood to Nurse Cathy Doan.

"I was humiliated," he explained. "Embarrassed. I'd known Cathy for nine or ten years. And those nurses are practical jokers, especially Cathy. They'd hide my hat, hide my paperwork."

He told McDaniel he had made the joke about using conditioner on his pubic hair "to break the tension." And he claimed that the comment about 'This is what they do to you when you kill your wife and kids' was misunderstood.

"But I think more true to the point was my next comment," he said, referring to his remark that his wife was looking down on him from heaven. "[I knew] Then, just as I know now, where my wife and babies are. And she's probably still up there shaking her head."

The following morning it was the prosecution's turn to cross-examine David Camm, and the questions would not be as easy. Stan Faith had been waiting almost eighteen months for this day. Since the murders he had become extremely close to the Renn family, believing he was now Kim, Brad and Jill's defender in the quest to bring their murderer to justice.

In his long career as a criminal prosecutor, Stan Faith had never met anyone like David Camm. Although he would not admit it, it had become personal.

"He's a sociopath," Faith declared, questioning the

defendant's public display of emotions the previous day. "When he tried to cry, it was hollow."

When Camm walked into the courtroom that Friday morning, he seemed unsteady on his feet, like he was drunk. After he was sworn in, Prosecutor Faith looked him straight in the eye, and asked his first question.

"Mr. Camm," he began, "are you on medication this morning?"

"Yes, sir, I am," slurred the defendant, looking to be in some danger of falling off the podium.

When asked exactly what he had taken, Camm said Klonopin and another prescribed drug, even providing the exact amounts and how many times a day he took them.

"I noticed you were sort of wobbling," said Faith. "Are you able to understand?"

"I've got a bit of a headache this morning, Mr. Faith," he said. "It started yesterday and I just haven't been able to get rid of it. That's not unusual for me."

Judge Striegel called a bench conference to decide how to proceed.

"This is what they prescribed for him," said Mike McDaniel. "You want me to have him looked at by a doc?"

The prosecutor said he "hated" to do it, but a doctor needed to be called in.

"I'm worried about the witness's competence," Faith told the judge, after the jury had been dismissed. "I observed him. He was wobbling, he was unsteady and he had his eyes closed at points. It's somebody on dope."

The judge ordered the court doctor be sent for as soon as possible. And as they waited, McDaniel asked his client how long he'd been on anti-anxiety pills.

"Ever since the night of the murders," replied Camm, adding that crying often triggers his migraine headaches.

When asked if the narcotics he'd taken were responsible for him having his eyes shut on the stand, Camm had another explanation.

"Well, when I had my eyes closed, I was praying," he explained.

He said his headache was "not real bad" and he felt competent to continue the cross-examination.

"I feel fully functional," he declared. "Adequately ready to go this morning. If I were to get to the point where I did not think I could fully function, and couldn't answer the questions properly, I would let the court know."

Then Stan Faith, worried what the impact of Camm testifying under the influence of drugs would have on any future appeal, warned the judge to be very careful.

"[We have] to make sure we're doing the constitutional thing here," he said. "And this is not something that will later come up."

The judge then called a recess until the defendant could be examined by a doctor.

An hour later the doctor declared David Camm fully competent and fit to continue the trial. He had given him a shot of Imitrex for a migraine, which he expected would start working soon.

At 10:30 a.m., after the shot took effect, the court reconvened and the jury was brought back.

For the rest of the day, Stan Faith peppered David Camm with questions about the murder scene, and what Faith referred to as Camm's "dime novel" life.

Going for the jugular, he asked about Kim's final conversation with her best friend, Marcy McLeod, and the inflammatory comment "History is repeating itself."

"I don't know why she would have made that remark," said the defendant.

Faith then moved straight on to Stephanie McCarty, the girlfriend Camm had left Kim for, when she was pregnant with Jill. He asked how Kim would have felt about him still calling her, long after their reconciliation.

"I know that she wouldn't have had a problem with that," he replied smugly.

"How do you know that?" asked Faith.

"You just have to know Kim," he explained. "I know my wife."

The prosecutor then turned his attention to Trooper Shelley Romero, asking why Camm was sexually propositioning her a month before the murders. Camm then became combative, asking Faith to let him explain the context of his phone call to her.

"Can you just answer the question?" Faith snapped. "It's a yes or no."

"I'm not sure exactly what I said to her," he said defensively. "But I did not blurt out the words, 'Shelley, do you want to have sex?'"

One by one, Faith questioned his quarry about his extramarital affairs, asking how Kim and his children would have felt about his behavior. Mentioning the weekend he'd spent in Atlanta with Stephanie in the early 1990s, Faith asked Camm to define a marital relationship.

"It's a bond between people that involves feelings and emotions," he replied, adding that he had had feelings for Kim but was beginning to fall in love with Stephanie.

"Just like in a dime novel, isn't it?" said Faith scornfully. "You've lived that kind of life."

"No, no, that's not true," Camm protested. "You want to take three or four years out of my entire life."

Then Faith asked the real reason why Camm had reconciled with Kim, after Stephanie had dumped him, when he'd pulled a gun and threatened suicide.

"That happened the night after my grandfather prayed for me to have a vision," he explained.

"Now you're not trying to manipulate this court with your images now?" mocked the prosecutor.

"Sir, I'm . . ."

"You have images that manipulate the emotions and tug at the heartstrings, don't you? You hide behind them, don't you, Mr. Camm?"

"Some," he began, before being cut off by the next question.

"You use them as a shield, don't you, Mr. Camm?"

"I'm a very emotional person," was the best he could come up with.

Then the prosecutor moved in, saying that everything in David Camm's life revolved around him. Camm disputed that, and began to sob, saying it was about Brad, Jill and Kim.

"You're working yourself up now to some tears," said the prosecutor. "Let me ask you something."

Faith asked if Camm had propositioned a female corrections officer three months ago, asking if "she'd like to have a little romp before she got married."

McDaniel got up to object to "this histrionic stuff from the prosecution," and Judge Striegel immediately dismissed the jury, calling both attorneys over to his table.

Mike McDaniel was now visibly angry. After nearly two months in the courtroom, the trial was becoming personal between Floyd County's two legal warhorses.

McDaniel told the judge that he didn't know whether this latest accusation fell under the 404(b) rule.

"It's an attempt to smear David," he said. "The State is attempting just one more incident of 'We ain't got much of a case, so let's just hammer David on behaving badly.' "

"You know, I'm sick of this smearing and crap," Faith told Judge Striegel, fast losing his temper. "He was a hypocrite in 1994 and he's still the same hypocrite that he was, today. He hasn't changed one iota. He wants everybody to feel sorry for him. He's the center of all attention. And when he said everything in his life is about Brad, Jill and Kim, he opened this particular door for that question."

Then Mike McDaniel said he was "pretty sick" of this crap too.

"I'm tired, I'm tired, I'm tired," said the defender, "of hearing about every comment that David may have ever made. The fellow is not a married man anymore . . . I mean, he isn't cheating on his wife."

Once again Judge Striegel overruled McDaniel's objection, allowing the prosecutor to ask the question, as long as the corrections officer agreed to take the stand later to testify. Camm said that he could not recall ever saying that.

Soon after the court reconvened following lunch, Mike McDaniel complained of chest pains. The judge then recessed for the weekend, as the ailing defense attorney was helped out of the courtroom by his wife and secretary, Debbie, to go straight to Floyd Memorial Hospital. After undergoing an EKG, doctors gave him a clean bill of health, ruling the pains were just stress and fatigue, brought on by the lengthy trial.

On Monday morning, Mike McDaniel was back in court for his client's final day of testimony. That morning Stan Faith led David Camm through the two police interviews he had given in the days following the murders, pointing out several inconsistencies. Notably, whether he'd made the emergency call to the ISP post before or after he'd tried to revive Brad with CPR.

Throughout the day Camm looked exhausted, studiously avoiding the prosecutor's withering gaze, answering every question in a flat monotone.

Time after time Stan Faith returned to Jill's blood on his tee-shirt, repeatedly asking Camm how it had gotten there.

"I've done my best to try and explain it to you," said the defendant. "Beyond that, I don't know."

At several crucial points in the cross-examination, Camm requested a drink of water and for extra time to review his previous statements. When the prosecutor questioned him about his expertise as a sharp-shooting marksman, he shrugged his shoulder, saying, "It doesn't make me a murderer."

During the afternoon session Stan Faith suddenly changed his line of questioning.

"Mr. Camm, I hate to get into this," he said. "But we're gonna have to. When's the last time you had sex with Kim?"

"Sunday night," said Camm.

Getting him to admit his wife had been a "very clean" person, he asked how his sperm had been found on Kim's panties by his own defense expert, four days after they had had sex.

"I don't know how long they can stay there," said Camm. "I'm not a DNA expert."

At the end of his two-day-long cross-examination, Stan Faith accused Camm of lying, and deliberately "adjusting" his testimony. Getting emotional, Camm maintained he had given the same account of his movements on the night of the murders to police and on the stand. He explained that the stress and shock of finding his family dead had caused him to block certain parts of the evening from his mind.

"It's easy for you to second-guess me," he told Faith defiantly. "I did what I could for my family."

Rumor has it that one night during the trial, the jury returned to the Holiday Inn to find a windup toy gorilla in their room, declaring "Not Guilty! Not Guilty!"

Allegedly, the next day the incident was reported to Judge Striegel, who immediately summoned both attorneys into his chambers. No one seemed to know where the toy gorilla had come from and the matter stopped there.

35

"In God's Hands Now"

The defense rested its case on Wednesday, March 13. It was the fortieth day of the nearly nine-week trial, and the jury had heard from 108 witnesses, viewing more than four hundred exhibits. The defense and prosecution had both wanted to call more blood-spatter experts as rebuttal witnesses, but in the end decided not to. They agreed the jury had endured enough, and there was no need to prolong things any further.

At 10:00 a.m. Judge Striegel called a recess to give Stan Faith and Mike McDaniel more than a day to prepare their closing arguments, to be delivered on Friday. The word among the reporters, many of whom had become friends over the duration of the trial, was that it would all end in a hung jury and mistrial.

When asked about this, Stan Faith agreed it was a real possibility.

"We'll try it again," he said, apparently with little thought of the Floyd County taxpayers, who would end up paying more than half-a-million dollars to prosecute David Camm.

Mike McDaniel said he was confident the jury had now made up its mind, and would find his client innocent in two or three hours.

"We've debunked a whole lot of stuff," he said. "The only thing that's left is the disputed blood-spatter evidence. We've got that, we've got character assassination."

That day Janice Renn wore a locket to court, containing

pictures of her murdered daughter and grandchildren. She sadly pointed out that tomorrow would have been Kim's thirty-eighth birthday, and the family would attend a special memorial Mass.

"I just want justice for them," she said. "I'm going to church and the cemetery and just pray that this is in God's hands now."

On Friday morning Stan Faith took the podium for the final time to deliver his forty-minute closing argument, which was illustrated by slides.

"Yesterday would have been Kim's thirty-eighth birthday," he told the jury, wearing his fire-engine red shirt, which would match his fiery prose. "He [David Camm] betrayed not only the honor of his family, but the trust of his badge and the honor of his profession. He used his power to prey upon vulnerable women."

Looking like an evangelical preacher, Faith continually pointed at the defendant during his speech, telling the jury that Camm had sought only "his pleasures," caring for no one else.

"The defendant is a devourer," he raged. "He cares nothing for his immediate family, or extended family. He is willing to bring down upon their heads a holocaust of extermination and destruction."

Then the prosecutor called the jury's attention to the "darkest" of all the pathology reports—the suggestion that Jill had been sexually abused.

"It is there we see the ultimate betrayal," said Faith, as a female juror nodded her head. "Think of the horror, the last of Jill's life. A world turned upside down, wrong side out. Words cannot tell the abuse and fear that she must have felt. The last thing Jill saw was her daddy pointing a .380 at her head . . . and wondered why."

He told the jury that no one else but David Camm "is the killer of the family," and he'd been waiting for them "with the perversion of hell" in the garage that Thursday night when they'd arrived home.

"He planned the perfect crime," declared Faith, describing the murders as a "hail of gunfire ending in an orgy of annihilation. He had a throwaway gun and an alibi. What he didn't know was that the very blood of the victims would be a witness against him. That the blood of the victims would cry out across the gulf of death and convict him."

Summing up, he warned the jury that if they did not convict David Camm, he would "pursue and devour" more women and become a rich man, by collecting the $681,000 from Kim and the children's life insurance policies.

"Don't let this man walk among us again," he demanded.

Then, after a fifteen-minute break, Mike McDaniel took the podium to deliver his closing argument. Once again his style was in complete contrast to the heated rhetoric of the prosecutor.

Wearing a radio microphone so he didn't have to raise his voice, the defender slowly retraced all his arguments, trying to explain why his client had acted the way he had after the murders.

"As humans we have defense mechanisms to protect our minds from what we can't deal with," he explained in his syrupy Southern drawl. "David's mechanisms started to block the horror that he'd seen. He's not sure about what he did. He's told his daughter was sexually assaulted. One more overload for his senses."

McDaniel maintains the reason for Camm's discrepancies in the two police interviews is that his interrogators lied during the second one to try to force a confession.

"They're trying to trick and trap him," he explained, "trying to get him to make terrible misstatements, which of course he did not do."

Then McDaniel attacked the prosecution for exaggerating his client's infidelities by misusing the 404(b) evidence rule.

"David's life has been put under a microscope in hopes that you will dislike him enough to convict him," said Mc-Daniel. "It's been done under disguise and under the rules of 'This is motive.'"

Finally, he called the jury's attention to the telephone call that the prosecution had originally used to try to prove their client was home when Kim and the children returned.

"There was no seven-nineteen phone call," he declared. "There was a six-nineteen phone call. The State counted upon that phone call to convince you that everybody else at the gym was wrong, that he sneaked out.

"There is no evidence, no evidence, that David ever left that gymnasium before they shut her down and locked her up, and set the alarm and pulled out of the lot about nine-twenty-two in the evening."

McDaniel said that it may never be known who murdered Kim, Brad and Jill, but one thing was certain—David Camm didn't do it, as he was somewhere else.

"Your job is not to figure out who did it," he told the jury. "Your job is to look at the evidence that's been presented and determine if you can say, beyond a reasonable doubt, that David ever left the gymnasium and went home and killed his family. If you can say beyond a reasonable doubt that David's the murderer.

"It's not about David being a philanderer. It's not about inheriting money. It's not about molesting his daughter, that's smoke. I'm going to ask you to decide this case on the facts. Thank you."

At 1:45 p.m., after giving the jury its final instructions, Judge Striegel sent them back to the deliberation room to decide David Camm's fate.

While the jury took lunch, Sheriff Randy Hubbard's deputies set up a display of the 400-plus exhibits inside the courtroom, for them to study at their leisure. Under the judge's orders, only the twelve jurors would actually deliberate, with the three alternates standing in the wings to take over if needed.

The Renn family waited in a courtroom in another part of the building, while the Lockharts and Camms set up camp in the magistrates' courtroom, across the hall from the deliberation room. And as all the prosecutors went back to their offices, a battery of reporters encamped outside their doors, awaiting the jury's decision.

It would be a long wait. At 5:35 p.m. the jury sent a message to the court bailiff asking to see Detective Sean Clemons' probable cause affidavit, listing the reasons why Camm was originally charged. Judge Striegel refused, on the grounds that it had never been officially put into evidence.

At 6:00 p.m. a local restaurant brought in dinner for the jurors, who ate in the deliberation room. Then at 8:15 p.m.—after almost six-and-a-half hours of deliberation—they finished for the day, returning to the Holiday Inn under strict guard.

At 9:00 on Saturday morning, the jury was back in their room to start the second day of deliberations. Once again all the various family members and press retook their places to wait. At 10:20 a.m. the foreman of the jury requested a magnifying glass, without any further explanation. Stan Faith speculated that they probably wished to take a closer look at the eight drops of blood on Area 30 of David Camm's teeshirt. That was encouraging, he told a reporter.

The core group of reporters, who had been covering the entire trial, all had their own opinions as to David Camm's guilt. Among them, one female television news reporter had definite doubts about it.

"The whole thing's just beyond bizarre," she said. "The basic logic of it, if he didn't do it, who did?"

She believed it was "a witch hunt from the get-go," but says there are still so many unanswered questions that pointed to his guilt.

"But, I mean, it was the kitchen-sink prosecution, and they threw everything at him," she said. "And I'd be really surprised if he doesn't get a new trial, just because of the 404(b) stuff."

Like many, she believed David Camm was his own worst enemy when he took the stand, alienating the jury with his arrogance.

Mat Herron alternated between thinking Camm was guilty and innocent.

"There are some days that I wake up and he's guilty," he said. "And others when there's no way he could have done it."

Sheriff Randy Hubbard, who had known the defendant since he was a teenager, had observed almost the entire trial from the vantage point of supervising court security.

After seeing David's performance on the stand and talking to him in jail, the sheriff had formed his own theories.

"You ask me and I'll tell you straight up," he explained in his office a few months later. "One part of his story that bothers me more than anything was his explanation as to why he got Bradley out of the vehicle. The time of death is very important. He told me he thought Bradley was breathing, OK?"

Hubbard makes the point that Brad was the only member of his family David thought was still alive, and the only one he ever checked for signs of life.

"Why would he lift Bradley out?" he asked. "He wasn't sure, but very careful not to disturb the trail of blood."

The sheriff also found the high-velocity blood-spatter evidence compelling.

"I think the evidence was there that he killed them. There were things that he did not explain away."

The sheriff also thought Dr. Tracey Corey's testimony was "pretty strong" evidence that Jill had been molested.

"Assuming that David did it," he theorized, "what would motivate him to kill Kim and his two children?

What would push that button to the point that he had no option?

"With his personality and ego at the time, if Kim had found out he had molested her daughter, that would push the button. If you knew David and his personality and his ego, you'd understand what I'm trying to say. That's the one thing that you don't want to accuse him of is a crime like that."

But inside the deliberation room, where it mattered, the jurors were deeply divided. Soon after they began deliberating, they voted eight to four in favor of convicting Camm. But as they went back to study the evidence, two changed their minds and it was ten to two in favor of finding him guilty.

And that's the way it stayed for the next couple of days, as the two holdout jurors stuck to their guns, leading to a deadlock.

Downstairs, in a holding cell at Floyd County Jail, David Camm waited hour after hour to learn his fate. Facing a possible 195 years in prison if convicted, he played it down, telling *48 Hours* he was "a little nervous [with] a whole lot of butterflies."

The only family member allowed to see David Camm in his cell was his Uncle Leland, who spent hours with him in prayer. Mike McDaniel was also a frequent visitor, explaining the various possibilities of what would happen if he was acquitted, convicted or there was a hung jury.

"He looks like shit," McDaniel told reporters. "Just frustration, I guess, really deeper than that. He really wants it to be over."

At 8:35 p.m., after a full sixteen hours of deliberation, the jurors were bused back to the Clarksville Holiday Inn. There they tried to unwind and relax, before resuming the next morning, but already tempers were frayed and there was little sleep that night.

"I'm so tired now, I can't think about anything," Frank Renn told Mat Herron. "I'm not sure of the questions they're asking. I think they might want to punish us for making them stay nine weeks."

On Sunday morning at 9:13 a.m., the jurors were back in their seats in the deliberation room. There were still hold-outs who refused to back down and join the majority, who thought Camm guilty.

At 12:10 p.m. the jury asked for lunch to be brought in, signifying that they had no immediate hopes of reaching a verdict.

Four hours later, the foreman of the jury, John Fredenburg, handed the court bailiff a note, saying they were deadlocked and could not reach a unanimous decision. Suddenly, everybody descended on an empty courtroom and the tortured, specter-like figure of David Camm appeared from an elevator, escorted by two deputies.

When the fifteen members of the jury filed in, they looked tired and exhausted, as if they'd been arguing.

"First of all," began Judge Striegel, "without revealing any numbers, do you think the jury is close to reaching a verdict?"

"No, sir," replied the foreman.

Then the judge asked each member of the jury if they thought a verdict could be reached. The first six all said yes, but juror seven, a middle-aged woman who was close to tears, said she was not sure.

"Basically, I don't want to give up," she told the judge. Juror number eight also agreed with her, but the four remaining ones didn't.

In line with Indiana legal procedure, Striegel ordered them back to the jury room to individually reread his twenty-four final instructions, and then try again.

Ten minutes after returning to the deliberation room, the foreman sent another note to the judge, via the bailiff, saying they wished to know about dinner arrangements. One jury member, it said, suffered from diabetes and needed to eat by 6:00 p.m. They also wished to know if the judge planned to discharge them and let them return to Clarksville to eat, or to make them stay longer that night to reach a verdict.

Then, warning the judge of growing tensions in the deliberation room, the foreman wrote: "Honestly Sir, the jury has some anger and frustration and together this may worsen the situation."

Mike McDaniel told the judge he was concerned they were at an impasse, urging him to declare a hung jury. But Stan Faith was in favor of letting them go to dinner and then return for more deliberations. As usual Judge Striegel sided with the prosecutor and the jury was bused back to Clarksville to dine together at the Sunset Grill.

At 7:45 p.m. they returned to continue discussions. Soon afterwards one of the holdouts changed her mind to guilty. But that still left one sole female juror, Judy Price, who refused to budge.

"There was a lot of yelling," she later told *48 Hours*. "I'm not comfortable with the way I acted."

Once again the jurors wearily sifted through the now-familiar evidence. They dissected the basketball games minute by minute and then returned to the blood-spatter evidence and the eight drops of Jill's blood on Area 30 of the defendant's tee-shirt.

"I wasn't convinced that was high-velocity blood spatter," Price explained.

But the other jurors were becoming increasingly frustrated with Price, and some were yelling so loudly that people in an adjoining courtroom could hear. After nine weeks away from home living in a hotel, and nearly twenty-nine hours of grueling deliberations, they'd had enough.

"They were saying some quite ugly things about me," remembered Price.

Finally, after three hours' further deliberation following dinner, a jury colleague she highly respected told Price he was so convinced that David Camm murdered his family that he would stake both his and his daughter's life on him being guilty.

And that simple argument persuaded Judy Price of Greenwood, Indiana, that David Camm was guilty, and to send him to prison for the rest of his life.

"That was high-velocity," she told the rest of the jury. "He's guilty."

So at 10:47 p.m. Sunday night the foreman sent out a note with the words everyone had been waiting for.

A VERDICT HAS BEEN REACHED.

36

The Verdict

It was well after midnight, and Judge Richard Striegel was taking no chances. After the lawyers and press had taken their seats, and the defendant had been brought in, Striegel addressed the court.

"There's to be no outbursts in the courtroom when I read the verdict," he instructed. "Try to keep yourself under control as best you can."

He also gave orders that the Renn family should leave first, so they could be interviewed by the press if they wished. Then, after they'd left the building, it would be the Lockharts' and Camms' turn to speak to the media.

"That's the way we want to handle it," said the judge. "So there's least conflict and least problems. Let's bring in the jury."

Then everybody rose as the twelve-member jury, looking exhausted, slowly filed into the courtroom. David Camm looked at them anxiously, but not one of them looked in his direction at the defense table. As the court sat down, a warden by Camm's side clutched a pair of handcuffs at the ready.

Directly behind him, in the second row, sat family, looking anxious and apprehensive; his father, Don, brother Donnie, sister, Julie, and uncles, Sam, Nelson and Leland.

"Would the foreman please rise?" said the judge "And have you reached a verdict?"

"Yes, sir, we have," replied Foreman John Fredenburg.

"Would you deliver that to the bailiff, please?" said the judge. "After I read the verdict we will poll the jury."

Donnie Camm, who had brought his eldest daughter, Kara, along, was so optimistic he even gave Mat Herron the thumbs-up, silently mouthing, "We've won."

The judge took the verdict from the bailiff and glanced at it, before reading it out loud.

"All three counts are identical," he began. " 'We the jury find the defendant, David R. Camm, guilty of murder, a felony.' "

The courtroom went into slow motion, as the verdict slowly sank in.

David Camm looked totally blank, shaking his head in disbelief.

"But I was playing basketball," he said incredulously, to no one in particular, as a deputy sheriff handcuffed and shackled him.

"It's wrong!" screamed Julie, rising to her feet and clenching her fists. "It's wrong! You know it's wrong. It's wrong!"

Donnie was yelling at the jury too: "He was at the game! Eleven witnesses! What is wrong with you people?"

Across the aisle the Renn family hugged each other, all breathing a sigh of relief that it was finally over, and Kim, Brad and Jill's murders had been avenged. Camm's first wife, Tammy Lynch, and his surviving daughter, Whitney, were with them.

The New Albany *Tribune*'s City Editor Amany Ali was so overcome with emotion at the press bench, she burst into tears.

Then, after Judge Striegel ordered a deputy to remove Julie, who was still screaming at the jurors, from the court, he polled each member of the jury, before discharging them.

Then, as previously agreed in the event of a guilty verdict, David Camm was to be allowed to spend thirty minutes alone with his family, while his jubilant in-laws were interviewed outside in the hallway.

Outside the courtroom stood a small army of reporters, waiting for interviews. The strong television lights blinded everyone as they came out. Tammy Lynch tried to shield 19-year-old Whitney from the cameras, as she led her in a daze into the county commissioner's office. A few minutes later Whitney collapsed and had to be carried out to an ambulance on a stretcher, an oxygen mask muffling her desperate sobs.

"This is justice," declared Stan Faith triumphantly. "Justice for society."

Complimenting the jury on their conscientiousness, he said they had done a great job.

"That took guts," he said, "and I think they cared. There is no reasonable doubt that he killed them."

As the jurors were escorted out by Sheriff Hubbard's deputies, they refused to speak to the press.

"You are the guilty ones!" a David Camm supporter shouted after them. "You are the guilty ones!"

Like the rest of Camm's family, Mike McDaniel was totally surprised about the verdict.

"The only thing I can say is that I look forward to retrying the case, without all the character assassination," he said gamely. "I think we'll probably be back here in eighteen months."

Sam Lockhart said he was in "total shock," and amazed at how the single hold-out juror had suddenly changed her mind.

"Unbelievable," he declared. "That a jury after nine weeks comes in undecided and then somebody changes their mind from not guilty to guilty."

When she had finally calmed down, Julie Hogue questioned whether Judy Price had been intimidated by the other jurors.

"I think someone caved in to what they believed in," she

said angrily. "They caved in to pressure from the other jurors. We have a hard time believing that someone who thought he was not guilty, now believes that he's guilty."

She vowed to carry on the battle to free her brother.

"We will not stop fighting," she declared. "[Dave's] an innocent man. We're not going to go away."

After all the Camms and Lockharts had left the court, Kim's family came out to address the media.

"We still don't have the kids back and we never will," said Kim's sister, Debbie. "We won't have Kim back in our family and that can't be changed. But at least he's not out."

Frank Renn, his big arms around his wife and daughter, told reporters his family felt relief at last and "a little bit satisfied" with the verdict.

"I know Kim is looking down now shaking her head at David Camm," he said sadly.

Eight days after David Camm was found guilty of murdering his family, his grandfather Amos Lockhart died at Floyd Memorial Hospital, at the age of 94. The Lockhart family patriarch had been determined to live until he knew the outcome of the trial, said family members, who think he then died of a broken heart.

As Amos' body lay in Gehlbach & Royse Funeral Home in Georgetown, Sheriff Randy Hubbard secretly allowed his grandson to pay his final respects early one morning, on his way to the Plainfield Correctional Facility outside Indianapolis, for a thirty-day psychological evaluation.

"We were in the process of transporting him to the Department of Corrections," explained the sheriff, who would later be accused of giving Camm preferential treatment. "He was there probably ten minutes or less."

On Thursday, April 11, David Camm was back in Floyd County Superior Court for sentencing. The former state trooper, who had just turned 38, now faced up to sixty-five years for each of the three first-degree murder counts—a total of 195 years.

First, Judge Richard Striegel placed a gag order on the jurors, five of whom were in the courtroom, to prevent them from talking any further to the press about how the verdict was reached.

"I think it's time for a little privacy," said Striegel. "Unless I approve them [talking publicly]."

Both the prosecution and defense could call family members who wished to address the judge, before sentencing was passed. Kim's mother, Janice Renn, was the first to address the court, calling for the maximum punishment for her son-in-law. David Camm looked on blankly, her emotional words hardly seemed to register.

"Since the night of September twenty-eight, 2000, I have felt mostly emptiness and pain," she said. "My pain came when I think about the brutal way they died, how scared they must have been."

Finally she asked Judge Striegel to give David Camm the maximum sentence allowed under Indiana law.

Then Kim's sister, Debbie, walked up to the podium to tell her brother-in-law exactly how she felt about him.

"All we ever wanted from you from the beginning of this whole nightmare was truth," she told him. "Just the simple truth."

She accused him of hiding behind religion, by casting himself as a martyr.

"I don't feel you'll ever be man enough or strong enough to give us the closure that we really need," she said. "At least we have the solace of knowing that we will see Kim, Brad and Jill again. And you, you'll have a far greater Judgment Day ahead."

She admitted that she had been "very disappointed" on learning about her brother's infidelities during the trial.

"However, making the leap from his behaviors to murderer and sociopath is a big one."

The last family member to take the stand was Donnie Camm.

"David wasn't the best husband," he said, "but he wasn't on trial for being a bad husband."

He then attacked the judge for allowing evidence of his brother's prior affairs to be admitted into evidence, saying it had poisoned the jury against David.

"The jury wanted to convict David before they ever got to the real evidence," he told the court. "David did not commit these crimes and the person that did this is still walking among us."

Then, facing a total of 195 years behind bars, David Camm walked to the stand in handcuffs, holding a yellow legal pad with his three-page handwritten statement.

"My heart is broken," he told the court. "I hurt inside until I'm twisted and turned."

Then he proclaimed his innocence, declaring that Kim, Brad and Jill were "walking this walk" with him and he was certain God would help him "endure this madness."

"Judge," he said defiantly, "you can imprison my body, but you have no control over my spirit."

Julie Hogue then stood up to plead for her brother, claiming her family had been victimized and her brother was totally innocent in a terrible miscarriage of justice. Emphasizing that what she had to say would not be typical, she noted that she had not rushed to support her brother.

"I believed Sean Clemons when he told me that I would understand why he had arrested Dave when I saw what he saw. I alienated my mother by believing Sean. I ended up having to apologize to my brother for doubting him and believing Sean.

"I'm now aware of the evidence in its undistorted form and I don't understand what Sean did. I have not seen what Sean saw."

She hoped her brother's experience wasn't typical. For him, she said, the truth had become lies and lies had become truth. "What is important here is that a man came home to find his family murdered by a criminal, then had his life further destroyed by those who are suppose to protect us from criminals . . .

Is Dave a hero? No. Is Dave a saint? No. Is he a murderer? No. Is he a victim? Yes."

The last member of the family to address the judge was his brother Donnie, who raised the matter of the controversial Rule 404(b), being allowed at the trial. And already the family were planning to use this as the main thrust of David's Camm's appeal.

"You need to understand that no one in our family would do anything to cover for David had he committed these crimes. We would not lie for him, we would not bend the truth. To believe that David committed these crimes is to believe that our family would lie to cover it up. Nothing could be further from the truth. In fact, our family believes that whoever committed these crimes deserves the severest of penalties, but we know that it wasn't David."

Donnie cautioned those in the packed courtroom who felt that justice had been served not to feel too comfortable. "The person that did this is still walking among us."

Then facing a total of 195 years behind bars, David Camm walked to the stand in handcuffs, holding a yellow legal pad on which he had handwritten his three-page statement. It would be his last chance to talk to Kim's family and he was totally unrepentant, casting himself in the biblical role of a tearful martyr.

"You may have gotten your wish and had me imprisoned in my body, but I will always be free on the inside and you can never take that away from me. Regardless of where I am, I can lay my head down in good conscience, conscience, knowing that Kim, Brad, and Jill are walking this walk with me, because they know I am innocent, and God will strengthen me . . .

"Judge, you do what you want. You can imprison my body, but you have no control over my spirit."

Judge Richard Striegel sentenced David Camm to the maximum sentence of 195 years in prison. That meant he'd be eligible for parole when he was 143 years old.

But before handing down the sentence, the judge finally had the chance to address Camm, and tell him exactly what he thought of him.

"By the murder of his wife and children," began the judge, "David Camm demonstrated his complete disregard for civilized society. In these cruel acts he exercised no restraint on his impulses and intentionally failed to conform his conduct with the law. Such behavior indicates there is a risk that the defendant will commit another crime."

Calling the killings "cold and unmerciful," Judge Striegel said that the evidence showed Camm confronted his wife in the garage when she arrived home with their children, and shot them dead one after the other.

"Civilized people cannot identify with this kind of thinking and behavior," he said. "These killings devastated and shattered the lives of all family members."

The judge said he found Camm's explanation of events the night of the murder "contrived and incredible," as he desperately tried to make his story fit the physical evidence. And he was not surprised that the jury had not believed David Camm's alibi.

"The details of his testimony," said the judge, "his mannerisms, and his demeanor on the stand were consistent with him being guilty of the murders.

"The killing of a spouse is certainly repugnant, but to

kill one's own children is something any civilized person would struggle with even believing. Each time the gun was fired the defendant had the choice to refrain from the act. He chose not to, and Kim, Brad and Jill's blood has convicted him.

"The Court finds that the crimes committed justify imposing the maximum sentence."

After sentencing, a tearful David Camm was led out of court in handcuffs and shackles, to begin his sentence at Plainfield Correctional Facility, until the Indiana Department of Correction could decide a suitable facility for him to spend the rest of his life in.

37

A Model Prisoner

Two months later David Camm was transferred to the Indiana State maximum security prison in Michigan City, where he was placed in protective custody. Prison Superintendent Cecil Davis ordered the former state trooper to be housed with a special group of high-risk prisoners. Camm would have little contact with the general population, but was allowed to receive mail, make phone calls and exercise in the gymnasium.

On May 13, Camm wrote a three-page letter to Louisville television reporter Abby Miller, who had covered his trial, striking up a rapport with her.

"I am still so confused, perplexed and angry," he wrote from his cell. "I can't begin to describe my despair. The system doesn't work. It is a failure. I thought it worked. I thought the jury would be balancing weight to tip the scales back. I was wrong."

And Prisoner 113866 complained of being sent to Michigan City instead of the Pendleton jail, which he had requested, as it was closer to his family.

Sam Lockhart visited him regularly and said his nephew had no television or radio, although he was allowed reading material.

"He's in a cell by himself," said Lockhart. "He's lonely. He misses his kids, misses Kim, his family."

A few days later, Mike McDaniel filed an appeal against David Camm's sentence, citing a "multitude of errors" at the trial. His motion listed thirteen reasons for a retrial, including Judge Striegel's decision on the 404(b) evidence rule, opening the doors for his client's extramarital affairs and Jill's alleged molestation to be heard by the jury. It had also emerged that three of the jurors' spouses had been allowed to attend parts of the trial and stay at the sequestered Holiday Inn.

"There's a lot of crap here," the defender told *The Courier-Journal.* "The guy didn't get a fair shot."

On May 23, McDaniel filed a motion in Floyd County Superior Court, demanding Judge Striegel remove himself from an appeal hearing scheduled for early June, so he could be called to the stand to testify about irregularities in the Camm trial.

"[The judge] told the jury their spouses could attend the trial unbeknownst to us," claimed McDaniel. "And he was aware juror's [sic] wives sat with victims and had a conversation with Faith."

The chief prosecutor said he saw nothing wrong with jurors' families attending the trial, denying that he had ever spoken to anyone.

"They say they never discussed the case with their spouses," said Faith. "I'm sure they obeyed the rules."

Six days later an angry Judge Striegel refused to step down, accusing McDaniel of spreading "rumors and innuendo."

At a bizarre hearing in Floyd County Superior Court, McDaniel found himself on the stand, being questioned by Chief Deputy Prosecutor Susan Orth, when the judge suddenly rose from his chair to publicly defend himself.

"This has been going on for almost three months," shouted Striegel, losing his temper. "I need a name. And I need a witness."

He said there was no reason to prolong the hearing, without evidence the jury had been tainted by spouses.

"If some jury misconduct occurred in that jury room, we want to know about it," said the judge. "But the fact that a juror's spouse was in the courtroom is meaningless. It's a public trial."

Mike McDaniel, who conceded he had no proof the three spouses had talked to Stan Faith, then withdrew his motion for Judge Striegel to step down.

At the next hearing in late June to discuss the fifteen alleged errors at the David Camm trial, Mike McDaniel failed to turn up, without giving a reason. Repeated phone calls to McDaniel and his wife and watchdog Debbie, were not returned. Sam Lockhart and other members of the family were in court and reportedly very angry about the lead defense attorney's conduct.

A week later, McDaniel officially withdrew from the David Camm appeal, after apologizing for not attending the hearing due to a misunderstanding. From now on, he told reporters, Public Defender Pat Biggs would be taking over and writing up all the appeals.

Sam Lockhart, now devoting himself full-time to his nephew's appeal, said McDaniel had almost had a heart attack during the trial and no attorney in America could have won the case, given the circumstances.

"Could he have done better? Yes," said Lockhart. "Would we use him again? Probably, at this point, not. And I don't think he would want to do it again."

In late July, Judge Striegel threw out the motion to grant David Camm a new trial, clearing the way for it to go up to the Indiana Court of Appeal. The judge denied all of the defense's thirteen points criticizing how he had run the murder trial.

Defending his decision to allow testimony about the defendant's prior sexual affairs into court, the judge maintained that the evidence showed "a history of marital infidelity" with "numerous women." Coupled with the fact that Camm had told investigators his marriage was "perfect," it was enough to subject him to credibility questions. And again he repeated he'd had no power to bar jurors' spouses from sitting in the courtroom of a public trial.

Straight after Judge Striegel's ruling, Sam Lockhart went shopping for a new defense lawyer to handle the appeal. He selected the high-profile Bloomington law offices of Liell & McNeil, and attorneys Katharine Liell and Stacy Uliana began work on preparing a brief for the Indiana Court of Appeal.

On September 27, 2002—one day before the second anniversary of the murders—Frank and Janice Renn filed a wrongful death lawsuit in Floyd Circuit Court against David Camm, demanding punitive damages.

The complaint, filed by the Renn family lawyer Nicholas Stein, stated that their son-in-law had wrongfully killed their daughter Kim and grandchildren, Brad and Jill.

"The acts of the Defendant, David Camm," it read, "were willful, wanton, reckless and intentional and warrant the imposition of punitive damages."

Stein claimed that David and Kim Camm had few assets, and the majority of the money was the $400,000 life insurance policy for Kim and her children. That money is now sitting in an escrow account, awaiting the outcome of the appeal.

Stein said the Renns were also suing David's younger brother Daniel, over a third policy worth $150,000, which he had originally brokered for them in Florida and now may be entitled to as a beneficiary, though he says he would never try to take the money from the family.

A month later, David Camm hit back with his own bizarre cross-claim for damages against John/Jane Doe, a.k.a., "Backbone," who he claimed was the still-to-be-identified murderer of his wife and children. The papers were filed in Floyd Circuit Court by David Camm's new civil attorney, David E. Mosley of Jefferson, Indiana.

In it Camm totally denied the Renns' accusations that he had murdered Kim and his children. And it included David Camm's own demand for compensation by the true killer, "Backbone," for causing him emotional distress, by his wrongful conviction.

"On the evening of September 28, 2000," read the nine-point counter claim, "David Camm's home was trespassed in by cross-claim defendant 'Backbone' who willfully, wantonly and intentionally killed Kimberly, Jill and Bradley, at a time when David Camm was miles away at a church basketball gym. The cross-claim defendant left behind at the Camm residence his Hanes sweatshirt which contained his/her hair and DNA evidence from his person and the handwritten inscription inside the collar, 'Backbone.'"

It then accused the Indiana State Police of failing to follow up leads and conduct a proper investigation, "so the current whereabouts of the cross-claim defendant are currently unknown to David Camm."

In the future, demanded David Camm, the Renns should direct all their demands for financial restitution to "Backbone."

In an accompanying press release, David Camm's family wrote that they hoped in the passage of time cooler heads would prevail, and people would realize he had been wrongfully charged and convicted.

"We believe David Camm is innocent beyond a shadow of a doubt," said the release. "We believe that his conviction was reached by a jury inflamed by lurid depictions of David's past sins so they were prejudiced against him."

On October 11, CBS-TV's *48 Hours* finally aired its one-hour in-depth investigation of the David Camm case, featuring an exclusive interview with the defendant. The show, which gave the case the *CSI* treatment, had the full cooperation of all parties, including the Indiana State Police.

CBS correspondent Richard Schlesinger, who had made four trips to New Albany, sitting in on some of the trial, told *The Courier-Journal* that he "loved" this story and found it "fascinating, because it had so many twists and turns."

Sam Lockhart said he hoped the program would raise doubts about the prosecution's tactics at the trial.

In November Stan Faith was defeated in the Floyd County elections, losing his job as chief prosecutor to his rival Keith Henderson. Faith then started a private practice as a defense attorney, taking an office across the same New Albany street as Mike McDaniel.

"God has a sense of humor," joked Faith.

Over the next year, as his appeal was placed in the interminably slow pipeline of the Indiana Court of Appeals, David Camm resigned himself to prison life, at least for the immediate future.

By all accounts he became a model prisoner, making friends among the other Michigan City segregated inmates, who didn't seem to mind his past career in law enforcement. He also earned a desirable job as a porter, allowing him to leave his cell several times a day, to deliver food and mop the floors.

"Mom and Dad would send him money," said his sister, Julie, who was a frequent visitor. "The other prisoners in his cell block considered him rich, because people gave him money so he could buy things."

David was allowed a television in his small cell, which he had to pay for, and now spent much of his free time working out in the prison gymnasium.

"He's a survivor," said his Uncle Sam, who also visited him. "Some of the guards up there told me that they knew he didn't do it."

On Wednesday, January 14, 2004, David Camm's new attorney Stacy Uliana couriered his appeal off to the Indiana Court of Appeal, as well as to State Attorney General Steve Carter. In it she claimed the controversial 404(b) testimony about her client's character had proven so damaging, it had been impossible for him to get a fair trial. She also criticized Judge Striegel for allowing the prosecution to introduce any evidence that Camm had molested his daughter Jill.

But former Chief Prosecutor Stan Faith told a reporter he doubted the conviction would be overturned.

In March, David Camm was transferred to the Wabash Valley Correctional Center in western Indiana. There he was handcuffed and shackled in a tiny solitary confinement cell.

"It was a mistake," said Sam Lockhart, who compared it to the notorious Abu Ghraib Prison in Baghdad. "They had no place for him. It's a punishment type similar to what they have in Iraq. They'd lead him by a chain to take a shower."

He spent six torturous weeks at Wabash Valley, spending his time killing flies with a homemade catapult and doing hundreds of push-ups to keep sane. But he was finally transferred back to Michigan City, after Sam Lockhart complained to the prison administrator in Indianapolis.

"Dave's pretty strong," said Lockhart. "He's hanging in there and he's hopeful that we'll be successful in the appeal and everything will turn out right. That's what he's living for right now."

In April, Judge Richard Striegel retired as Floyd County's sole superior court judge, a position which was created in 1979 after he was first elected. In his place, Indiana Governor Joe Kernan appointed prosecutor Susan Orth, 45, who had played a major role in the David Camm trial.

"[It's such] a tremendous honor," she said. "I feel like I grew up in that courtroom."

And some speculated on the ramifications of David Camm winning a retrial and finding himself before the court of his one-time prosecutor.

Epilogue

On Tuesday, August 10, 2004, the Indiana Court of Appeal reversed David Camm's three convictions for murder by unanimous decision. The three appellant judges ruled Judge Striegel should not have allowed evidence of Camm's extra-marital affairs into the trial.

In a landmark decision that could change Indiana law and the 404(b) Evidence Rule, the Court of Appeal concluded Camm was "unfairly prejudiced by the introduction of extensive evidence and argument regarding his poor character."

In the scathing twenty-nine-page opinion, Judge Michael Barnes and his two colleagues on the appeals panel sharply criticized Judge Striegel for his handling of the trial.

"The trial court abused its discretion in allowing the State to introduce evidence of Camm's adulterous conduct," it said, adding there was no evidence Camm was having an affair at the time of the murder.

It also noted the Indiana Supreme Court had never ruled on the admission evidence of adultery as a motive in the murder of a spouse.

"There was no evidence of a violent or hostile relationship between Camm and his wife," read the decision. "Nor any evidence that he ever threatened her with harm. Although we are cognizant of the great financial and emotional expense invested in the first nine-week trial, we cannot allow these convictions to stand."

The Court noted the powerful alibi evidence offered by the eleven witnesses who testified that Camm was in the church gymnasium during the entire time his wife and children most likely were murdered. It also noted the evidence showing that the seemingly damning phone call from the Camm home was actually placed at 6:19 p.m., not an hour later as the phone records seemed to indicate. And it focused on the unexplained crime scene evidence, including the presence of unidentified DNA on Kim and Brad's pants and the mysterious "Backbone" sweatshirt, also with unidentified DNA on it.

Finding that the jury's determination of Camm's guilt had come down to a "battle of the experts," the three Appeal Court judges believed it a strong possibility that "improper admission of evidence" had led to the guilty verdict, noting that the evidence against Camm was "far from overwhelming."

They were also highly critical of Stan Faith, trusting that some of the claimed instances of "prosecutorial misconduct were unintentional and will not be repeated in any retrial."

Among other "guidance" offered in the event of a retrial, the panel urged the judge to carefully "consider whether the highly inflammatory nature" of the evidence regarding Jill's possible molestation substantially outweighs the probative value of any evidence that Camm molested Jill." It also ruled that the admission of testimony regarding Camm's alleged sexual propositioning of Corrections Officer Diane Heavrin was inadmissible, as was the testimony of Kim's friend Marcy McLeod that Kim had allegedly told Marcy, just a few weeks before Kim's murder, "History is repeating itself."

Defense Attorney Katherine Liell said David Camm had dropped to his knees and thanked God when she telephoned him in prison with the news.

"What a great day it is today," she said triumphantly.

"Lady Justice will not stand blindly aside while people's rights are being trampled on in Floyd County."

And former Defense Attorney Mike McDaniel said he was "ecstatic," calling the ruling "some vindication."

Not surprisingly Stan Faith found it "disappointing," while retired Judge Striegel still maintained that he had been following the rules at the trial.

The Renn family were devastated by the Appeal Court ruling. Speaking through their attorney Nicholas Stein, they described it as "the nightmare that just won't end."

But there would still be a long way to go before David Camm was a free man again. Under Indiana law, Attorney General Steve Carter had thirty days to decide whether to appeal the ruling to the state Supreme Court.

The day after the ruling came down, the new Floyd County prosecutor, Keith Henderson, held a press conference, calling for the state Supreme Court to intervene and have David Camm serve out his sentence. Saying that 75 percent of the state's case against Camm would be inadmissible under the appeal judges' opinion, Henderson vowed to retry the case if necessary.

He also pledged to order a cold-case squad to reopen the whole murder investigation, if the attorney general passed the Camm case back to him.

"We will marshal every resource that we have," he told reporters. "David Camm is not going to walk out of prison today or anytime in the near future."

On September 10, Indiana Attorney General Steve Carter filed a thirteen-page appeal, asking the Indiana Supreme Court to reinstate David Camm's murder convictions. The attorney general argued that the appeals court ruling would set a precedent that "has no basis in Indiana law."

Writing that the Court of Appeal's ruling was "too narrow," Carter said the admissibility of adulterous behavior in a murder case involving a spouse should be evaluated on an individual case basis. And the 404(b) evidence, he claimed, was not important in the jury's decision to convict David Camm.

"The jury found the scientific evidence presented by the state to be compelling," Carter wrote, "and used that evidence along with the substantial circumstantial evidence of guilt to convict the defendant."

On November 5, the Indiana Supreme Court refused to reinstate David Camm's three murder convictions, passing it back to Floyd County prosecutor Keith Henderson to decide whether to refile charges for a second trial. Immediately Camm's attorney Katharine Liell lodged a motion, requesting his immediate release, as he currently had no charges against him.

A few days later David Camm was moved from the State Prison in Michigan City back to Floyd County to attend a court hearing. Once again he was placed in the custody of Sheriff Randy Hubbard.

Prosecutor Henderson was now under pressure over his decision whether to hold a second highly expensive trial. And he had assembled a team of cold-case investigators to reinvestigate the murders, searching for new evidence.

"It will be looked at with a new set of eyes," said Henderson. "I seek to have justice in this case. We will be ready."

A few days later the prosecutor held a news conference to announce David Camm would be retried for the murders of Kim, Brad and Jill, although he would not be able to use much of the evidence from the first trial.

"I would not retry this case if I did not think it could be won," he told reporters, adding that a new "confidential informant" would provide new damning evidence against Camm. The state's star witness was in fact a fellow inmate who claimed Camm had confessed to the murders in jail.

Calling the witness "a jailhouse snitch," Katharine Liell questioned how much credibility he could have with a jury.

At the press conference the prosecution also released a

new probable cause affidavit, explaining why there was enough evidence to retry the case. In it the state's lead investigator Gary Gilbert, who had conducted twenty new interviews with his team, wrote that Jill Camm's autopsy had found evidence the little girl had been sexually abused. There was also her "blood spray" on her father's shirt.

Inexplicably the prosecution still apparently maintained that Camm had made the 7:19 p.m. phone call from his house, even though a Verizon employee had testified it had been a mistake.

On Tuesday, November 16, David Camm was led into Floyd County Court for the first time since he was sentenced to 195 years for the murders of his family. He was wearing black-and-white checked prison garb, his hands shackled behind his back. And there was a dramatic change in his physical appearance. Although he had spent more than four years incarcerated he had put on a lot of weight and bore little resemblance to how he had looked at his trial.

And it was also the first time that members of the Camm, Lockhart and Renn families had seen each other since the first trial.

The hearing was to decide whether Camm would be freed until his second trial, a motion that prosecutors were strongly opposing. After hearing both defense and prosecution arguments, Judge J. Terrence Cody refused to allow Camm out on bail. But one thing both sides did agree about was that there must be a new venue for the upcoming trial.

"It's a sad day because David is not out," Sam Lockhart told reporters. "But it's a happy day because we think we have another chance."

In late November both sides agreed to move the second David Camm trial ninety-one miles west of New Albany to Warrick County, Indiana. It is now scheduled be held in the spring of 2005 in a modern 65-seat courtroom in Booneville, the county's seat, where it will be presided over by Warrick County Superior Court Judge Robert Aylsworth.

"It's going to start all over again," despaired Frank Renn to reporters. "We're prepared to take it as far as we can take it."

In late fall 2004, David Camm's daughter Whitney, 21, discovered she was pregnant. But it is doubtful that he will ever see his first grandchild, as Whitney has cut off all communications with her father since his arrest.

In the final week of January 2005, David Camm was released from Floyd County Jail, after Warrick Superior Court Judge Robert Aylsworth granted him bail on a $20,000 cash bond. Within hours Sam Lockhart presented a cashier's check to the Floyd County Clerk and Camm, having noticeably put on weight and looking dazed, was driven away as a free man and reunited with his family for the first time in more than four years.

Until his second trial, now scheduled for August 2005, Camm must remain at Sam Lockhart's house every night from 9:00 p.m. to 6:00 a.m. and wear an electronic monitoring device.

Postscript

In an amazing turn of events on Friday, March 4, 2005, just as this book was going to print, an ex-con from Louisville named Charles D. Boney was arrested and charged with the murders of Kim, Brad and Jill Camm. The arrest of the 35-year-old Boney came days after a national database had finally identified the mysterious DNA on the "Backbone" sweatshirt as his. Boney, who grew up in New Albany, had been released from jail in June 2000, three months before the murders, having served time for armed robbery and criminal confinement.

Initially, he denied any involvement in the murders and claimed he didn't even know Camm. But, according to prosecutors, he admitted under tough questioning that he had first met David Camm in Summer 2000 in a pick-up basketball game in New Albany. They had struck up a friendly conversation, he told investigators, and when Camm learned of Boney's criminal past, Boney says he asked if Boney could find him a "clean gun."

According to the prosecution's account, Boney says he brought the gun to Camm's house wrapped in the "Backbone" sweatshirt. Then he says he returned to Lockhart Road on September 28, 2000, the day of the murders. He told detectives that, when Kim came home with Brad and Jill, Camm rushed out to the garage. Then Boney heard gunshots and went in the garage, leaving his fingerprints on the Ford Bronco, as he leaned over to look inside. He also says he placed Kim Camm's shoes on top of the SUV.

Earlier, it had emerged from court records that Boney had been arrested in 1989 for attacking several young women, apparently in order to steal their shoes. He reportedly told police he had a "fetish for legs," although he now says these were just fraternity pranks.

Floyd County prosecutor Keith Henderson apparently buys Boney's story, now saying that Boney's case is so "intertwined" with Camm's that they should be tried together. So, on Wednesday, March 8, Henderson abruptly dropped the existing murder charges against David Camm and then immediately re-filed them with a new charge for conspiracy, a move than will return the case to Floyd County. Camm was immediately re-arrested and placed back in jail without bond. Boney was also officially charged with the three murders and one count of conspiracy and prosecutors will push for the two men to be tried together.

It's my contention that they were both present at the time of the murders," Prosecutor Henderson declared at a press conference, adding there had been no deals with either man "at this point."

On learning of the new developments, Kim's father, Frank Renn, said he was "ecstatic" that his ex–son-in-law was back in jail.

"I'm tickled to death about that," he told reporters. "Justice will be served, and it will easier to sleep at night."

But the Camm family was dumbfounded by the news, having assumed, as had many others, that Boney's arrest would soon lead to Camm's exoneration. That possibility still seems more real than ever, but for now gives little comfort to Camm's supporters.

"I thought they'd finally come to their senses when they released him on bond," said a crestfallen Sam Lockhart. "But [prosecutors] are just doing this to cover themselves. They can't admit they're wrong." According to Lockhart, "They're doing this because they made errors in the past and can't admit errors."